**Recommended**

# Country Inns & Pubs of Britain 2005

Accommodation, Food & Traditional Good Cheer, with details of Family & Pet Friendly Pubs

*Editorial Consultant Peter Stanley Williams*

For Contents see page 3

For Index of Towns & Counties see back of book

**FHG Publications
Paisley**

Part of IPC Country and Leisure Media

# ENGLAND and WALES Counties

**NORTH WALES**
1. Denbighshire
2. Flintshire
3. Wrexham

**SOUTH WALES**
4. Swansea
5. Neath and Port Talbot
6. Bridgend
7. Rhondda Cynon Taff
8. Merthyr Tydfil
9. Vale of Glamorgan
10. Cardiff
11. Caerphilly
12. Blaenau Gwent
13. Torfaen
14. Newport
15. Monmouthshire

**Please mention Recommended Country Inns & Pubs when enquiring**

# CONTENTS

## Recommended COUNTRY INNS & PUBS of Britain 2005

Colour Section ............................. 1-16
Tourist Board Gradings ................. 16

Vouchers ................................. 21-40

## ENGLAND

Bedfordshire .............................. 41
Berkshire .................................. 42
Buckinghamshire ........................ 43
Cheshire ................................... 45
Cornwall ................................... 46
Cumbria ................................... 50
Derbyshire ................................ 55
Devon ...................................... 58
Dorset ..................................... 65
Durham .................................... 67
Essex ...................................... 68
Gloucestershire ......................... 69
Hampshire ................................ 74
Herefordshire ............................ 77
Hertfordshire ............................. 79
Isle of Wight ............................. 80
Kent ....................................... 81
Lancashire ................................ 82
Leicestershire & Rutland .............. 84

Lincolnshire .............................. 85
Norfolk .................................... 87
Northamptonshire ...................... 90
Northumberland ........................ 91
Nottinghamshire ........................ 92
Oxfordshire .............................. 93
Shropshire ................................ 95
Somerset ................................. 97
Staffordshire ........................... 102
Suffolk .................................. 103
Surrey ................................... 104
East Sussex ............................ 106
Warwickshire .......................... 107
Wiltshire ................................ 109
Worcestershire ........................ 111
North Yorkshire ....................... 114
South Yorkshire ....................... 124
West Yorkshire ....................... 125

## SCOTLAND

Aberdeen, Banff & Moray .......... 128
Argyll & Bute .......................... 129
Ayrshire & Arran ..................... 131
Borders ................................. 132

Dumfries & Galloway ................ 133
Highlands ............................... 135
Perth & Kinross ....................... 139
Scottish Islands ....................... 140

## WALES

Anglesey & Gwynedd ................ 142
Ceredigion .............................. 143
Pembrokeshire ........................ 144

Powys ................................... 145
South Wales ........................... 147

Pet Friendly Pubs ..................... 149
Family Friendly Pubs ................. 163

Index of Town/Counties ....... 173-174

**Recommended Country Inns & Pubs 2005**                                    3

**Bedfordshire/Berkshire/Buckinghamshire**

## THE Globe INN

**Globe Lane, Stoke Road, Old Linslade, Leighton Buzzard, Bedfordshire LU7 7TA**

★ Canal-side location with access over own bridge.
★ Beer garden with outdoor eating facilities
★ Bar/Lounge open all day, every day
★ Children welcome ★ Children's play area
★ Dining area with non-smoking section
★ Excellent choice of food served
12 noon to 9pm daily
★ Booking Highly Recommended

**Tel: 01525 373338 • Fax: 01525 850551**

## THE DUNDAS ARMS

info@dundasarms.co.uk • www.dundasarms.co.uk

The inn's lovely position between the River Kennet and the canal makes it a most pleasant spot to stop for refreshment, and indeed for an overnight stay or weekend break. The comfortably furnished bedrooms are fully equipped with private bathroom, television and tea-making facilities, and enjoy relaxing views over the river. If your visit here is purely for refreshment, you will be delighted by the excellent bar food menu, which features really interesting "specials" alongside traditional favourites such as ploughmans and steak and kidney pie, and by the range of well kept real ales. For more leisurely dining, menus in the restaurant make full use of fresh local produce, and there is also an excellent wine list. CAMRA.

**Station Road, Kintbury, Berkshire RG17 9UT • Tel: 01488 658263/658559 • Fax: 01488 658568**

## THE GREYHOUND INN

Enjoy a delicious meal in our restaurant and sample wines from our extensive cellar. Relax with a drink at the bar or on the terrace. Rest in one of our twelve luxuriously appointed rooms. Celebrate your special day or private party.
Whatever the occasion you will find a very warm welcome awaits you at The Greyhound Inn.

High Street  Chalfont St. Peter  Buckinghamshire SL9 9RA
T: 01753 883404   F: 01753 891627   www.thegreyhoundinn.net

**Please mention Recommended Country Inns & Pubs when enquiring**

**Cornwall/Cumbria**

## Boscean Country Hotel
**St Just, Penzance, Cornwall TR19 7QP • Tel/Fax 01736 788748**

The Boscean Country Hotel, located amidst some of the most dramatic scenery in West Cornwall, is somewhere very special just waiting to be discovered. This country house offers a wonderful combination of oak panelled walls, a magnificent oak staircase and open log fires. The natural gardens, extending to nearly three acres, are a haven for wildlife including foxes and badgers. Situated on the Heritage Coast in an Area of Outstanding Natural Beauty close to Cape Cornwall and the coastal footpath, this is an ideal base from which to explore the Land's End Peninsula. The moors of Penwith are rich in Iron and Bronze Age relics dating back to 4OOOBC. Penzance, St Michael's Mount, St Ives, Land's End and the Minack Theatre are all a short distance away. 12 en suite rooms, centrally heated throughout, licensed bar. Excellent home cooking using fresh local produce. *Unlimited Desserts!!* Open all year. *ETC* ♦♦♦♦

Bed & Breakfast £23.00 • Dinner, Bed & Breakfast £36.00
E-mail: Boscean@aol.com • Website: www.bosceancountryhotel.co.uk

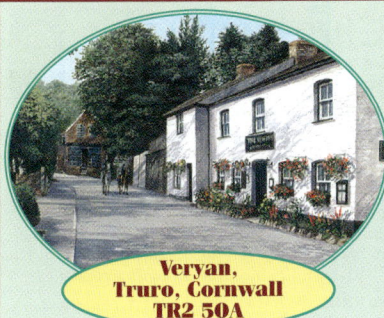

## THE *New Inn*
**Tel: 01872 501362 • Fax: 01872 501078**
**website: www.newinnveryan.co.uk**

Set in a picturesque village on the Roseland Peninsula, the New Inn is a small granite pub, originally consisting of two cottages and was built in the 16th century. Visitors are welcome to enjoy the atmosphere in our local village bar and we are locally renowned for our good food and cask ales, a wide range of food being served in the bar. Accommodation consists of spacious and comfortable rooms – one single with separate private facilities, and one double and one twin en suite. St Austell and Truro are nearby, and we are situated close to the beautiful sandy beaches of Pendower and Carne.

**Veryan, Truro, Cornwall TR2 5QA**

## SAWREY HOTEL
**Far Sawrey, Near Ambleside, Cumbria LA22 0LQ**

This fully licensed 18th century free house stands within easy reach of all parts of Lakeland, just one mile from Windermere car ferry and 2½ miles from Hawkshead. It is an ideal centre for touring, walking, pony trekking and sailing, and all the other activities that this beautiful area is renowned for.

There are 18 bedrooms, all with colour TV, tea/coffee facilities, telephone and private bathrooms. Excellent cuisine is available in the restaurant, and the Claife Crier Bar serves an extensive range of hot and cold snacks. Under the personal management of the proprietors.

**Tel & Fax: 015394 43425      ETC/RAC ★★**

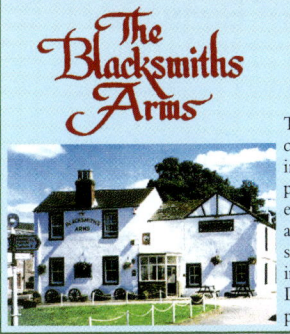

## The Blacksmiths Arms
**Talkin Village, Brampton, Cumbria CA8 1LE**
**Tel: 016977 3452 • Fax: 016977 3396**
e-mail: info@blacksmithstalkin.co.uk •
www.blacksmithstalkin.co.uk

The Blacksmith's Arms offers all the hospitality and comforts of a traditional country inn. Enjoy tasty meals served in the bar lounges, or linger over dinner in the well-appointed restaurant. The inn is personally managed by the proprietors, Anne and Donald Jackson, who guarantee the hospitality one would expect from a family concern. Guests are assured of a pleasant and comfortable stay. There are eight lovely bedrooms, all en suite. Peacefully situated in the beautiful village of Talkin, the inn is convenient for the Borders, Hadrian's Wall and the Lake District. There is a good golf course, walking and other country pursuits nearby.

Recommended Country Inns & Pubs 2005

**Cumbria/Derbyshire/Devon**

## BRACKENRIGG INN

With breathtaking views across Ullswater, this 18th century coaching inn is an informal port of call with a cheerful bar warmed by an open fire and a reputation for excellent food. A bar menu is available for lunch and dinner, with a table d'hôte menu added in the evenings; the chef-inspired fare can be enjoyed in the bar, lounge or restaurant. With so much to see and do in the area as nature intended, this is a rewarding place in which to stay. With the benefit of a fabulous panorama of lake and fells, the comfortable guest rooms have en suite facilities, colour television and tea and coffee-makers; all are centrally heated, including spacious suites and superior rooms. There is wheelchair access and a suite suitable for disabled guests is available.

**Watermillock, Ullswater, Penrith, Cumbria CA11 0LP**
**Tel: 01768 486206 • Fax: 01768 486945**
website: www.brackenrigginn.co.uk • e-mail: enquiries@brackenrigginn.co.uk

---

## Ye Olde Cheshire Cheese Inn
**How Lane, Castleton, Hope Valley S33 8WJ**
**Telephone: 01433 620330 • Fax: 01433 621847**
website: www.cheshirecheeseinn.co.uk • e-mail: kslack@btconnect.com

This delightful 17th century free house is situated in the heart of the Peak District and is an ideal base for walkers and climbers; other local attractions include cycling, swimming, gliding, horse riding and fishing. All bedrooms are en suite with colour TV and tea/coffee making facilities. A "Village Fayre" menu is available all day, all dishes home cooked in the traditional manner; there is also a selection of daily specials. Large car park. Full Fire Certificate. B&B from £25.00. All credit cards accepted.

**SPECIAL GOLF PACKAGES ARRANGED • PERSONAL TRAINING INSTRUCTOR AND GYM AVAILABLE ON PREMISES**

---

## THE TWISTED OAK
### PUBLIC HOUSE & RESTAURANT

Telephone: 01392 273666

Lunch 12pm until 2.30pm &
Dinner 6pm until 9.30pm every day

**Little John's Cross Hill, Ide, Exeter**

---

## the Ring of Bells inn
north bovey, devon tq13 8rb
tel: 01647 440375 • fax: 01647 440746
e-mail: info@ringofbellsinn.com • www.ringofbellsinn.com

For a real taste of Dartmoor, stay at the 13th century thatched Ring of Bells Inn in the delightfully unspoilt village of North Bovey. The Ring of Bells is surrounded by beautiful countryside, and is ideal as a base for exploring Dartmoor. The recently refurbished accommodation consists of five charming double/twin bedrooms, all with en suite bathrooms, tea and coffee facilities, and colour TV. Low beams and real fires add to the ambience, and as well as a variety of home-cooked bar meals, there is a cosy dining room where the chefs provide excellent fixed price and à la carte menus, which include local loin of venison, tender North Bovey steaks, Devon duckling, fresh Brixham fish, and some inspired vegetarian dishes. There is an interesting wine list, and a selection of well-kept local ales on tap. Featured as one of 'Devon's Finest', and awarded the 'Gold Seal' of excellence for quality and service, The Ring of Bells is simply enchanting.

**Devon/Dorset/Gloucestershire**

### THE CASTLE INN HOTEL & RESTAURANT
#### Lydford, Okehampton, Devon EX20 4BH
#### Tel: 01822 820241 • Fax: 01822 820454
#### info@castleinnlydford.com • www.castleinnlydford.com

One of the finest traditional wayside inns in the West Country, this romantic Elizabethan, family-run hotel simply oozes character. Featured in Conan Doyle's 'The Hound of the Baskervilles', it nestles on the western slopes of Dartmoor, offering first-class food in a bar and restaurant with slate floors, bowed ceilings, low, lamp-lit beams and fascinating antiques; dining by candlelight from imaginative à la carte menus is a memorable experience. Close by is Lydford Castle, built in 1195, and picturesque Lydford Gorge. Guest rooms, decorated in individual style, are beautifully furnished and equipped. This is a wonderful place to shake off the cobwebs of urban existence and appreciate the really worthwhile things of life.

### The Durant Arms
#### Ashprington, Totnes, Devon TQ9 7UP
#### Tel: 01803 732240/732471 • Fax: 01803 732471

Nestling amidst the verdant beauty of the Dart Valley, this attractive inn has all the virtues of a traditional English country inn with the comforts of the contemporary holiday-maker in mind. The cuisine is worthy of special mention with a wide range of main courses catering for all tastes plus an interesting selection of imaginative desserts. Just three miles past the Elizabethan town of Totnes, this is a fine overnight stop and several beautifully appointed bedrooms suit the purpose admirably.

e-mail: info@thedurantarms.com • website: www.thedurantarms.com

### THE POACHERS INN
#### Piddletrenthide, Near Dorchester DT2 7QX
#### Tel: 01300 348258 • Fax: 01300 348153
#### • Web: www.thepoachersinn.co.uk

Country Inn set in the heart of lovely Piddle Valley. Within easy reach of all Dorset's attractions. All rooms en suite with colour TV, tea and coffee, telephone; swimming pool (May-September). Riverside garden, restaurant where Half Board guests choose from à la carte menu at no extra cost.

*Bed and Breakfast – £30 per person per night.*
*Dinner, Bed and Breakfast – £45 per person per night. 10% discount for seven nights.*
*Low Season Breaks – two nights Dinner, Bed and Breakfast – £90 per person.*
*3rd night D,B&B – FREE (Oct - April) excl. Bank Holiday weekends*   Send for brochure.

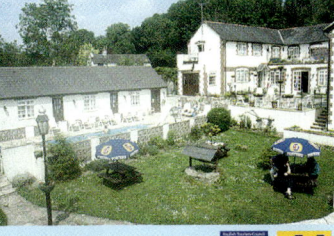

### The Falcon Inn
#### Painswick, Gloucestershire GL6 6UN
#### Tel: 01452 814222 • Fax: 01452 813377
#### e-mail: bleninns@clara.net • www.falconinn.com

Being situated right on the popular Cotswold Way, this fine 16th century coaching inn and posting house is a particular favourite with walkers and touring parties who appreciate the ambience of the bars with their stone floors, wood panelling and log fires; there is even a special drying room for ramblers should the weather disappoint. The inn has a fascinating history, having, in its time, served as a courthouse, the venue for cockfights and as an important coaching inn with stage coaches leaving regularly for destinations throughout the country. It also claims the world's oldest bowling green in the grounds. Excellent accommodation awaits guests, facilities being on a par with those offered by the restaurant which is renowned for its superb fare. There is a large car park.

**Recommended Country Inns & Pubs 2005**

## Gloucestershire/Hampshire/Hertfordshire

### THE FOUNTAIN INN & LODGE
**Parkend, Royal Forest of Dean, Gloucestershire GL15 4JD**

Traditional village inn, well known locally for its excellent meals and real ales. An extensive menu offers such delicious main courses as Lamb Steak In Woodland Berry Sauce and Gloucester Sausage in Onion Gravy, together with a large selection of curries, vegetarian dishes, and snacks.

Centrally situated in one of England's foremost wooded areas, the inn makes an ideal base for sightseeing, or for exploring some of the many peaceful forest walks nearby.

All bedrooms (including one specially adapted for the less able) are en suite, decorated and furnished to an excellent standard, and have television and tea/coffee making facilities. Various half-board breaks are available throughout the year.

Tel: 01594 562189 • Fax: 01594 564438 • e-mail: TheFountainInn@aol.com • www.thefountaininnandlodge.com

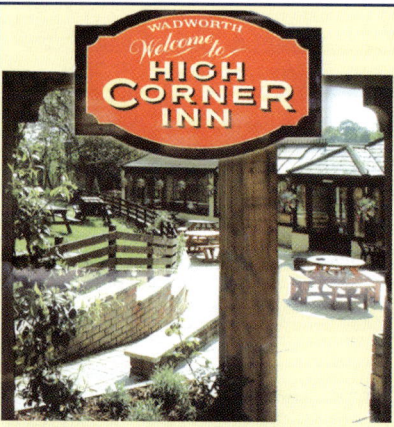

---

Nestled deep in the heart of the New Forest, the High Corner Inn is set in 7 beautiful acres of woodland. Both oak-beamed bars have open fireplaces and views across the patio and gardens. Children are welcome, and will delight in playing in the outdoor adventure playground.

A full range of Wadworth cask-conditioned ales is available, as well as an excellent selection of wines and spirits. We serve a wide range of quality home-cooked meals, bar snacks, plus a Sunday carvery.

*Accommodation is available in 7 en suite double bedrooms, all with colour TV and tea/coffee facilities.*

*Dogs and horses are welcome – stables and paddocks are available for DIY livery.*

### The High Corner Inn
**Near Linwood, Ringwood, Hampshire BH24 3QY**
**Tel: 01425 473973**
**www.highcornerinn.com**

---

### SALISBURY ARMS HOTEL
**Fore Street, Hertford, Hertfordshire SG14 1BZ**
**Tel: 01992 583091 • Fax: 01992 552510**
**www.salisbury-arms-hotel.co.uk**
**e-mail: reception@salisbury-arms-hotel.co.uk**

Hertford's oldest hostelry offers guests excellent food, traditional local ales and an extensive list of wines available by the glass and bottle in surroundings that have character and charm. This is complemented by great service. The two bars and the lounge are excellent for winding down and putting the world to rights. The wood panelled, air-conditioned restaurant offers an excellent value table d'hôte and à la carte menu that offers a combination of traditional and contemporary dishes and is well known for its superb food. The rooms are all en suite with satellite TV. Two rooms have been specially designed for those who require disabled facilities. The meeting room can accommodate up to 40 people for conferences/company dinners or celebration parties. The surrounding area has much to offer in terms of places of interest. Green fee discounts are available to guests with booked tee times at many of the surrounding golf clubs. Central London is 35 minutes away by train. ETC/AA ★★★

---

**Please mention Recommended Country Inns & Pubs when enquiring**

**Isle of Wight/Norfolk/Northumberland/Oxfordshire**

# THE NEW INN
## AWARD WINNING INN

Telephone: 01983 531314

Lunch 12pm until 2.30pm &
Dinner 6pm until 9.30pm every day

Main Road, Shalfleet, Isle of Wight

---

## The Lifeboat Inn

16th Century Smugglers' Ale House
Ship Lane, Thornham, Norfolk PE36 6LT
Tel: 01485 512236 • Fax: 01485 512423

A lovely sixteenth century traditional English inn, the Lifeboat, once the haunt of smugglers, has magnificent views over Thornham harbour to the sea beyond. The bar, with its low ceiling, pillars and uneven floor, conjured up visions of the unhurried life of years gone by as we sampled an excellent pint of real ale and tucked into our fisherman's pie. Daily specials increase the already excellent choice of freshly prepared dishes available in the bar; alternatively one may dine in the restaurant, where a frequently changing menu makes the best of local seasonal produce. All the comfortable bedrooms have en suite bathrooms and most enjoy views over the harbour to the sea.

website: www.lifeboatinn.co.uk

---

## The Red Lion Hotel

East Haddon, Northamptonshire NN6 8BU
Tel: 01604 770223 • Fax: 01604 770767
web: www.redlionhoteleasthaddon.co.uk

This traditional, stone-built inn sits snugly in the charming village of East Haddon, just eight miles from Northampton. Situated close to Althorp House, Home of Earl Spencer, and other notable houses and gardens. Warwick, Stratford and the Cotswolds 45 minute drive away. Golf, fishing, squash, swimming and snooker are all available locally. Those wishing to make the most of a relaxing weekend break will find comfortable, spick-and-span bedrooms with full en suite facilities, television, etc. Good English cooking is the basis of the carefully balanced à la carte menu and a comprehensive range of gourmet bar food is available at lunchtime and in the evening in the brass and copper bedecked bars, accompanied by one's choice from the well-kept ales, beers, wines and other refreshments.

**Egon Ronay • Good Food Guide**

---

## THE DOG HOUSE HOTEL

It is seldom that one would claim to be delighted to be 'in the dog house', but when the establishment in question is this sturdy stone-built inn, a stay here is a privilege, not a punishment! The attractively furnished bedrooms, all en suite, offer a full range of facilities, and special Friday and Saturday rates make a weekend break a particularly attractive proposition. The Hotel Restaurant offers an extensive choice of menu with the emphasis very firmly on quality and professional service; meals can be enjoyed in the light and airy conservatory or in the bar, where a range of blackboard specials prove excellent value for money. The golfing enthusiast will be delighted to find two 18-hole golf courses almost next door.

Frilford Heath, Abingdon, Oxfordshire OX13 6QJ
Tel: 01865 390830 • Fax: 01865 390860

---

**Recommended Country Inns & Pubs 2005**

**Oxfordshire/Shropshire/Somerset/Worcestershire**

## THE KING'S HEAD INN
FREE HOUSE • ACCOMMODATION • RESTAURANT
e-mail: kingshead@orr-ewing.com
www.kingsheadinn.net

**Bledington, Near Kingham, Oxon OX7 6XQ**
Tel: 01608 658365 • Fax: 01608 658902

Facing Bledington's village green with its brook and ducks stands the 15th century King's Head Inn, an establishment which has echoed with the sounds of convivial hospitality for over four centuries. Bledington nestles in the heart of the Cotswolds and is within easy reach of all top tourist attractions. The charming accommodation is in keeping with the atmosphere, all bedrooms (en suite) having television, telephone and hot drinks facilities. High quality and inventive bar fare is served, with full à la carte and table d'hôte menus in the award-winning restaurant in the evenings. A selection of real ales and interesting whiskies is served in the bar which has original old beams and an inglenook fireplace.

AA ♦♦♦♦ • Egon Ronay ★
Good Pub Guide Dining County Pub of the Year • Logis

## THE Crown COUNTRY INN

**Munslow, Near Craven Arms, Shropshire SY7 9ET**

Tel: 01584 841205
Fax: 01584 841255

Set below the rolling hills of Wenlock Edge, the Crown Country Inn is an ideal place to stay and explore the area. This Grade II Listed Tudor inn retains many historic features, including oak beams and flagstone floors.
• CAMRA •

www.crowncountryinn.co.uk
info@crowncountryinn.co.uk

Here you can sample traditional ales, fine food and a warm welcome from hosts, Richard and Jane Arnold. The menu offers a tempting variety of traditional and more exotic dishes, plus daily 'specials', all freshly prepared using the finest ingredients. Accommodation is available in three large bedrooms, all en suite, with television and tea/coffee making facilities. All rooms are non-smoking.

AA ♦♦♦♦

• Shropshire Good Eating Awards •
Restaurant of the Year 2001/2002/2003/2004

## The Talbot 15th Century Coaching Inn
### at Mells, Near Bath

On the edge of Somerset's Mendip Hills, this delightful retreat in a medieval village near Bath offers beautiful en suite rooms, wonderful freshly prepared food, and great real ale.

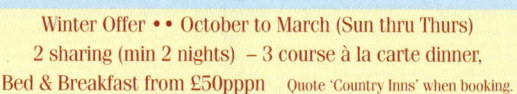

AA ♦♦♦♦

Winter Offer • • October to March (Sun thru Thurs)
2 sharing (min 2 nights) – 3 course à la carte dinner,
Bed & Breakfast from £50pppn    Quote 'Country Inns' when booking.

Tel: 01373 812254 • www.talbotinn.com

## The Manor Arms Country Inn
**Abberley Village, Worcestershire WR6 6BN**
Tel: 01299 896507 • Fax: 01299 896723
e-mail: info@themanorarms.co.uk
website: www.themanorarms.co.uk

Of great charm and character and gracing a sleepy English village high in the Abberley Hills, the Manor Arms is over 300 years old and retains much of its period ambience. The old oak beams in the walls and ceilings remain exposed and the imposing fireplace in the lounge bar was originally part of the private quarters. There is an excellent choice of Cask Marque award-winning traditional ales, along with a bar menu, grill menu, fresh fish menu, à la carte menu and sausage board. There are 11 individually furnished letting rooms, including a family suite (a double, twin and lounge area, accommodating up to 6 adults) and the Manor Suite which has a four-poster bed, luxury bathroom and sitting room.

**North Yorkshire**

## Golden Lion HOTEL
**Market Place, Leyburn, North Yorkshire DL8 5AS**

At the gateway to Wensleydale, this splendid hotel dates from 1765, although it has been tastefully modernised. Light meals and afternoon teas are served in the bars, and the restaurant with its picture windows and colourful murals is a popular venue. Excellent accommodation is available in rooms with bathrooms en suite, television, telephone, radio and tea and coffee-makers. A lift operates to all floors and many rooms are specially adapted to the needs of disabled guests. Within easy walking distance is the little town of Middleham on the River Ure which is well known as a racehorse training centre.

Tel: 01969 622161
Fax: 01969 623836
e-mail: annegoldenlion@aol.com

## The Foresters Arms
**MAIN STREET, GRASSINGTON, SKIPTON
NORTH YORKSHIRE BD23 5AA
Tel: 01756 752349 • Fax: 01756 753633**

The Foresters Arms, Grassington, once an old coaching inn, situated in the heart of the Yorkshire Dales. An ideal centre for walking or touring. A family-run business for over 35 years. Serving hand-pulled traditional ales. Bar meals served lunchtime and evenings. All bedrooms are en suite and have satellite TVs and tea/coffee making facilities. Prices £30 single; £60 double.

*Proprietor: Rita Richardson*

## The Angel Inn
❖ **TOPCLIFFE** ❖

The Angel Inn, steeped in tradition, dates back to the early 17th century. Travellers would rest, take ale, food and change horses at The Angel on their journey north and on their return south.
Tastefully extended in recent years into a charming quality country inn, renowned for a warm, friendly atmosphere, fine food and traditional Yorkshire ales.
En suite bedrooms, residents' lounge, three bar areas, games room, beer garden, water patio and large car park.

The Angel Inn, Country Inn, Hotel & Restaurant
Long Street, Topcliffe, Thirsk, North Yorkshire YO7 3RW
Tel: 01845 577237 • Fax: 01845 578000

---

The Branston Family are deservedly proud of their excellent reputation for providing good hospitality, good food, and a warm, friendly atmosphere. En suite bedrooms (double, twin, family and disabled) are tastefully furnished, with tea/coffee facilities and colour television, and there is a lounge for the exclusive use of guests. Drinks and meals can be enjoyed in the pleasant bar, where large open fireplaces and oak beams add to the welcoming ambience; meals are also available in the light and airy conservatory restaurant. Its location on the main A64 York to Scarborough road is ideal for exploring this scenic area; the North Yorkshire moors and several golf courses, including Ganton Championship Course, are within easy reach.

**THE GANTON GREYHOUND** Ganton, Near Scarborough, North Yorkshire YO12 4NX
Tel: 01944 710116 • Fax: 01944 712705 •
e-mail: gantongreyhound@supanet.com • www.gantongreyhound.com

**Recommended Country Inns & Pubs 2005**

## North Yorkshire/West Yorkshire

### GEORGE INN
Kirk Gill, Hubberholme,
Near Skipton,
North Yorkshire BD23 5JE
Tel: 01756 760223
www.thegeorge-inn.co.uk

A traditional Dales inn of flagstone floors, stone walls and mullioned windows, this homely, unpretentious retreat is a real jewel. It nestles beneath the fells in a seemingly remote hamlet alongside the River Wharfe; a picturesque and peaceful setting that will be of direct appeal to urban escapees. Here, in two cosy bars, one may revive body and spirit whilst enjoying an excellent range of no-nonsense, home-cooked meals and sweets as well as well-kept beers that include Black Sheep ale and a good selection of wines and spirits. Relax – there is no need to leave this tranquil paradise, for first-rate overnight accommodation is available in rooms with en suite facilities.

---

### The Hobbit
Hob Lane, Norland
Sowerby Bridge
W. Yorkshire HX6 3QL
Tel: 01422 832202
Fax: 01422 835381

Nestling on a hillside on the outskirts of Sowerby Bridge, overlooking the Calderdale Valley, these converted delvers' cottages are now **The Hobbit Hotel & Rivendell Restaurant**. 14 newly decorated en suite rooms, all with TV, telephone and tea/coffee making facilities, offer a perfect retreat from the daily hustle and bustle. There is always a friendly welcome, and the facility for bar food, a restaurant meal or a relaxed drink in the bar. Occasionally The Hobbit is a venue for weddings, murder mysteries, medieval banquets or tribute nights.

www.londonandedinburghinns.com

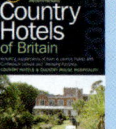

---

## FHG PUBLICATIONS 2005

- Recommended COUNTRY HOTELS
- Recommended COUNTRY INNS & PUBS
- BED & BREAKFAST STOPS • CHILDREN WELCOME!
- The Original FHG Guide to COAST & COUNTRY HOLIDAYS
- CARAVAN & CAMPING HOLIDAYS, England, Scotland, Wales & Ireland
- BRITAIN'S BEST HOLIDAYS
- THE GOLF GUIDE Where to Play / Where to Stay
- PETS WELCOME!
- Recommended SHORT BREAK HOLIDAYS in Britain
- SELF CATERING HOLIDAYS in Britain

**Available from bookshops or larger newsagents**

**FHG PUBLICATIONS LTD**
Abbey Mill Business Centre,
Seedhill, Paisley PA1 ITJ

www.holidayguides.com

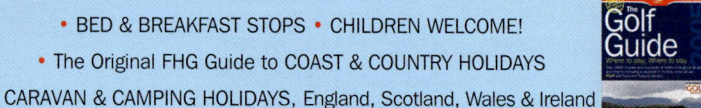

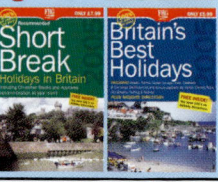

# SCOTLAND Counties

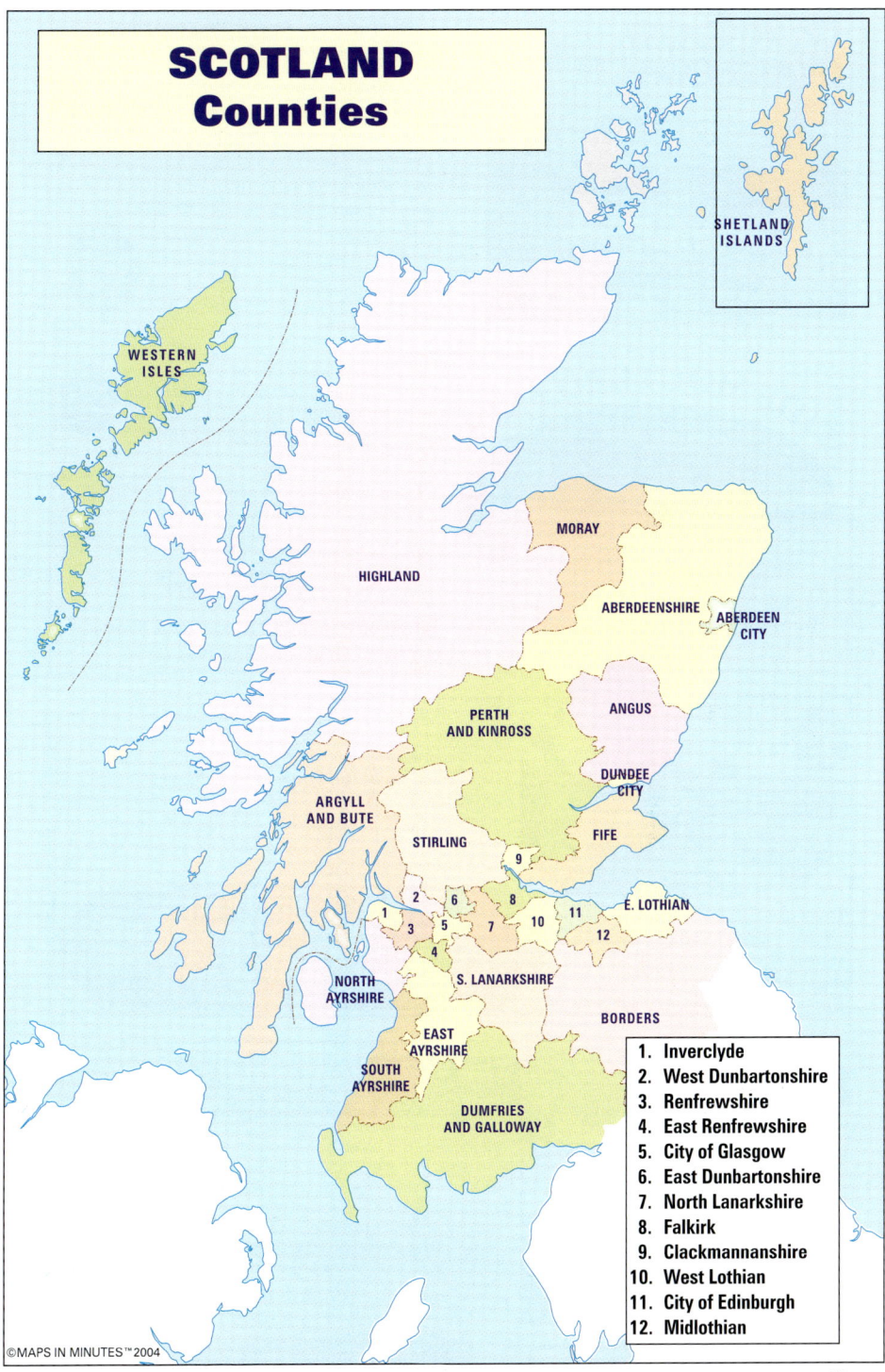

1. Inverclyde
2. West Dunbartonshire
3. Renfrewshire
4. East Renfrewshire
5. City of Glasgow
6. East Dunbartonshire
7. North Lanarkshire
8. Falkirk
9. Clackmannanshire
10. West Lothian
11. City of Edinburgh
12. Midlothian

Recommended Country Inns & Pubs 2005

**Argyll & Bute/Borders/ Dumfries & Galloway**

# CAIRNDOW STAGECOACH INN

**Cairndow, Argyll PA26 8BN**
**Tel: 01499 600286 • Fax: 01499 600220**

Across the Arrochar Alps at the head of Loch Fyne, this historic coaching inn enjoys a perfect position. All bedrooms are en suite with TV, radio, central heating, tea/coffee and direct-dial phone. Two de luxe bedrooms with king-size beds and two-person spa bath are available. Dine by candlelight in our Stables Restaurant; bar meals and drinks served all day. Ideal centre for touring Western Highlands and Trossachs. Amenities include a loch-side beer garden, sauna, multi-gym, solarium; half-price green fees at Inveraray Golf Course.

## WIDE MOUTHED FROG

The "Frog" is ideally situated at Dunstaffnage Marina, just three miles north of Oban and the ferry terminal to the Isles, and owners, Linda and Stuart Byron, concentrate on providing a casual and relaxed atmosphere. There is an all-day food service, with menus featuring the best of local produce and specialising in fresh seafood, and the bars offer a varied selection of refreshments. Accommodation is available in ten new en suite bedrooms, all with satellite colour television, direct-dial telephone and tea/coffee making facilities; bathrooms have bath and power shower. Major credit cards accepted.

**Dunstaffnage Bay, Near Oban PA37 1PX • Tel: 01631 567005 • Fax: 01631 571044**
**e-mail: frogenqs@aol.com • website: www.widemouthedfrog.com**

Nestling on the northern slopes of the Cheviots and but a mile from the Scotland–England border, this attractive hotel with its distinctive black and white facade is situated at the end of the 268-mile Pennine Way. The surrounding undulating countryside supports an abundance of wildlife, and nature lovers, be they walkers, cyclists or car drivers, find this a convenient and comfortable port of call and appreciate the recently upgraded refreshment and accommodation facilities.

Good ale and good company may be sought in a bright and friendly bar and there is a beer garden popular on sunny days. Delightfully furnished rooms with en suite facilities await overnight guests.

## THE BORDER HOTEL
**The Green, Kirk Yetholm, Kelso TD5 8PQ**
**Tel: 01573 420237 • Fax: 01573 420549**
**www.theborderhotel.com**
**BorderHotel@aol.com**

## The Waterfront Hotel & Bistro
**North Crescent, Portpatrick DG9 8SX**

The Waterfront is a stylish new hotel, furnished to a very high specification and situated opposite the picturesque harbour of Portpatrick. With eight en suite bedrooms and an elegant restaurant serving a delicious selection of dishes and wines, The Waterfront is perfectly located for that Golfing Break, with Portpatrick (Dunskey) and Lagganmore Golf Clubs being within 1 mile and Stranraer Golf Club within 8 miles. Individual or Group Golfing packages at favourable rates available on request. 'We look forward to welcoming you".

Bed & Breakfast from £28pppn (en suite, sharing)

**Tel: 01776 810800**
**Fax: 01776 810850**

e-mail: WaterfrontHotel@aol.com • website: www.waterfronthotel.co.uk

**Highlands** **Powys**

Where a warm Highland welcome waits for you

**THE NIP INN**

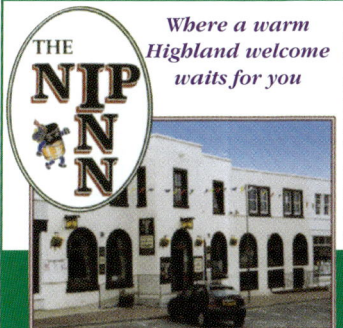

Lying in the centre of the village of Lairg, The Nip Inn is an ideal base from which to tour the North of Scotland. Superb, home-cooked food, using the best local ingredients, is served in the elegant restaurant and in the attractive setting of the lounge bar. All meals can be complemented by a bottle of wine from a comprehensive list. All six bedrooms are individual in character, and furnished to a high standard, with en suite facilities, colour TV and tea/coffee hospitality tray. The popular lounge bar, boasting some fine malt whiskies and good draught beers, is just the place to unwind and relax. Among the many attractions of this scenic area are fishing, boating, sailing and golf, including Royal Dornoch nearby. Local places of interest include the Falls of Shin, Dunrobin Castle and Clynelish Distillery.

**Main Street, Lairg, Sutherland IV27 4DB**
**Tel: 01549 402243 • Fax: 01549 402593**
**e-mail: info@nipinn.co.uk**

---

## The Gun Lodge Hotel
### High Street, Ardersier, Inverness-shire IV2 7QB
### Tel & Fax: 01667 462734
### e-mail: availability@gunlodgehotel.co.uk
### www.gunlodgehotel.com

Situated on the Moray Firth coast with easy access to rugged Highland scenery and forested areas to the south, this unpretentious family-run hotel offers food and shelter in a warm and friendly atmosphere. In addition to tasty bar food, there is a full à la carte menu in the cosy restaurant, prices being extremely reasonable. Fishing, shooting, hill walking and golf are activities that can be enjoyed locally and historians will be fascinated by the colossal fortress of Fort George, 1½ miles away and the famous battlefield of Culloden (10 miles) where Bonnie Prince Charlie was defeated in 1746. Comfortable overnight accommodation is available, including two en suite family rooms with a full range of support facilities for young children and babies.

---

## THE *Blue Bell* INN
### Llangurig, Powys SY18 6SG
### Tel: 01686 440254 • Fax: 01686 440337
### info@theblue-bellinn.com
### www.theblue-bellinn.com

**The Blue Bell Inn** is situated on the main A44 road to Aberystwyth, in an area ideal for angling, walking, cycling, birdwatching, clay pigeon shooting, horse riding and golf. The inn serves very good food and the menu extends from a sandwich to a Prime Welsh steak. Look out for Elsie's home-made specials on the blackboard. The menu also includes a good selection of vegetarian dishes. The inn is a free house and serves a wide variety of real ales and lagers. This friendly pub has a very good reputation for food and drink, and visitors always get a warm welcome from Gwlithyn, Jo and all the staff and regular customers.

---

# FHG

## Publisher's Note

While every effort is made to ensure accuracy, we regret that FHG Publications cannot accept responsibility for errors, omissions or misrepresentations in our entries or any consequences thereof. Prices in particular should be checked because we go to press early. We will follow up complaints but cannot act as arbiters or agents for either party.

Recommended Country Inns & Pubs 2005

# Ratings You Can Trust

## ENGLAND

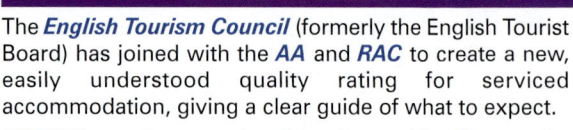

The **English Tourism Council** (formerly the English Tourist Board) has joined with the **AA** and **RAC** to create a new, easily understood quality rating for serviced accommodation, giving a clear guide of what to expect.

**HOTELS** are given a rating from One to Five **Stars** – the more Stars, the higher the quality and the greater the range of facilities and level of services provided.

**GUEST ACCOMMODATION**, which includes guest houses, bed and breakfasts, inns and farmhouses, is rated from One to Five **Diamonds**. Progressively higher levels of quality and customer care must be provided for each one of the One to Five Diamond ratings.

**HOLIDAY PARKS, TOURING PARKS and CAMPING PARKS** are now also assessed using **Stars**. Standards of quality range from a One Star (acceptable) to a Five Star (exceptional) park.

Look out also for the new **SELF-CATERING** Star ratings. The more **Stars** (from One to Five) awarded to an establishment, the higher the levels of quality you can expect. Establishments at higher rating levels also have to meet some additional requirements for facilities.

NB Some self-catering properties had not been assessed at the time of going to press and in these cases the old-style **KEY** symbols will still be shown.

## SCOTLAND

**Star Quality Grades** will reflect the most important aspects of a visit, such as the warmth of welcome, efficiency and friendliness of service, the quality of the food and the cleanliness and condition of the furnishings, fittings and decor.

### THE MORE STARS, THE HIGHER THE STANDARDS.

The description, such as Hotel, Guest House, Bed and Breakfast, Lodge, Holiday Park, Self-catering etc tells you the type of property and style of operation.

## WALES

Places which score highly will have an especially welcoming atmosphere and pleasing ambience, high levels of comfort and guest care, and attractive surroundings enhanced by thoughtful design and attention to detail

### STAR QUALITY GUIDE FOR

**HOTELS, GUEST HOUSES AND FARMHOUSES**
**SELF-CATERING ACCOMMODATION**
(Cottages, Apartments, Houses)
**CARAVAN HOLIDAY HOME PARKS**
(Holiday Parks, Touring Parks, Camping Parks)

| | |
|---|---|
| ★★★★★ | Exceptional quality |
| ★★★★ | Excellent quality |
| ★★★ | Very good quality |
| ★★ | Good quality |
| ★ | Fair to good quality |

In England, Scotland and Wales, all graded properties are inspected annually by Tourist Authority trained Assessors.

Recommended

# Country Inns & Pubs of Britain 2005

Accommodation, Food & Traditional Good Cheer, with details of Pet Friendly and Family Friendly Pubs

Editorial Consultant: Peter Stanley Williams

**For Contents see Page 3**
**For Index of towns/counties see pages 173-174**

FHG Publications
Paisley

Part of IPC Country & Leisure Media Ltd

## Other FHG Publications

*Recommended Country Hotels of Britain*
*Recommended Short Break Holidays in Britain*
*Pets Welcome!*
*The Golf Guide: Where to Play/Where to Stay*
*Farm Holiday Guide to Coast & Country Holidays in England/Scotland/Wales/Ireland*
*Self-Catering Holidays in Britain*
*Britain's Best Holidays*
*Guide to Caravan and Camping Holidays*
*Bed and Breakfast Stops*
*Children Welcome! Family Holiday and Days Out Guide*


ISBN 185055 363 7
© IPC Media Ltd 2005

**Cover photograph**:
The White Horse Inn at Shere, Surrey, supplied by Andy Williams, Photo Library
**Cover design**: Focus Network

No part of this publication may be reproduced by any means or transmitted without the permission of the Publishers.

Maps: ©MAPS IN MINUTES™. ©Crown Copyright, Ordanance Survey 2004.
Typeset by FHG Publications Ltd. Paisley.
Printed and bound in Great Britain by BemroseBooth Ltd, Derby

Distribution. Book Trade: ORCA Book Services, Stanley House,
3 Fleets Lane, Poole, Dorset BH15 3AJ
(Tel: 01202 665432; Fax: 01202 666219)
e-mail: mail@orcabookservices.co.uk
News Trade: Market Force (UK) Ltd, 5th Floor Low Rise, King's Reach Tower,
Stamford Street, London SE1 9LS
Tel: 0207 633 3450; Fax: 0207 633 3572

Published by FHG Publications Ltd,
Abbey Mill Business Centre, Seedhill, Paisley PA1 1TJ
Tel: 0141-887 0428; Fax: 0141-889 7204
e-mail: fhg@ipcmedia.com

US ISBN 1-58843-498 2
Distributed in the United States by
Hunter Publishing Inc., 130 Campus Drive, Edison, N.J. 08818, USA

*Recommended Country Inns & Pubs of Britain* is an FHG publication,
published by IPC Country & Leisure Media Ltd,
part of IPC Media Group of Companies.

# THE FHG DIPLOMA

## HELP IMPROVE BRITISH TOURIST STANDARDS

You are choosing holiday accommodation from our very popular FHG Publications. Whether it be a hotel, guest house, farmhouse or self-catering accommodation, we think you will find it hospitable, comfortable and clean, and your host and hostess friendly and helpful.

Why not write and tell us about it?

As a recognition of the generally well-run and excellent holiday accommodation reviewed in our publications, we at FHG Publications Ltd. present a diploma to proprietors who receive the highest recommendation from their guests who are also readers of our Guides. If you care to write to us praising the holiday you have booked through FHG Publications Ltd. – whether this be board, self-catering accommodation, a sporting or a caravan holiday, what you say will be evaluated and the proprietors who reach our final list will be contacted.

The winning proprietor will receive an attractive framed diploma to display on his premises as recognition of a high standard of comfort, amenity and hospitality. FHG Publications Ltd. offer this diploma as a contribution towards the improvement of standards in tourist accommodation in Britain. Help your excellent host or hostess to win it!

---

## FHG DIPLOMA

We nominate


Because




Name  ............................................................................................................................

Address............................................................................................................................

............................................................................................................................

Telephone No.............................................

# Recommended
# Wayside & Country Inns
## OF BRITAIN 2005

## PUBLISHER'S FOREWORD

Since Roman times, there have been inns and taverns to provide travellers with a meal and some shelter for the night, more often than not in very basic rooms, often shared with strangers.

Today, the weary traveller is more likely to find country pubs with well-stocked bars, and excellent, if not always luxurious accommodation, with clean and comfortable bedrooms and probably en suite bathrooms too.

Recommended Country Inns and Pubs 2005 offers a fine selection of such hostelries, each with its own special atmosphere. Good quality food will be on offer, and there is often a restaurant for evening meals. There may even be some form of entertainment, and the chance to exchange a few pleasantries with the locals.

Children are welcome in some establishments, and you may find special facilities for them such as family rooms, smaller portions, play areas and even outdoor playgrounds. More details can be found in our FAMILY FRIENDLY PUBS SUPPLEMENT starting on page 163. The separate PET-FRIENDLY PUBS SUPPLEMENT starts on page 149, and we hope this will prove useful.

Our READERSí OFFER VOUCHERS on pages 21- 40 should help you plan your outings, should you decide to stay and explore the area.

Our selection of pubs, inns and small hotels is 'recommended" on the basis of reputation, written descriptions, facilities and long association rather than through personal inspection. We cannot accept responsibility for errors, misrepresentations or the quality of hospitality but we are always interested to hear from readers about their own experiences. Fortunately complaints are few, and rarely serious, but if you do have a problem which cannot be settled on the spot (the best solution, by the way), please let us know. We cannot act as intermediaries or arbiters, but we will record your complaint and follow it up with the establishment.

As far as we can establish, the details for all our entries are accurate as we go to press. We do suggest, however, that you confirm prices and other specific points while you are making enquiries and bookings.

Please mention Recommended Country Inns & Pubs when you make enquiries or bookings. Whether this latest edition is your touring companion, a source of holiday ideas or a handy outings guide, we hope that you will find high quality fare, good value and a warm welcome. We would be happy to receive your recommendations and particulars of any pub or inn which you may judge worthy of inclusion – see page 94 for details.

Anne Cuthbertson
Editor

**FHG READERS' OFFER 2005**

## Leighton Buzzard Railway
Page's Park Station, Billington Road,
Leighton Buzzard, Bedfordshire LU7 4TN
Tel: 01525 373888
e-mail: info@buzzrail.co.uk • website: www.buzzrail.co.uk

One free adult/child with full-fare adult ticket

valid from 20/3/05 – 30/10/05

NOT TO BE USED IN CONJUNCTION WITH ANY OTHER OFFER

---

**FHG READERS' OFFER 2005**

## Bekonscot Model Village
Warwick Road, Beaconsfield, Buckinghamshire HP9 2PL
Tel: 01494 672919 • e-mail: info@bekonscot.co.uk
website: www.bekonscot.com

One child FREE when accompanied by full-paying adult

valid February to October 2005

NOT TO BE USED IN CONJUNCTION WITH ANY OTHER OFFER

---

**FHG READERS' OFFER 2005**

## Geevor Tin Mine
Pendeen, Penzance, Cornwall TR19 7EW
Tel: 01736 788662 • Fax: 01736 786059
e-mail: bookings@geevor.com • website: www.geevor.com

TWO for the price of ONE or £3.25 off a family ticket

valid 02/01/2005 to 20/12/2005

NOT TO BE USED IN CONJUNCTION WITH ANY OTHER OFFER

---

**FHG READERS' OFFER 2005**

## Cars of the Stars Motor Museum
Standish Street, Keswick, Cumbria CA12 5HH
Tel: 017687 73757
e-mail: cotsmm@aol.com • website: www.carsofthestars.com

One child free with two paying adults

Valid 2005

NOT TO BE USED IN CONJUNCTION WITH ANY OTHER OFFER

---

**FHG READERS' OFFER 2005**

## Windermere Steamboats & Museum
Rayrigg Road, Windermere, Cumbria LA23 1BN
Tel: 015394 45565 • e-mail: steamboat@ecosse.net
website: www.steamboat.co.uk

Two for the price of one (adults)

valid March to October 2005

NOT TO BE USED IN CONJUNCTION WITH ANY OTHER OFFER

*A 70-minute journey into the lost world of the English narrow gauge light railway. Features historic steam locomotives from many countries.*

**PETS MUST BE KEPT UNDER CONTROL AND NOT ALLOWED ON TRACKS**

**Open:** Sundays and Bank Holiday weekends 13 March to 30 October. Additional days in summer.

**Directions:** on A4146 towards Hemel Hempstead, close to roundabout junction with A505.

FHG PUBLICATIONS, ABBEY MILL BUSINESS CENTRE, PAISLEY PA1 1TJ

---

*Be a giant in a magical miniature world of make-believe depicting rural England in the 1930s. "A little piece of history that is forever England."*

**Open:** 10am to 5pm daily mid February to end October.

**Directions:** Junction 16 M25, Junction 2 M40.

FHG PUBLICATIONS, ABBEY MILL BUSINESS CENTRE, PAISLEY PA1 1TJ

---

*Geevor is the largest mining history site in the UK in a spectacular setting on Cornwall's Atlantic coast. Guided underground tour, many surface buildings, museum, cafe, gift shop. Free parking.*

**Open:** daily except Saturdays 10am to 5pm

**Directions:** 7 miles from Penzance beside the B3306 Land's End to St Ives coast road

FHG PUBLICATIONS, ABBEY MILL BUSINESS CENTRE, PAISLEY PA1 1TJ

---

*A collection of cars from film and TV, including Chitty Chitty Bang Bang, James Bond's Aston Martin, Del Boy's van, Fab1 and many more.*

**PETS MUST BE KEPT ON LEAD**

**Open:** daily 10am-5pm. Closed February half term. Weekends only in December.

**Directions:** in centre of Keswick close to car park.

FHG PUBLICATIONS, ABBEY MILL BUSINESS CENTRE, PAISLEY PA1 1TJ

---

*World's finest steamboat collection and premier all-weather attraction. Swallows and Amazons exhibition, model boat pond, tea shop, souvenir shop. Free guided tours. Model boat exhibition.*

**Open:** 10am to 5pm 3rd weekend in March to last weekend October.

**Directions:** on A592 half-a-mile north of Bowness-on-Windermere.

FHG PUBLICATIONS, ABBEY MILL BUSINESS CENTRE, PAISLEY PA1 1TJ

## FHG Crich Tramway Village
**READERS' OFFER 2005**

Crich, Matlock, Derbyshire DE4 5DP
Tel: 0870 758 7267 • Fax: 0870 753 4321
e-mail: enquiry@tramway.co.uk • website: www.tramway.co.uk

One child FREE with every full paying adult

valid during 2005

**NOT TO BE USED IN CONJUNCTION WITH ANY OTHER OFFER**

---

## FHG Living Coasts
**READERS' OFFER 2005**

Harbourside, Beacon Quay, Torquay, Devon TQ1 2BG
Tel: 01803 202470 • Fax: 01803 202471
e-mail: info@livingcoasts.org.uk • website: www.livingcoasts.org.uk

40p OFF standard ticket price for each person

valid during 2005

**NOT TO BE USED IN CONJUNCTION WITH ANY OTHER OFFER**

---

## FHG The Big Sheep
**READERS' OFFER 2005**

Abbotsham, Bideford, Devon EX39 5AP
Tel: 01237 472366
e-mail: info@thebigsheep.co.uk • website: www.thebigsheep.co.uk

Admit one child FREE with each paying adult

valid during 2005

**NOT TO BE USED IN CONJUNCTION WITH ANY OTHER OFFER**

---

## FHG Coldharbour Mill Museum
**READERS' OFFER 2005**

Coldharbour Mill, Uffculme, Cullompton, Devon EX15 3EE
Tel: 01884 840960 • e-mail: info@coldharbourmill.org.uk
website: www.coldharbourmill.org.uk

TWO adult tickets for the price of ONE

valid during 2005

**NOT TO BE USED IN CONJUNCTION WITH ANY OTHER OFFER**

---

## FHG Killhope Lead Mining Museum
**READERS' OFFER 2005**

Cowshill, Upper Weardale, Co. Durham DL13 1AR
Tel: 01388 537505
e-mail: killhope@durham.gov.uk • website: www.durham.gov.uk/killhope

One child FREE with full-paying adult (not valid for Park Level Mine)

valid April to October 2005

**NOT TO BE USED IN CONJUNCTION WITH ANY OTHER OFFER**

A superb family day out in the atmosphere of a bygone era. Explore the recreated period street and fascinating exhibitions. Unlimited tram rides are free with entry. Play areas, shops, tea rooms, pub, restaurant and lots more.

**Open:** daily April to October 10 am to 5.30pm, weekends in winter.

**Directions:** eight miles from M1 Junction 28, follow brown and white signs for "Tramway Museum".

FHG PUBLICATIONS, ABBEY MILL BUSINESS CENTRE, PAISLEY PA1 1TJ

---

Features a range of fascinating coastal creatures from penguins to fur seals, puffins to sea ducks. Reconstructed beaches, cliff faces and an estuary. A huge meshed aviary allows birds to fly free over your head, while special tunnels give stunning crystal-clear views of the birds and seals underwater.

**Open:** all year from 10am to 6pm (summer) or dusk (winter)

**Directions:** follow brown tourist signs from Torquay. Situated right on the harbour front.

FHG PUBLICATIONS, ABBEY MILL BUSINESS CENTRE, PAISLEY PA1 1TJ

---

"England for Excellence" award-winning family entertainment park. Highlights: hilarious shows including the famous sheep-racing and the duck trials; the awesome Ewetopia indoor adventure playground for adults and children; brewery; mountain boarding; great local food.

**Open:** daily, 10am to 6pm April - Oct Phone for Winter opening times and details.

**Directions:** on A39 North Devon link road, two miles west of Bideford Bridge.

FHG PUBLICATIONS, ABBEY MILL BUSINESS CENTRE, PAISLEY PA1 1TJ

---

A picturesque 200-year old woollen mill with machinery that spins yarn and weaves cloth. Mill machinery, restaurant, exhibition gallery, shop and gardens in a waterside setting.

**Open:** Museum open March to October daily 10.30am to 5pm. Mill Shop and restaurant open all year round.

**Directions:** Two miles from Junction 27 M5; follow signs to Willand (B3181) then brown tourist signs to Working Woollen Mill.

FHG PUBLICATIONS, ABBEY MILL BUSINESS CENTRE, PAISLEY PA1 1TJ

---

Voted 'Most Family-Friendly Museum 2004', Killhope is Britain's best preserved lead mining site, with lots to see and do. Underground Experience is something not to be missed.

**Open:** March 19th to October 31st 10.30am to 5pm daily.

**Directions:** alongside A689, midway between Stanhope and Alston in the heart of the North Pennines.

FHG PUBLICATIONS, ABBEY MILL BUSINESS CENTRE, PAISLEY PA1 1TJ

**FHG READERS' OFFER 2005**

# BARLEYLANDS FARM
Barleylands Road, Billericay, Essex CM11 2UD
Tel: 01268 290229 • e-mail: info@barleylands.co.uk
website: www.barleylands.co.uk

FREE adult ticket when accompanied by one child

Valid 1st March to 31st October. Not special event days

NOT TO BE USED IN CONJUNCTION WITH ANY OTHER OFFER

---

**FHG READERS' OFFER 2005**

# Noah's Ark Zoo Farm
Failand Road, Wraxall, Bristol BS48 1PG
Tel: 01275 852606 • Fax: 01275 857080
website: www.noahsarkzoofarm.co.uk

one FREE child for each group of 4 or more persons

valid until October 2005 (closed in winter)

NOT TO BE USED IN CONJUNCTION WITH ANY OTHER OFFER

---

**FHG READERS' OFFER 2005**

# NATIONAL WATERWAYS MUSEUM
Llanthony Warehouse, Gloucester Docks, Gloucester GL1 2EH
Tel: 01452 318200 • website: www.nwm.org.uk
e-mail: bookingsnwm@thewaterwaystrust.org

20% off museum admission (excludes combination tickets)

valid during 2005

NOT TO BE USED IN CONJUNCTION WITH ANY OTHER OFFER

---

**FHG READERS' OFFER 2005**

# Cider Museum & King Offa Distillery
21 Ryelands Street, Hereford HR4 0LW
Tel: 01432 354207 • Fax: 01432 371641
e-mail: info@cidermuseum.co.uk • www.cidermuseum.co.uk

50p reduction on entry fee

valid during 2005

NOT TO BE USED IN CONJUNCTION WITH ANY OTHER OFFER

---

**FHG READERS' OFFER 2005**

# Verulamium Museum
St Michael's, St Albans, Herts AL3 4SW
Tel: 01727 751810 • e-mail: museum@stalbans.gov.uk
web: www.stalbansmuseums.org.uk

"Two for One"

valid until 31/12/05

NOT TO BE USED IN CONJUNCTION WITH ANY OTHER OFFER

| | |
|---|---|
| Craft Village with animals, museum, blacksmith, glassblowing, miniature railway (Sundays and August), craft shops, tea room and licensed restaurant.<br>**DOGS MUST BE KEPT ON LEAD** | **Open:** Craft Village open all year. Farm open 1st March to 31st October.<br>**Directions:** M25, A127 towards Southend. Take A176 junction off A127, 3rd exit Wash Road, 2nd left Barleylands Road. |

FHG PUBLICATIONS, ABBEY MILL BUSINESS CENTRE, PAISLEY PA1 1TJ

| | |
|---|---|
| Fantastic 'hands-on' adventure zoo farm for all ages and all weathers. 60 different species from chicks and lambs to camels and bison. New indoor and outdoor mazes (longest in world and educational). Family-friendly Cafe & Shop. | **Open:** from February half-term to end October 10.30am to 5pm Monday to Saturday (closed Mon + Sun in term time)<br>**Directions:** on B3128 between Bristol and Clevedon or Exit 19 or 20 from M5 |

FHG PUBLICATIONS, ABBEY MILL BUSINESS CENTRE, PAISLEY PA1 1TJ

| | |
|---|---|
| On three floors of a Listed Victorian warehouse telling 200 years of inland waterway history. • Historic boats • Boat trips available (Easter to October)<br>• Painted boat gallery • Blacksmith<br>• Archive film • Hands-on displays<br>"A great day out" | **Open:** every day 10am to 5pm (excluding Christmas Day). Last admissions 4pm<br>**Directions:** Junction 11A or 12 off M5 – follow brown signs for Historic Docks. Railway and bus station - 15 minute walk. Free coach parking. |

FHG PUBLICATIONS, ABBEY MILL BUSINESS CENTRE, PAISLEY PA1 1TJ

| | |
|---|---|
| Discover the fascinating history of cider making. There is a programme of temporary exhibitions and events plus free samples of Hereford cider brandy. | **Open:** April to Oct 10am to 5.30pm (daily) Nov to Dec 11am to 3pm (daily) Jan to Mar 11am to 3pm (Tues to Sun)<br>**Directions:** situated west of Hereford off the A438 Hereford to Brecon road. |

FHG PUBLICATIONS, ABBEY MILL BUSINESS CENTRE, PAISLEY PA1 1TJ

| | |
|---|---|
| The museum of everyday life in Roman Britain. An award-winning museum with re-created Roman rooms, hands-on discovery areas, and some of the best mosaics outside the Mediterranean. | **Open:** Monday to Saturday 10am-5.30pm Sunday 2pm-5.30pm.<br>**Directions:** St Albans. |

FHG PUBLICATIONS, ABBEY MILL BUSINESS CENTRE, PAISLEY PA1 1TJ

**FHG READERS' OFFER 2005**

## Chislehurst Caves
Old Hill, Chislehurst, Kent BR7 5NB
Tel: 020 8467 3264 • Fax: 020 8295 0407
e-mail: info@chislehurstcaves.co.uk • website: www.chislehurstcaves.co.uk

one FREE entry with one full-paying adult

valid until 31st December 2005

NOT TO BE USED IN CONJUNCTION WITH ANY OTHER OFFER

---

**FHG READERS' OFFER 2005**

## Docker Park Farm
Arkholme, Carnforth, Lancashire LA6 1AR
Tel & Fax: 015242 21331
e-mail: info@dockerparkfarm.co.uk • website: www.dockerparkfarm.co.uk

One FREE child per one paying adult (one voucher per child)

valid from January to December 2005

NOT TO BE USED IN CONJUNCTION WITH ANY OTHER OFFER

---

**FHG READERS' OFFER 2005**

## Snibston Discovery Park
Ashby Road, Coalville, Leicestershire LE67 3LN
Tel: 01530 278444 • Fax: 01530 813301
e-mail: snibston@leics.gov.uk • website: www.leics.gov.uk/museums

One FREE child with every full paying adult

valid until June 2005

NOT TO BE USED IN CONJUNCTION WITH ANY OTHER OFFER

---

**FHG READERS' OFFER 2005**

## Skegness Natureland Seal Sanctuary
North Parade, Skegness, Lincolnshire PE25 1DB
Tel: 01754 764345
e-mail: natureland@fsbdial.co.uk • website: www.skegnessnatureland.co.uk

Free entry for one child when accompanied by full-paying adult.

Valid during 2005

NOT TO BE USED IN CONJUNCTION WITH ANY OTHER OFFER

---

**FHG READERS' OFFER 2005**

## PLEASURELAND
Marine Drive, Southport, Merseyside PR8 1RX
Tel: 08702 200204 • Fax: 01704 537936
e-mail: mail@pleasurelandltd.freeserve.co.uk • website: www.pleasureland.uk.com

3 for 2 – if two all day wristbands purchased, third provided FREE
offer not valid on Bank Holiday Weekends

valid from March to November 2005

NOT TO BE USED IN CONJUNCTION WITH ANY OTHER OFFER

Miles of mystery and history beneath your feet! Grab a lantern and get ready for an amazing underground adventure. Your whole family can travel back in time as you explore this labyrinth of dark mysterious passageways. See the caves church, Druid altar and more. Under 16s must be accompanied by an adult.

**Open:** Wednesday to Sunday from 10am. Last tour 4pm. Open daily during local school holidays.

**Directions:** take A222 between A20 and A21; at Chislehurst railway bridge turn into station approach; turn right at end, then right again.

FHG PUBLICATIONS, ABBEY MILL BUSINESS CENTRE, PAISLEY PA1 1TJ

---

We are a working farm, with lots of animals to see and touch. Enjoy a walk round the Nature Trail or refreshments in the tearoom. Lots of activities during school holidays.

**Open:** Summer: daily 10.30am to 5pm
Winter: weekends only 10.30am to 4pm.

**Directions:** Junction 35 off M6, take B6254 towards Kirkby Lonsdale, then follow the brown signs.

FHG PUBLICATIONS, ABBEY MILL BUSINESS CENTRE, PAISLEY PA1 1TJ

---

Located in 100 acres of landscaped grounds, Snibston is a unique mixture, with historic mine buildings, outdoor science play areas, wildlife habitats and an exhibition hall housing five hands-on galleries. Cafe and gift shop.
Plus new Toy Box gallery for under 5s & 8s.

**Open:** seven days a week 10am to 5pm.

**Directions:** Junction 22 from M1, Junction 13 from M42. Follow brown Heritage signs.

FHG PUBLICATIONS, ABBEY MILL BUSINESS CENTRE, PAISLEY PA1 1TJ

---

Well known for rescuing and rehabilitating orphaned and injured seal pups found washed ashore on Lincolnshire beaches. Also: penguins, aquarium, pets' corner, reptiles, Floral Palace (tropical birds and butterflies etc).

**Open:** daily from 10am. Closed Christmas/Boxing/New Year's Days.

**Directions:** at the north end of Skegness seafront.

FHG PUBLICATIONS, ABBEY MILL BUSINESS CENTRE, PAISLEY PA1 1TJ

---

Over 100 rides and attractions, including the Traumatizer suspended looping coaster and the Lucozade Space Shot.
New for 2004 -
Lost Dinosaurs of the Sahara

**Open:** March to November, times vary.

**Directions:** from North: M6 (Junction 31), A59, A565
from South: M6 (Junction 26), M58 (Junction 3), A570

FHG PUBLICATIONS, ABBEY MILL BUSINESS CENTRE, PAISLEY PA1 1TJ

## FHG READERS' OFFER 2005

**DINOSAUR ADVENTURE PARK**
Weston Park, Lenwade, Norwich, Norfolk NR9 5JW
Tel: 01603 876310 • Fax: 01603 876315
e-mail: info@dinosaurpark.co.uk • website: www.dinosaurpark.co.uk

50p off standard admission prices for up to six people

*valid until end of October 2005*

**NOT TO BE USED IN CONJUNCTION WITH ANY OTHER OFFER OR GROUP PRICES**

---

## FHG READERS' OFFER 2005

**The White Post Farm Centre**
Farnsfield, Nottingham, Notts NG22 8HL
Tel: 01623 882977 • e-mail: tim@whitepostfarmcentre.co.uk
Fax: 01623 883499 • website: www.whitepostfarmcentre.co.uk

10% off entry to the farm with voucher

*valid during 2005*

**NOT TO BE USED IN CONJUNCTION WITH ANY OTHER OFFER**

---

## FHG READERS' OFFER 2005

**Galleries of Justice**
Shire Hall, High Pavement, Lace Market, Nottingham NG1 1HN
Tel: 0115 9520555 • e-mail: info@galleriesofjustice.org.uk
Fax: 0115 9939828 • website: www.galleries of justice.org.uk

TWO for ONE with full paying adult one free visit per voucher

*Valid from Jan to Dec 2005, not Bank Holidays*

**NOT TO BE USED IN CONJUNCTION WITH ANY OTHER OFFER**

---

## FHG READERS' OFFER 2005

**Didcot Railway Centre**
Didcot, Oxfordshire OX11 7NJ
Tel: 01235 817200 • Fax: 01235 510621
e-mail: didrlyc@globalnet.co.uk • website: www.didcotrailwaycentre.org.uk

one child FREE when accompanied by full-paying adult

*valid until end 2005 except during Day Out With Thomas events*

**NOT TO BE USED IN CONJUNCTION WITH ANY OTHER OFFER**

---

## FHG READERS' OFFER 2005

**The Helicopter Museum**
The Heliport, Locking Moor Road, Weston-Super-Mare BS24 8PP
Tel: 01934 635227 • Fax: 01934 645230
e-mail: office@helimuseum.fsnet.co.uk • website: www.helicoptermuseum.co.uk

One child FREE with two full-paying adults

*valid from April to October 2005*

**NOT TO BE USED IN CONJUNCTION WITH ANY OTHER OFFER**

| | |
|---|---|
| *It's time you came-n-saurus for a monster day out of discovery, adventure and fun. Enjoy the adventure play areas, dinosaur trail, secret animal garden and lots more.* | **Open:** Please call for specific opening times or see our website.<br><br>**Directions:** 9 miles from Norwich, follow the brown signs to Weston Park from the A47 or A1067 |

FHG PUBLICATIONS, ABBEY MILL BUSINESS CENTRE, PAISLEY PA1 1TJ

| | |
|---|---|
| *A modern working farm with displays indoors and outdoors designed to help visitors listen, feel and learn whilst having fun. Daily baby animal holding sessions plus a large indoor play barn.* | **Open:** daily from 10am<br><br>**Directions:** 12 miles from Nottingham on A614 or follow Robin Hood signs from J27 of M1. |

FHG PUBLICATIONS, ABBEY MILL BUSINESS CENTRE, PAISLEY PA1 1TJ

| | |
|---|---|
| *Journey with us through 300 years of Crime and Punishment on this unique atmospheric site. Witness a real trial in the authentic Victorian courtroom. Prisoners and gaolers act as guides as you become part of history.* | **Open:** Tuesday to Sunday 10am to 5pm peak season 10am to 4pm off-peak.<br><br>**Directions:** from Nottingham city centre follow the brown tourist signs. |

FHG PUBLICATIONS, ABBEY MILL BUSINESS CENTRE, PAISLEY PA1 1TJ

| | |
|---|---|
| *See the steam trains from the golden age of the Great Western Railway. Steam locomotives in the original engine shed, a reconstructed country branch line, and a re-creation of Brunel's original broad gauge railway. On Steam Days there are rides in the 1930s carriages.* | **Open:** Sat/Sun all year; daily 30 Apr to 25 Sept. 10am - 5pm weekends and Steam Days, 10am - 4pm other days and in winter.<br><br>**Directions:** at Didcot Parkway rail station; on A4130, signposted from M4 (Junction 13) and A34 |

FHG PUBLICATIONS, ABBEY MILL BUSINESS CENTRE, PAISLEY PA1 1TJ

| | |
|---|---|
| *The world's largest helicopter collection - over 70 exhibits, includes two royal helicopters, Russian Gunship and Vietnam veterans plus many award-winning exhibits. Cafe, shop. Flights.*<br><br>PETS MUST BE KEPT UNDER CONTROL | **Open:** Wednesday to Sunday 10am to 5.30pm. Daily during school Easter and Summer holidays and Bank Holiday Mondays. (10am to 4.30pm November to March)<br><br>**Directions:** Junction 21 off M5 then follow the propellor signs. |

FHG PUBLICATIONS, ABBEY MILL BUSINESS CENTRE, PAISLEY PA1 1TJ

**FHG READERS' OFFER 2005**

# Easton Farm Park
Easton, Woodbridge, Suffolk IP13 0EQ
Tel: 01728 746475 • e-mail: easton@eastonfarmpark.co.uk
website: www.eastonfarmpark.co.uk

£1 per person OFF for up to 4 full paying admissions

*Valid until end 2005*

NOT TO BE USED IN CONJUNCTION WITH ANY OTHER OFFER

---

**FHG READERS' OFFER 2005**

# PARADISE PARK & GARDENS
Avis Road, Newhaven, East Sussex BN9 0DH
Tel: 01273 512123 • Fax: 01273 616000
e-mail: enquiries@paradisepark.co.uk • website: www.paradisepark.co.uk

Admit one FREE adult or child with one adult paying full entrance price

*valid during 2005*

NOT TO BE USED IN CONJUNCTION WITH ANY OTHER OFFER

---

**FHG READERS' OFFER 2005**

# Buckleys Yesterday's World
High Street, Battle, East Sussex TN33 0AQ
Tel: 01424 775378 • e-mail: info@yesterdaysworld.co.uk
website: www.yesterdaysworld.co.uk

50p OFF each admission

*Valid until end 2005*

NOT TO BE USED IN CONJUNCTION WITH ANY OTHER OFFER

---

**FHG READERS' OFFER 2005**

# The New Metroland
39 Garden Walk, Metrocentre, Gateshead NE11 9XY
Tel: 0191 4932048 • e-mail: enquiries@metroland.uk.com
Fax: 0191 4932904 • website: www.metroland.uk.com

buy one all-day GOLD PASS and get one for £1.50

*valid until 31/12/05 except Bank Holiday Weekends*

NOT TO BE USED IN CONJUNCTION WITH ANY OTHER OFFER

---

**FHG READERS' OFFER 2005**

# Wildfowl & Wetlands Trust
Pattinson, Washington, Tyne & Wear NE38 8LE
Tel: 0191 416 5454
e-mail: val.pickering@wwt.org.uk • website: www.wwt.org.uk

One FREE admission with full-paying adult

*valid from 1st Jan 2005 to 30th Sept 2005*

NOT TO BE USED IN CONJUNCTION WITH ANY OTHER OFFER

Come and meet the farm animals. Pony rides, pat-a-pet, indoor and outdoor play areas, woodland and river walks. Gift shop, tearoom. Monthly farmers' market.

**DOGS MUST BE KEPT ON LEADS**

**Open:** March to September 10.30am to 6pm

**Directions:** follow brown tourist signs off A12 and other roads

FHG PUBLICATIONS, ABBEY MILL BUSINESS CENTRE, PAISLEY PA1 1TJ

---

Discover 'Planet Earth' for an unforgettable experience. A unique Museum of Life, Dinosaur Safari, beautiful Water Gardens with fish and wildfowl, planthouses, themed gardens, Heritage Trail, miniature railway. Playzone includes crazy golf and adventure play area. Garden Centre and Terrace Cafe.

**Open:** open daily, except Christmas Day and Boxing Day.

**Directions:** signposted off A26 and A259.

FHG PUBLICATIONS, ABBEY MILL BUSINESS CENTRE, PAISLEY PA1 1TJ

---

The past is brought to life at one of the best loved family attractions in the South East. Step back in time and wander through over 30 shop and room settings.

**PETS NOT ALLOWED IN CHILDREN'S PLAY AREA**

**Open:** 9.30am to 6pm (last admission 4.45pm, one hour earlier in winter).

**Directions:** just off A21 in Battle High Street opposite the Abbey.

FHG PUBLICATIONS, ABBEY MILL BUSINESS CENTRE, PAISLEY PA1 1TJ

---

Europe's largest indoor family funfair, with exciting rides such as the New Rollercoaster, Disco Dodgems and Swashbuckling Pirate Ship. There's something for everyone whatever the weather!

**Open:** daily except Christmas Day and New Year's Day.
Mon-Sat 10am to 8pm,
Sun 11am to 6pm
(open from 12 noon Monday to Friday during term time).

**Directions:** signposted from the A1.

FHG PUBLICATIONS, ABBEY MILL BUSINESS CENTRE, PAISLEY PA1 1TJ

---

100 acres of parkland, home to hundreds of duck, geese, swans and flamingos. Discovery centre, cafe, gift shop; play area.

**Open:** every day except Christmas Day

**Directions:** signposted from A19, A195, A1231 and A182.

FHG PUBLICATIONS, ABBEY MILL BUSINESS CENTRE, PAISLEY PA1 1TJ

## FHG READERS' OFFER 2005

# The Deep
Hull, HU1 4DP
Tel: 01482 381000 • Fax: 01482 381018
e-mail: info@thedeep.co.uk • website: www.thedeep.co.uk

One FREE child for each two full paying adults

valid until Dec 2005

**NOT TO BE USED IN CONJUNCTION WITH ANY OTHER OFFER**

---

## FHG READERS' OFFER 2005

# Yorkshire Dales Falconry & Wildlife Conservation Centre
Crow's Nest, Near Giggleswick, Settle, N. Yorks LA2 8AS
Tel: 01729 822832 • Fax: 01729 825160
e-mail: info@falconryandwildlife.com • www.falconryandwildlife.com

one child FREE with 2 full-paying adults

valid until end 2005

**NOT TO BE USED IN CONJUNCTION WITH ANY OTHER OFFER**

---

## FHG READERS' OFFER 2005

# World of James Herriot
23 Kirkgate, Thirsk, North Yorkshire YO7 1PL
Tel: 01845 524234 • Fax: 01845 525333
website: www.worldofjamesherriot.org

admit TWO for the price of ONE (one voucher per transaction only)

valid until October 2005

**NOT TO BE USED IN CONJUNCTION WITH ANY OTHER OFFER**

---

## FHG READERS' OFFER 2005

# MAGNA SCIENCE ADVENTURE CENTRE
Sheffield Road, Templeborough, Rotherham S60 1DX
Tel: 01709 720002 • Fax: 01709 820092
e-mail: info@magnatrust.co.uk • website: www.visitmagna.co.uk

one FREE adult or child ticket with each full-paying adult/child
not valid with family tickets

valid until 31st Dec 2005

**NOT TO BE USED IN CONJUNCTION WITH ANY OTHER OFFER**

---

## FHG READERS' OFFER 2005

# The Colour Museum
Perkin House, PO Box 244, Providence Street, Bradford BD1 2PW
Tel: 01274 390955 • Fax: 01274 392888
e-mail: museum@sdc.org.uk • website: www.sdc.org.uk

TWO for ONE

valid during 2005

**NOT TO BE USED IN CONJUNCTION WITH ANY OTHER OFFER**

*The Deep is the world's only submarium. Discover the story of the world's oceans on a dramatic journey from the beginning of time and into the future. Explore the wonders of the oceans, from the tropical lagoon to the icy waters of Antarctica, including 40 sharks and over 3000 other fish.*

**Open:** daily 10am to 6pm
(last entry at 5pm).
Closed Christmas Eve and Christmas Day
**Directions:** from the North take A1/M, M62/A63. From the South take A1/M, A15/A63 follow signs to Hull city centre, then local signs to The Deep.

FHG PUBLICATIONS, ABBEY MILL BUSINESS CENTRE, PAISLEY PA1 1TJ

---

*All types of birds of prey exhibited here, from owls and kestrels to eagles and vultures. Special flying displays 12 noon, 1.30pm and 3pm. Bird handling courses arranged for either half or full days.*

**Open:** 10am to 4.30pm summer
10am to 4pm winter

**Directions:** on main A65 trunk road outside Settle.
Follow brown direction signs.

FHG PUBLICATIONS, ABBEY MILL BUSINESS CENTRE, PAISLEY PA1 1TJ

---

*Visit James Herriot's original house recreated as it was in the 1940s. Television sets used in the series 'All Creatures Great and Small'. A new children's interactive gallery with life-size model farm animals and three rooms dedicated to the history of veterinary medicine.*

**Open:** daily.
April to October 10am-6pm
November to March 11am to 4pm
**Directions:** follow signs off A1 or A19 to Thirsk, then A168,
off Thirsk market place

FHG PUBLICATIONS, ABBEY MILL BUSINESS CENTRE, PAISLEY PA1 1TJ

---

*The UK's first Science Adventure Centre. Explore the elements - Earth, Air, Fire and Water - and have fun firing a giant water cannon, launching rockets, exploding rock faces and working real JCBs. Two spectacular shows - The Big Melt and The Face of Steel; also new Sci Tek Playground.*

**Open:** daily 10am to 5pm
(closed 24th-26th Dec and 1st Jan)

**Directions:** from M1 take Junction 33 (from south) or Junction 34 (from north), and follow signs. One mile from Meadowhall Shopping Centre

FHG PUBLICATIONS, ABBEY MILL BUSINESS CENTRE, PAISLEY PA1 1TJ

---

*The Colour Museum is unique. Dedicated to the history, development and technology of colour, it is the ONLY museum of its kind in Europe. A truly colourful experience for both kids and adults, it's fun, it's informative and it's well worth a visit.*

**Open:** Tuesday to Saturday
10am to 4pm
(last admission 3.30pm).
**Directions:** just off Westgate on B6144 from the city centre to Haworth.

FHG PUBLICATIONS, ABBEY MILL BUSINESS CENTRE, PAISLEY PA1 1TJ

**FHG READERS' OFFER 2005**

## Inveraray Jail
Church Square, Inveraray, Argyll PA32 8TX
Tel: 01499 302381 • Fax: 01499 302195
e-mail: inverarayjail@btclick.com • website: www.inverarayjail.co.uk

one child FREE with one full-paying adult

valid until end 2005

**NOT TO BE USED IN CONJUNCTION WITH ANY OTHER OFFER**

---

**FHG READERS' OFFER 2005**

## Kelburn Castle & Country Centre
Fairlie, Near Largs, Ayrshire KA29 0BE
Tel: 01475 568685 • e-mail: admin@kelburncountrycentre.com
website: www.kelburncountrycentre.com

One child FREE for each full paying adult

Valid until October 2005

**NOT TO BE USED IN CONJUNCTION WITH ANY OTHER OFFER**

---

**FHG READERS' OFFER 2005**

## Scottish Seabird Centre
The Harbour, North Berwick, East Lothian EH39 4SS
Tel: 01620 890202 • Fax: 01620 890222
e-mail: info@seabird.org • website: www.seabird.org

any TWO admissions for the price of ONE

valid until 1st October 2005

**NOT TO BE USED IN CONJUNCTION WITH ANY OTHER OFFER**

---

**FHG READERS' OFFER 2005**

## Edinburgh Butterfly & Insect World
Dobbies Garden World, Melville Nursery, Lasswade EH18 1AZ
Tel: 0131-663 4932 • Fax: 0131 654 2774
info@edinburgh-butterfly-world.co.uk • www.edinburgh-butterfly-world.co.uk

one child FREE with each full-paying adult

valid from 1st Jan 2005 to 30th April 2005

**NOT TO BE USED IN CONJUNCTION WITH ANY OTHER OFFER**

---

**FHG READERS' OFFER 2005**

## The Scottish Mining Museum
Lady Victoria Colliery, Newtongrange, Midlothian EH22 4QN
Tel: 0131-663 7519 • Fax: 0131-654 0952
visitorservices@scottishminingmuseum.com • www.scottishminingmuseum.com

one child FREE with full-paying adult

valid January to December 2005

**NOT TO BE USED IN CONJUNCTION WITH ANY OTHER OFFER**

19th century prison with fully restored 1820 courtroom and two prisons. Guides in uniform as warders, prisoners and matron. Remember your camera!

**Open:** April to October 9.30am - 6pm (last admission 5pm)
November to March 10am - 5pm (last admission 4pm)

**Directions:** A83 to Campbeltown

**FHG PUBLICATIONS, ABBEY MILL BUSINESS CENTRE, PAISLEY PA1 1TJ**

---

The historic home of the Earls of Glasgow. Waterfalls, gardens, famous Glen, unusual trees. Riding school, stockade, play areas, exhibitions, shop, cafe and The Secret Forest. Falconry Centre.
**PETS MUST BE KEPT ON LEAD**

**Open:** daily 10am to 6pm Easter to October.

**Directions:** on A78 between Largs and Fairlie, 45 minutes' drive from Glasgow.

**FHG PUBLICATIONS, ABBEY MILL BUSINESS CENTRE, PAISLEY PA1 1TJ**

---

Get close to Nature with a visit to this stunning award-winning Centre. With panoramic views across the islands of the Firth of Forth and the sandy beaches of North Berwick, the area is a haven for wildlife. Live 'Big Brother' cameras zoom in really close to see a variety of wildlife including gannets, puffins, seals and sometimes even dolphins. Wildlife boat safaris and passenger ferry to Fife in summer.

**Open:** daily from 10am

**Directions:** from A1 take road for North Berwick; near the harbour; Centre signposted.

**FHG PUBLICATIONS, ABBEY MILL BUSINESS CENTRE, PAISLEY PA1 1TJ**

---

It's Creeping, It's Crawling, It's a Jungle in there!
Free-flying exotic butterflies, roaming iguanas, giant pythons, 'glow in the dark' scorpions, and 'Bugs and Beasties' handling and phobia-curing sessions. Incredible leaf-cutting ants.

**Open:** summer 9.30am to 5.30pm winter 10am to 5pm

**Directions:** just off Edinburgh City Bypass at Gilmerton exit or Sheriffhall Roundabout

**FHG PUBLICATIONS, ABBEY MILL BUSINESS CENTRE, PAISLEY PA1 1TJ**

---

visitscotland 5-Star Attraction with two floors of interactive exhibitions and a 'Magic Helmet' tour of the pithead, re-created coal road and coal face. Largest working winding engine in Britain.

**Open:** daily. Summer: 10am to 5pm (last tour 3.30pm). Winter: 10am to 4pm (last tour 2.30pm)

**Directions:** 5 minutes from Sherrifhall Roundabout on Edinburgh City Bypass on A7 south

**FHG PUBLICATIONS, ABBEY MILL BUSINESS CENTRE, PAISLEY PA1 1TJ**

**FHG**
**READERS' OFFER 2005**

# Scottish Deer Centre
Cupar, Fife KY15 4NQ
Tel: 01337 810391 • Fax: 01337 810477

TWO for ONE

*valid from 1st Jan 2005 to 31st Dec 2005*

NOT TO BE USED IN CONJUNCTION WITH ANY OTHER OFFER

---

**FHG**
**READERS' OFFER 2005**

# the scottish fisheries museum
Harbourhead, Anstruther, Fife KY10 3AB
Tel: 01333 310628
e-mail: info@scottish-fisheries-museum.org

Accompanied children FREE - maximum 5 per party

*valid until end 2005*

NOT TO BE USED IN CONJUNCTION WITH ANY OTHER OFFER

---

**FHG**
**READERS' OFFER 2005**

# Landmark Forest Theme Park
Carrbridge, Inverness-shire PH23 3AJ
Tel: 01479 841613 • Freephone 0800 731 3446
e-mail: landmarkcentre@btconnect.com • website: www.landmark-centre.co.uk

10% DISCOUNT for pet owners. Free admission for pets!
Maximum of four persons per voucher

*Valid during 2005*

NOT TO BE USED IN CONJUNCTION WITH ANY OTHER OFFER

---

**FHG**
**READERS' OFFER 2005**

# Highland and Rare Breeds Farm
Elphin, Near Ullapool, Sutherland IV27 4HH
Tel: 01854 666204

One FREE adult or child with adult paying full entrance price

*valid May to September 2005*

NOT TO BE USED IN CONJUNCTION WITH ANY OTHER OFFER

---

**FHG**
**READERS' OFFER 2005**

# New Lanark World Heritage Site
New Lanark Mills, New Lanark, Lanarkshire ML11 9DB
Tel: 01555 661345• Fax: 01555 665738
e-mail: visit@newlanark.org • website: www.newlanark.org

One FREE child with every full price adult

*valid until 31st October 2005*

NOT TO BE USED IN CONJUNCTION WITH ANY OTHER OFFER

8 species of deer from around the world. Birds of prey flying demonstrations, indoor and outdoor play areas.
Visit our Wolfwood.
Courtyard shopping and coffee shop.

**Open:** daily except Christmas and New Year's Day.
Summer 10am to 5pm
Winter 10am to 4pm
**Directions:** on the A91 just 12 miles from St Andrews

FHG PUBLICATIONS, ABBEY MILL BUSINESS CENTRE, PAISLEY PA1 1TJ

---

In the heart of the Fife fishing community, the Museum tells and researches the story of the Scottish fishing industry and its people from the earliest times to the present. The comprehensive collection includes ships, models, paintings, photographs, equipment and the written word.

**Open:** daily. Apr-Sept 10am to 5.30pm (4.30pm Sun); Oct-Mar 10am to 4pm (12 to 4pm Sun)

**Directions:** on coast road, 10 miles south of St Andrews

FHG PUBLICATIONS, ABBEY MILL BUSINESS CENTRE, PAISLEY PA1 1TJ

---

Great day out for all the family.
Wild Water Coaster*, Microworld exhibition, Forest Trails, Viewing Tower, Climbing Wall*, Tree Top Trail, Steam powered Sawmill*, Clydesdale Horse*. Shop, restaurant and snackbar.
(* Easter to October)
**DOGS MUST BE KEPT ON LEADS**

**Open:** daily (except Christmas Day and attractions marked*).

**Directions:** 23 miles south of Inverness at Carrbridge, just off the A9.

FHG PUBLICATIONS, ABBEY MILL BUSINESS CENTRE, PAISLEY PA1 1TJ

---

Highland croft open to visitors for "hands-on" experience with over 30 different breeds of farm animals "stroke the goats and scratch the pigs". Farm information centre and old farm implements.
For all ages, cloud or shine!

**Open:** July and August 10am to 5pm.

**Directions:** On A835
15 miles north of Ullapool

FHG PUBLICATIONS, ABBEY MILL BUSINESS CENTRE, PAISLEY PA1 1TJ

---

A beautifully restored cotton mill village close to the Falls of Clyde. Explore the fascinating history of the village, try the 'New Millennium Experience', a magical ride which takes you back in time to discover what life used to be like.

**Open:** 11am to 5pm daily.
Closed Christmas Day
and New Year's Day.

**Directions:** 25 miles from Glasgow and 35 miles from Edinburgh; well signposted on all major routes.

FHG PUBLICATIONS, ABBEY MILL BUSINESS CENTRE, PAISLEY PA1 1TJ

**FHG READERS' OFFER 2005**

## MUSEUM OF CHILDHOOD MEMORIES
1 Castle Street, Beaumaris, Anglesey LL58 8AP
Tel: 01248 712498
website: www.aboutbritain.com/museumofchildhoodmemories.htm

One child FREE with two adults

*valid during 2005*

**NOT TO BE USED IN CONJUNCTION WITH ANY OTHER OFFER**

---

**FHG READERS' OFFER 2005**

## Llanberis Lake Railway
Gilfach Ddu, Llanberis, Gwynedd LL55 4TY
Tel: 01286 870549 • e-mail: info@lake-railway.co.uk
website: www.lake-railway.co.uk

One pet travels FREE with each full fare paying adult

*Valid Easter to October 2005*

**NOT TO BE USED IN CONJUNCTION WITH ANY OTHER OFFER**

---

**FHG READERS' OFFER 2005**

## Alice in Wonderland Centre
3/4 Trinity Square, Llandudno, Conwy, North Wales LL30 2PY
Tel: 01492 860082 • e-mail: alice@wonderland.co.uk
website: www.wonderland.co.uk

One child FREE with two paying adults. Guide Dogs welcome

*valid during 2005*

**NOT TO BE USED IN CONJUNCTION WITH ANY OTHER OFFER**

---

**FHG READERS' OFFER 2005**

## Felinwynt RAINFOREST & BUTTERFLY CENTRE
Felinwynt, Cardigan, Ceredigion SA43 1RT
Tel: 01239 810882
website: www.butterflycentre.co.uk

TWO for the price of ONE (one voucher per party only)

*valid until end October 2005*

**NOT TO BE USED IN CONJUNCTION WITH ANY OTHER OFFER**

---

**FHG READERS' OFFER 2005**

## Rhondda Heritage Park
Lewis Merthyr Colliery, Coed Cae Road, Trehafod, Near Pontypridd CF37 7NP
Tel: 01443 682036 • e-mail: info@rhonddaheritagepark.com
website: www.rhonddaheritagepark.com

Two adults or children for the price of one when accompanied by a full paying adult

*Valid until end 2005 for full tours only. Not valid on special event days.*

**NOT TO BE USED IN CONJUNCTION WITH ANY OTHER OFFER**

| | |
|---|---|
| Nine rooms in a Georgian house filled with items illustrating the happier times of family life over the past 150 years. Joyful nostalgia unlimited. | **Open:** March to end October<br><br>**Directions:** opposite Beaumaris Castle |

**FHG PUBLICATIONS, ABBEY MILL BUSINESS CENTRE, PAISLEY PA1 1TJ**

| | |
|---|---|
| A 60-minute ride along the shores of beautiful Padarn Lake behind a quaint historic steam engine. Magnificent views of the mountains from lakeside picnic spots.<br><br>**DOGS MUST BE KEPT ON LEAD AT ALL TIMES ON TRAIN** | **Open:** most days Easter to October. Free timetable leaflet on request.<br><br>**Directions:** just off A4086 Caernarfon to Capel Curig road at Llanberis; follow 'Country Park' signs. |

**FHG PUBLICATIONS, ABBEY MILL BUSINESS CENTRE, PAISLEY PA1 1TJ**

| | |
|---|---|
| Walk through the Rabbit Hole to the colourful scenes of Lewis Carroll's classic story set in beautiful life-size displays. Recorded commentaries and transcripts available in several languages. | **Open:** all year 10am to 5pm but closed Sundays in winter and Christmas/Boxing Day/New Year's Day.<br><br>**Directions:** situated just off the main street, 250 yards from coach and rail stations. |

**FHG PUBLICATIONS, ABBEY MILL BUSINESS CENTRE, PAISLEY PA1 1TJ**

| | |
|---|---|
| Mini-rainforest full of tropical plants and exotic butterflies. Personal attention of the owner, Mr John Devereux. Gift shop, cafe, video room, exhibition. Suitable for disabled visitors. WTB Quality Assured Visitor Attraction.<br><br>**PETS NOT ALLOWED IN TROPICAL HOUSE ONLY** | **Open:** daily Easter to end October 10.30am to 5pm<br><br>**Directions:** 7 miles north of Cardigan on Aberystwyth road. Follow brown tourist signs on A487. |

**FHG PUBLICATIONS, ABBEY MILL BUSINESS CENTRE, PAISLEY PA1 1TJ**

| | |
|---|---|
| Make a pit stop whatever the weather! Join an ex-miner on a tour of discovery, ride the cage to pit bottom and take a thrilling ride back to the surface. Multi-media presentations, period village street, children's adventure play area, restaurant and gift shop. Disabled access with assistance. | **Open:** Open daily 10am to 6pm (last tour 4.30pm). Closed Mondays October to Easter, also Dec 25th to 3rd Jan inclusive.<br><br>**Directions:** Exit Junction 32 M4, signposted from A470 Pontypridd. Trehafod is located between Pontypridd and Porth. |

**FHG PUBLICATIONS, ABBEY MILL BUSINESS CENTRE, PAISLEY PA1 1TJ**

# Bedfordshire

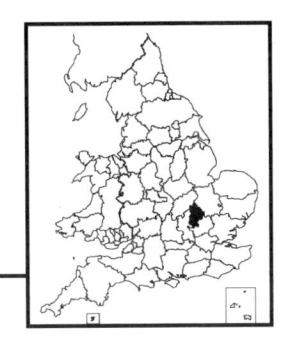

## THE KNIFE & CLEAVER
The Grove, Houghton Conquest, Bedford, Bedfordshire MK45 3LA
Tel: 01234 740387 • Fax: 01234 740900
e-mail: info@knifeandcleaver.com • website: www.knifeandcleaver.com

Deep in the heart of rural Bedfordshire, this friendly country inn offers a warm welcome to locals and visitors alike, and proves equally popular with both. One of the main reasons for its enviable reputation is the quite exceptional Victorian-style conservatory restaurant, where the finest of fresh ingredients are prepared with care and imagination by first-class chefs and where the accompanying wine list has been selected with quality and value as the highest priorities. Nine well-appointed en suite bedrooms, all with power shower, satellite television and a full range of amenities, provide comfortable accommodation for those wishing to explore this lovely area. *ETC* ◆◆◆◆

9 BEDROOMS, ALL WITH PRIVATE BATHROOM; FREE HOUSE WITH REAL ALE; HISTORIC INTEREST; CHILDREN WELCOME; PETS BY ARRANGEMENT; BAR AND RESTAURANT MEALS; AMPTHILL 2 MILES; S££££, D££.

## THE GLOBE INN
Off Stoke Road, Old Linslade, Leighton Buzzard, Bedfordshire LU7 7TA
Tel: 01525 373338 • Fax: 01525 850551

Situated on the edge of the Grand Union Canal, The Globe Inn is an idyllic pub/restaurant for all age groups to enjoy, for a special occasion or just a casual meeting. Entertain the little ones on our outside play area, and feed them with their own special menu. Our traditional and friendly atmosphere warms everyone's hearts, as does our exceptional quality food. Our restaurant is open seven days a week, and booking is highly recommended. Seafood dishes are our speciality, and our chef ensures the home-cooked aspect is kept with his pies and puddings. Our evenings are enhanced by candlelight, and during the winter months open fires add to the warm welcome. Enjoy our range of well-kept cask-conditioned ales with a meal in the bar, or some fine wine in our traditional restaurant. *See also Colour Advertisement.*

NO ACCOMMODATION; GREENE KING HOUSE WITH REAL ALE; CHILDREN WELCOME; BAR AND RESTAURANT MEALS; LUTON 11 MILES.

---

The £ symbol when appearing at the end of the italic section of an entry shows the anticipated price, during 2005, for full Bed and Breakfast.

*Normal Bed & Breakfast rate per person (in single room)*

| PRICE RANGE | CATEGORY |
| --- | --- |
| Under £25 | S£ |
| £26-£35 | S££ |
| £36-£45 | S£££ |
| Over £45 | S££££ |

*Normal Bed & Breakfast rate per person (sharing double/twin room)*

| PRICE RANGE | CATEGORY |
| --- | --- |
| Under £25 | D£ |
| £26-£35 | D££ |
| £36-£45 | D£££ |
| Over £45 | D££££ |

This is meant as an indication only and does not show prices for Special Breaks, Weekends, etc. Guests are therefore advised to verify all prices on enquiring or booking.

# Berkshire

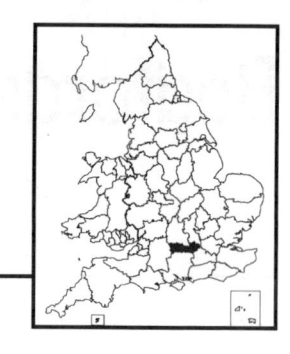

## THE DUNDAS ARMS
Station Road, Kintbury, Berkshire RG17 9UT
Tel: 01488 658263/658559 • Fax: 01488 658568 • e-mail: info@dundasarms.co.uk
website: www.dundasarms.co.uk

The inn's lovely position between the River Kennet and the canal makes it a most pleasant spot to stop for refreshment, and indeed for an overnight stay or weekend break. The comfortably furnished bedrooms are fully equipped with private bathroom, television and tea-making facilities, and enjoy relaxing views over the river. If your visit here is purely for refreshment, you will be delighted by the excellent bar food menu, which features really interesting "specials" alongside traditional favourites such as ploughmans and steak and kidney pie, and by the range of well kept real ales. For more leisurely dining, menus in the restaurant make full use of fresh local produce, and there is also an excellent wine list. CAMRA. *See also Colour Advertisement.*

5 BEDROOMS, ALL WITH PRIVATE BATHROOM; FREE HOUSE WITH REAL ALE; CHILDREN WELCOME; BAR MEALS, RESTAURANT EVENINGS ONLY; NON-SMOKING AREAS; HUNGERFORD 3 MILES; S£££££, D££.

## THE BELL AT BOXFORD
Lambourn Road, Newbury, Berkshire RG20 8DD
Tel: 01488 608721 • Fax: 01488 608749 • e-mail: info@bellatboxford.com
website: www.bellatboxford.com

The smart exterior of this traditional country inn between Newbury and Lambourn will attract the attention of passers by, maybe and possibly disciples of the turf. To venture within is to discover homely comforts in the form of log fires and real ales as well as bags of character. Widely recommended, the international fare on offer in the candlelit restaurant is a lure in itself, there being a mouth-watering choice of reasonably-priced dishes on the à la carte menu, not forgetting the daily 'blackboard specials'. Excellent accommodation is available at this hostelry run in distinguished style by Paul and Helen Lavis, bedrooms having en suite facilities, direct-dial telephone and modern appointments including internet access. *ETC* ♦♦♦

10 BEDROOMS, ALL WITH PRIVATE BATHROOM; FREE HOUSE WITH REAL ALE; CHILDREN AND PETS WELCOME; BAR AND RESTAURANT MEALS; NEWBURY 4 MILES; S££££, D£££.

# Buckinghamshire

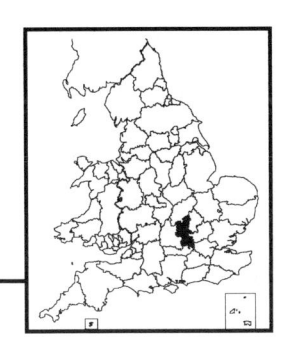

## THE WHITE HART
**Three Households, Chalfont St Giles, Buckinghamshire HP8 4LP**
**Tel: 01494 872441• Fax: 01494 876375 • www.thewhitehartstgiles.co.uk**
**e-mail: enquiries@thewhitehartstgiles.co.uk**

The answer is yes! - what's the question? Eleven en suite bedrooms. Cask ales, Dom Perignon, New World wines, Pinot Grigio, Cava. A la carte menu, bouillabaisse, desserts to die for, foie gras, lobster, just a sandwich, king scallops, latte, monkfish and parma ham, langoustine risotto, Tournedos Rossini, innovative specials, vegetarian options, and summer salads. And just that bit extra! We are serious about what we do. Chef patron Scott MacRae. *ETC* ♦♦♦♦, *Les Routiers*.

11 BEDROOMS, ALL WITH PRIVATE BATHROOM; CHILDREN AND PETS WELCOME; BAR LUNCHES AND RESTAURANT MEALS; NON-SMOKING AREAS; AMERSHAM 3 MILES; S£££next, D££££.

## THE GREYHOUND INN
**High Street, Chalfont St Peter, Buckinghamshire SL9 9RA**
**Tel: 01753 883404 • Fax: 01753 891627 • website: www.thegreyhoundinn.net**

Enjoy a delicious meal in our restaurant and sample wines from our extensive cellar. Relax with a drink at the bar or on the terrace. Rest in one of our twelve luxuriously appointed rooms. Celebrate your special day or private party. Whatever the occasion you will find a very warm welcome awaits you at The Greyhound Inn. *ETC* ★★★★ *See also Colour Advertisement.*

12 BEDROOMS, ALL WITH PRIVATE BATHROOM; UNIQUE PUB CO. (SUPPLYLINE) HOUSE; HISTORIC INTEREST; CHILDREN WELCOME; BAR AND RESTAURANT MEALS; NON-SMOKING AREAS; UXBRIDGE 6 MILES; D££££.

# DIFFERENT DRUMMER HOTEL
**94 High Street, Stony Stratford, Milton Keynes, Buckinghamshire MK11 1AH**
**Tel: 01908 564733 • Fax: 01908 260646 • e-mail: info@hoteldifferentdrummer.co.uk**
**website: www.hoteldifferentdrummer.co.uk**

Until 1982 known as 'The Swan with Two Nicks', this is an ancient inn, dating back to 1476, with a noble history that has been transformed by the Keswani family into a superbly furnished hotel where the refinements of the present blend happily with the aura of the past. Today, the traditions of a town distinguished by its hospitality and beautifully preserved coaching hostelries are well maintained at this splendid 'inn of the modern happiness'. Travellers in the staging era would marvel at the luxury of en suite bathrooms, fitted carpets, central heating, colour television with satellite channels in their rooms but although guest rooms have been designed with the present-day visitor in mind, a sympathetic eye has been cast at the building's history. The elegant Georgian facade remains unchanged from 1743 when it replaced an earlier frontage following the great fire of Stony Stratford; the old stables still exist and fine antique furniture graces the rooms. These days, all is light, warmth and comfort on the highest plane. A special reference to the magnificent, oak-panelled Al Tamborista Restaurant is reserved and fully deserved; here, diners may experience by candlelight Italian and seafood cuisine at its very best and most inventive. Also very deserving of mention is the recently opened winebar and restaurant, The Vine, where top international cuisine and quality wines combine with London-style contemporary chic. An absolute must for those looking for something different in style and cuisine. *ETC/AA* ★★

23 BEDROOMS, ALL WITH PRIVATE BATHROOM; FREE HOUSE; HISTORIC INTEREST; CHILDREN AND PETS WELCOME; BAR AND RESTAURANT MEALS; NON-SMOKING AREAS; BUCKINGHAM 8 MILES; S£££users, D££££.

---

## • • *Some Useful Guidance for Guests and Hosts* • •

Every year literally thousands of holidays, short breaks and overnight stops are arranged through our guides, the vast majority without any problems at all. In a handful of cases, however, difficulties do arise about bookings, which often could have been prevented from the outset.

*It is important to remember that when accommodation has been booked, both parties – guests and hosts – have entered into a form of contract. We hope that the following points will provide helpful guidance.*

**GUESTS:**
- When enquiring about accommodation, be as precise as possible. Give exact dates, numbers in your party and the ages of any children.
- State the number and type of rooms wanted and also what catering you require – bed and breakfast, full board etc. Make sure that the position about evening meals is clear – and about pets, reductions for children or any other special points.
- Read our reviews carefully to ensure that the proprietors you are going to contact can supply what you want. Ask for a letter confirming all arrangements, if possible.
- If you have to cancel, do so as soon as possible. Proprietors do have the right to retain deposits and under certain circumstances to charge for cancelled holidays if adequate notice is not given and they cannot re-let the accommodation.

**HOSTS:**
- Give details about your facilities and about any special conditions. Explain your deposit system clearly and arrangements for cancellations, charges etc. and whether or not your terms include VAT.
- If for any reason you are unable to fulfil an agreed booking without adequate notice, you may be under an obligation to arrange suitable alternative accommodation or to make some form of compensation.

*While every effort is made to ensure accuracy, we regret that FHG Publications cannot accept responsibility for errors, omissions or misrepresentations in our entries or any consequences thereof. Prices in particular should be checked because we go to press early. We will follow up complaints but cannot act as arbiters or agents for either party.*

# Cheshire

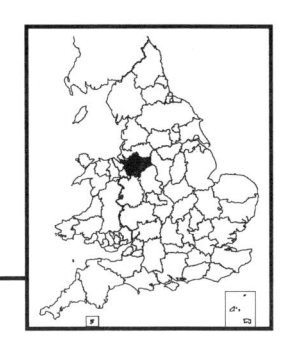

## THE ALVANLEY ARMS
**Cotebrook, Near Tarporley, Cheshire CW6 9DS**
**Tel: 01829 760200 • e-mail: info@alvanleyarms.co.uk**
**website: www.alvanleyarms.co.uk**

The adjacent Cotebrook Shire Horse Centre and Countryside Park has a close relationship with this most attractive hostelry, for both are owned by the King family. A splendid blaze of colour from hanging baskets and window boxes greets the eye and within, pictures, photographs and tack relating to the noble Shire horse adorn the walls of the oak-beamed bar where good ale and malts may be enjoyed before a welcoming log fire. An intimate restaurant presents an appetising range of chef-created home-cooked food, with fresh fish regularly delivered from the seaports. All around is the tranquil beauty of the Cheshire countryside, yet historic Chester is only 10 miles away. Dating from the 16th century, the inn, just north of Tarporley on the A49, offers accommodation of innate character, delightfully decorated, originally beamed rooms being appointed to a high degree of comfort with en suite bath and shower, colour television, hairdryer and tea and coffee-making facilities. Business folk with contacts with the commercial centres of the North-West make this a popular port of call and there is much of sporting interest in the area; Oulton Park is just a mile away and Portal Golf and Country Club is close by. The Shire Horse Centre and Countryside Park extends over 50 acres and incorporates a nature trail, a variety of birdlife and British wild and domestic animals. *AA* ◆◆◆◆

7 BEDROOMS, ALL WITH PRIVATE BATHROOM; ROBINSONS HOUSE WITH REAL ALE; HISTORIC INTEREST; CHILDREN WELCOME; BAR AND RESTAURANT MEALS; NON-SMOKING AREAS; TARPORLEY 2 MILES; S£££, D££.

## THE PLOUGH AT EATON
**Macclesfield Road, Eaton, Near Congleton, Cheshire CW12 2NR**
**Tel: 01260 280207 • Fax: 01260 298377**

Traditional oak beams and blazing log fires in winter reflect the warm and friendly atmosphere of this half-timbered former coaching inn which dates from the 17th century. The heart of the 'Plough' is the kitchen where food skilfully prepared is calculated to satisfy the most discerning palate. Luncheons and dinners are served seven days a week with traditional roasts on Sundays. In peaceful, rolling countryside near the Cheshire/Staffordshire border, this is a tranquil place in which to stay and the hostelry has elegantly colour-co-ordinated guest rooms, all with spacious bathrooms, colour television, direct-dial telephone and tea and coffee-making facilities amongst their impressive appointments. *ETC/RAC* ★★★★

8 BEDROOMS, ALL WITH PRIVATE BATHROOM; FREE HOUSE WITH REAL ALE; HISTORIC INTEREST; CHILDREN WELCOME; BAR AND RESTAURANT MEALS; NON-SMOKING AREAS; CONGLETON 2 MILES; S£££, D££££.

---

Visit the **FHG** website
**www.holidayguides.com**
for details of the wide choice of accommodation
featured in the full range of FHG titles

# Cornwall

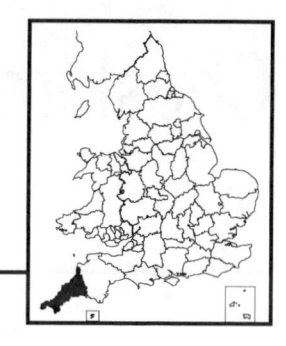

### THE SHIP INN
Fore Street, Lerryn, Lostwithiel, Cornwall PL22 0PT
Tel: 01208 872374 • Fax: 01208 872614 • e-mail: shiplerryn@aol.com
website: www.cornwall-online.co.uk/shipinn-lerryn

This charming and traditional Cornish country inn can be found in what must surely be the prettiest riverside village in Cornwall. Popular with walkers and sailors alike, it offers a warm welcome to all. A log fire and central heating ensure year round comfort and make this a cosy choice for an out of season break. The attractive guest rooms all have en suite bathrooms, beverage-making facilities, colour television and radio. One bedroom is on the ground floor, making it ideal for elderly or disabled visitors. Excellent home-cooked fare is available in the restaurant lunchtimes and evenings, when you can choose from an extensive menu which also includes a good choice for vegetarians. The bar offers a choice of real ales and a large selection of malt whiskies. *AA* ★★★★

5 BEDROOMS, ALL WITH PRIVATE BATHROOM; FREE HOUSE WITH REAL ALE; HISTORIC INTEREST;
CHILDREN AND PETS WELCOME; BAR AND RESTAURANT MEALS; NON-SMOKING AREAS; LOSTWITHIEL 3 MILES; D£££.

## PUBLISHER'S NOTE

**FHG**

While every effort is made to ensure accuracy, we regret that FHG Publications cannot accept responsibility for errors, misrepresentations or omissions in our entries or any consequences thereof. Prices in particular should be checked because we go to press early. We will follow up complaints but cannot act as arbiters or agents for either party.

## ROYAL OAK INN
Duke Street, Lostwithiel, Cornwall PL22 0AG
Tel: 01208 872552 • website: www.royaloaklostwithiel.co.uk

Full of character and with two beautifully kept bars, one of which does duty as a restaurant where splendid and reasonably priced meals are served nightly, the 13th century Royal Oak is tucked away just off the main road. An underground tunnel is said to connect its cellar to the dungeons of nearby 12th and 13th century Restormel Castle, providing a smuggling and, possibly, an escape route. No-one will surely wish to escape from this warmly welcoming hostelry with its log fire and friendly atmosphere. Overnight guests are accommodated in attractively decorated bedrooms, all appointed with en suite facilities, television, radio and tea-makers. *RAC Two Tankards, Les Routiers.*

6 BEDROOMS, ALL WITH PRIVATE BATHROOM; FREE HOUSE WITH REAL ALE; HISTORIC INTEREST; CHILDREN WELCOME; BAR LUNCHES, RESTAURANT EVENINGS ONLY; NON-SMOKING AREAS; BODMIN 5 MILES; S£££, D£££.

## THE GODOLPHIN ARMS
West End, Marazion, Cornwall TR17 0EN
Tel: 01736 710202 • Fax: 01736 710171 • website: www.godolphinarms.co.uk
e-mail: reception@godolphinarms.co.uk

An imposing building dominating magnificent views of St Michael's Mount and across Mounts Bay, delightfully furnished in bright and cheerful mode, this is both an attractive holiday venue in its own right and a recommended port of call for a casual drink and a meal. The main restaurant on the first floor takes full advantage of the spectacular views and presents a mouthwatering menu, fish dishes figuring prominently. The popular Gig Bar, which leads directly on to a superb beach, specialises in Continental snacks and light lunches and offers a wide choice of real ales. Guest rooms are stylishly appointed; all are en suite and have colour television and tea and coffee-making facilities. *AA* ★★

10 BEDROOMS, ALL WITH PRIVATE BATHROOM; FREE HOUSE WITH REAL ALE; CHILDREN AND PETS WELCOME; BAR AND RESTAURANT MEALS; NON-SMOKING AREAS; PENZANCE 3 MILES; S££££, D££££.

## BOSCEAN COUNTRY HOTEL
St Just, Penzance, Cornwall TR19 7QP
Tel & Fax: 01736 788748 • e-mail: Boscean@aol.com
website: www.bosceancountryhotel.co.uk

The Boscean Country Hotel, located amidst some of the most dramatic scenery in West Cornwall, is somewhere very special just waiting to be discovered. This country house offers a wonderful combination of oak panelled walls, a magnificent oak staircase and open log fires. The natural gardens, extending to nearly three acres, are a haven for wildlife including foxes and badgers. Situated on the Heritage Coast in an Area of Outstanding Natural Beauty close to Cape Cornwall and the coastal footpath, this is an ideal base from which to explore the Land's End Peninsula. The moors of Penwith are rich in Iron and Bronze Age relics dating back to 4OOOBC. Penzance, St Michael's Mount, St Ives, Land's End and the Minack Theatre are all a short distance away. 12 en suite rooms, centrally heated throughout, licensed bar. Excellent home cooking using fresh local produce. Unlimited Desserts!! Open all year. *ETC* ♦♦♦ *See also Colour Advertisement.*

LICENSED; 12 BEDROOMS, ALL WITH PRIVATE BATHROOMS; TRURO 24 MILES.

*Cornwall* 47

## THE CORNISH ARMS
**Pendoggett, Port Isaac, Cornwall PL30 3HH**
**Tel: 01208 880263 • Fax: 01208 880335**

A delightful 16th century coaching inn in the small rural village of Pendoggett, just one mile from the coast. Anyone who makes The Cornish Arms a base for exploring the area will not be disappointed by the attractive accommodation or the warmth of the welcome extended. Whilst retaining the character of a traditional coaching inn, The Cornish Arms offers all modern amenities in every bedroom: colour and satellite television, telephone, tea and coffee making facilities etc. The highly recommended restaurant specialises in locally caught seafood and an extensive range of other dishes. Complement your meal with wine from the extensive cellars of The Cornish Arms. With Bass straight from the barrel, together with other real ales, you will see why it is worth visiting The Cornish Arms. *ETC/RAC* ★★

7 BEDROOMS, ALL WITH PRIVATE BATHROOM; FREE HOUSE WITH REAL ALE; RESTAURANT AND BAR MEALS; WADEBRIDGE 5 MILES.

## COLLIFORD TAVERN
**Colliford Lake, Near St Neot, Liskeard, Cornwall PL14 6PZ**
**Tel: 01208 821335 • e-mail: info@colliford.com**
**website: www.colliford-tavern.co.uk**

Set in attractive grounds which include a children's play area, ponds and a working waterwheel, this delightfully furnished free house run by the Cooper family offers excellent à la carte fare and bar snacks. Sprucely-appointed guest rooms are spacious and have en suite shower, colour television, radio alarm, beverage maker and numerous thoughtful extras. An unusual feature of the tavern is a 37' deep granite well. In the midst of the scenic splendour of Bodmin Moor, this is a relaxing country retreat only a few minutes' walk from Colliford Lake, so popular with fly fishermen. Both north and south coasts are within easy driving distance and terms are most reasonable. *ETC* ◆◆◆◆

6 BEDROOMS, ALL WITH PRIVATE BATHROOM; FREE HOUSE WITH REAL ALE; HISTORIC INTEREST; CHILDREN WELCOME; BAR LUNCHES, RESTAURANT EVENINGS ONLY; NON-SMOKING AREAS; BODMIN 7 MILES; s£££, D££.

## CORNISHMAN INN
**Tintagel, Cornwall PL34 0DB**
**Tel: 01840 770238 • Fax: 01840 770078**
**e-mail: info@cornishmaninn.com • website: www.cornishmaninn.com**

A simple but heartwarming pleasure is to sit on the terrace of this traditional wayside hostelry surrounded by blooms that would be the envy of Kew Gardens, enjoying a glass of one's favourite nectar and perhaps, one of the home-made 'specials' from the comprehensive menu. Should the sun not oblige, there are three charismatic bars featuring a proud display of rural bygones. Within easy reach of the mythical home of King Arthur at Tintagel Castle and a romantically rugged coast, the inn has all the attributes of a wonderful holiday base with the coastal footpath, several surfing beaches and facilities for golf and boating near at hand.

10 BEDROOMS, ALL WITH PRIVATE BATHROOM; FREE HOUSE WITH REAL ALE; CHILDREN WELCOME; BAR LUNCHES, RESTAURANT EVENINGS ONLY; NON-SMOKING AREAS; CAMELFORD 4 MILES; D££.

## THE NEW INN
**Tresco, Isles of Scilly, Cornwall TR24 0QE**
**Tel: 01720 422844 • Fax: 01720 423200 • e-mail: newinn@tresco.co.uk**
**website: www.tresco.co.uk**

Calling those with a penchant for adventure and romance, this spruce inn is the social centre of this wonderful, verdant, away-from-it-all island. Main topics of conversation tend to be about fishing, anything to do with boats and what the tide has washed up. Practical considerations prompt conjecture on how to satisfy sea-breeze sharpened appetites. Guests may choose between tasty bar fare or the more formal menu in the restaurant. The inn has a fine swimming pool and other attractions include regular live music, and two annual beer festivals – and 'flowers, flowers everywhere'. A multi-faceted jewel set in an azure sea, this paradise can be reached by helicopter or ship from Penzance or by Skybus from various mainland locations.

16 BEDROOMS, ALL WITH PRIVATE BATHROOM; FREE HOUSE WITH REAL ALE; HISTORIC INTEREST; CHILDREN WELCOME; BAR MEALS, RESTAURANT EVENINGS ONLY; NON-SMOKING AREAS; D,B&B: s££££, D££££.

## NEW INN
### Veryan, Truro, Cornwall TR2 5QA
### Tel: 01872 501362 • Fax: 01872 501078 • website: www.newinnveryan.co.uk

Set in a picturesque village on the Roseland Peninsula, the New Inn is a small granite pub, originally consisting of two cottages and was built in the 16th century. Visitors are welcome to enjoy the atmosphere in our local village bar and we are locally renowned for our good food and cask ales, a wide range of food being served in the bar. Accommodation consists of spacious and comfortable rooms - one single with separate private facilities, and one double and one twin en suite. St Austell and Truro are nearby, and we are situated close to the beautiful sandy beaches of Pendower and Carne. *See also Colour Advertisement.*

3 BEDROOMS, ALL WITH PRIVATE BATHROOM; REAL ALE; HISTORIC INTEREST; BAR MEALS; NON-SMOKING AREAS; MEVAGISSEY 7 MILES; S££, D££.

## THE RISING SUN
### The Square, St Mawes, Truro, Cornwall TR2 5DJ
### Tel: 01326 270233 • Fax: 01326 270198 • e-mail: therisingsun@btclick.com
### website: www.innsofcornwall.co.uk

Regular patrons of this friendly establishment in the centre of St Mawes make a beeline for the window seats, for they know that from here they get the best (and most comfortable) view of the ever-changing panorama of harbour and waterfront. The light and airy conservatory provides an equally good vantage point, as do those of the pleasantly decorated en suite bedrooms which look to the front. The inn's location on the unspoiled Roseland Peninsula makes it extremely popular with sailors and walkers, who know that they will find here a warm welcome, lively conversation, good food and a first-rate choice of beers, wines and spirits, which in fine weather can be enjoyed on the neat terrace. AA ★★ *and Rosette.*

8 BEDROOMS, ALL WITH PRIVATE BATHROOM; ST AUSTELL BREWERY HOUSE WITH REAL ALE; CHILDREN AND PETS WELCOME; BAR MEALS, RESTAURANT EVENINGS ONLY; NON-SMOKING AREAS; TRURO 20 MILES; S££££, D££££.

## DRIFTWOOD SPARS HOTEL
### Trevaunance Cove, St Agnes, Cornwall TR5 0RT
### Tel: 01872 552428/553323 • website: www.driftwoodspars.com

Situated only a hundred yards from the beach, the building which is now the popular Driftwood Spars Hotel is over 300 years old and has seen active service as a tin miners' store, a chandlery, a sailmaker's workshop and a fish cellar. But nowadays the emphasis is strictly on providing guests with good food, ale and atmosphere. There are three bars serving a selection of real local ales, including one brewed on the premises, and appetising home-cooked food; there is also an upstairs dining area. Driftwood Spars offers 18 bedrooms, all with private facilities, colour television, telephone, and tea-making equipment; some with stunning sea views. Food available all day during main holiday season. Please telephone or write for brochure. *See also Colour Advertisement on Outside Back Cover.*

18 BEDROOMS, ALL WITH PRIVATE FACILITIES; FREE HOUSE WITH REAL ALE; HISTORIC INTEREST; CHILDREN WELCOME; BAR AND RESTAURANT MEALS; NEWQUAY 12 MILES, TRURO 8, REDRUTH 7; S££, D££.

# Cumbria

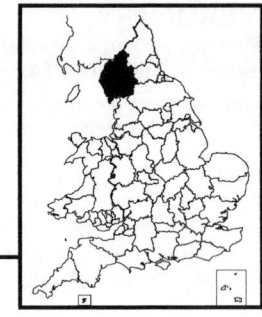

## DRUNKEN DUCK INN
**Barngates, Ambleside, Cumbria LA22 0NG**
**Tel: 015394 36347 • Fax: 015394 36781 • e-mail: info@drunkenduckinn.co.uk**
**website: www.drunkenduckinn.co.uk**

Dating from the 16th century, this unique establishment was known originally as the 'Barngates Inn'. Its present name appears to have been acquired less than a century ago when a barrel on stillage in the cellar slipped its hoops and the contents seeped into the ducks' feeding ditch. Thus was born a name which is as memorable and unusual as the inn itself. Veritably, this is a mellow place with the bars offering a variety of real ales, including the inn's own popular brews, and over 60 whiskies. The restaurant has a relaxed and informal atmosphere. At night the candlelit rooms provide a perfect setting for the excellent, imaginative food and good selection of wines. Set in 60 acres of enchanting Cumbrian scenery and with all the pleasures of Lakeland within easy reach, the Drunken Duck offers splendid accommodation, guest rooms being furnished in traditional style but with such modern conveniences as en suite facilities, colour television and hair dryer. Definitely, delightfully different! *ETC* ♦♦♦♦ *Silver Award, AA Four Red Diamonds and Rosette.*

16 BEDROOMS, ALL WITH PRIVATE BATHROOM; FREE HOUSE WITH REAL ALE; CHILDREN WELCOME, PETS IN BAR ONLY; BAR AND RESTAURANT MEALS; NON-SMOKING AREAS; AMBLESIDE 2 MILES; S£££users, D££££.

## SAWREY HOTEL
**Far Sawrey, Near Ambleside, Cumbria LA22 0LQ**
**Tel & Fax: 015394 43425**

This fully licensed 18th century free house stands within easy reach of all parts of Lakeland, just one mile from Windermere car ferry and 2½ miles from Hawkshead. It is an ideal centre for touring, walking, pony trekking and sailing, and all the other activities that this beautiful area is renowned for. There are 18 bedrooms, all with colour television, tea/coffee facilities, telephone and private bathrooms. Excellent cuisine is available in the restaurant, and the Claife Crier Bar serves an extensive range of hot and cold snacks between noon and 2pm. Under the personal management of the proprietors. *ETC/RAC* ★★.
*See also Colour Advertisement.*

18 BEDROOMS, ALL WITH PRIVATE BATHROOM; FREE HOUSE WITH REAL ALE; HISTORIC INTEREST; CHILDREN AND PETS WELCOME; BAR LUNCHES, RESTAURANT EVENINGS ONLY; NON-SMOKING AREAS; HAWKSHEAD 2 MILES; S££, D££.

## DUKE'S HEAD HOTEL
**Armathwaite, Near Carlisle, Cumbria CA4 9PB**
**Tel: 016974 72226**

Serene and secure in the unspoilt Eden Valley, the Duke's Head claims to be the house of "probably the best roast duckling in Cumbria" and few will be disposed to argue or insist on the "probably". Excellent and moderately-priced meals are served in the bar and restaurant daily. Peacefully situated between the Border Country and the Lake District, yet easily accessible from the M6, A1, A6 and A69, this hospitable inn is also in demand for its comfortable accommodation and bookings are advisable. There are numerous country pursuits to be enjoyed in the immediate vicinity, including walking, fishing, shooting, canoeing and rock climbing. The scenic Settle to Carlisle railway provides a delightful way to view the enchanting countryside.

5 BEDROOMS, ALL WITH PRIVATE BATHROOM; REAL ALE; CHILDREN AND PETS WELCOME; BAR AND RESTAURANT MEALS; NON-SMOKING AREAS; CARLISLE 9 MILES; D££.

## THE WHITE MARE COUNTRY HOUSE HOTEL, PUB & RESTAURANT
**Beckermet, Cumbria CA21 2XS**
**Tel: 01946 841246 • Fax: 01946 841100 • e-mail: phil@whitemare.co.uk**
**website: www.whitemare.co.uk**

A small, friendly country pub and hotel happily placed between the Lakeland mountains and the sea, the wide and inviting facade of this well-organised retreat holds the promise of good company and refreshment within. Those acting upon this impression will not be disappointed; an open fire bids welcome in an attractive bar which offers the choice of several real ales and a variety of tempting dishes, either by way of the popular home-made 'daily specials' or on the interesting restaurant menu. Afternoon teas are served each Sunday between 3pm and 5.30pm. A games room opens up the possibility of a challenge at darts or pool. This is a lovely area in which to stay and the inn provides first-class accommodation in centrally-heated (non-smoking) en suite bedrooms, all with television, video, modem point and tea and coffee-makers. Wedding packages including full ceremony (civil wedding licence held) and accommodation are available.

8 BEDROOMS, ALL WITH PRIVATE BATHROOM; FREE HOUSE WITH REAL ALE; HISTORIC INTEREST; CHILDREN WELCOME; BAR AND RESTAURANT MEALS; NON-SMOKING AREAS; WHITEHAVEN 7 MILES; D£/££.

**FHG** **FHG PUBLICATIONS** publish a large range of well-known accommodation guides. We will be happy to send you details or you can use the order form at the back of this book.

## THE BURNMOOR INN
Boot, Eskdale, Cumbria CA19 1TG
Tel: 019467 23224 • Fax: 019467 23337 • e-mail: enquiries@burnmoor.co.uk
website: www.burnmoor.co.uk

Situated in this stunning valley close to amazing walks, including Scafell, Harter and Gable to name but a few. Both you and your hounds can enjoy en suite luxury in one of our nine bedrooms, all with tea and coffee making facilities and comfortable furnishings. We offer good food in both restaurant and bar where you can enjoy one of our real ales (CAMRA Guide) and discuss your next day's assault. Well-behaved pets are welcome - please arrange when booking. Special bargain breaks are available October to April. Well-equipped self-catering accommodation is situated opposite the inn. Resident Proprietors: Harry and Paddington Berger. *ETC* ♦♦♦

9 BEDROOMS, ALL WITH PRIVATE BATHROOM; FREE HOUSE WITH REAL ALE; HISTORIC INTEREST; CHILDREN AND PETS WELCOME; BAR MEALS, RESTAURANT EVENINGS ONLY; NON-SMOKING AREAS; RAVENGLASS 6 MILES; S££, D££.

## THE BLACKSMITH'S ARMS
Talkin Village, Brampton, Cumbria CA8 1LE
Tel: 016977 3452 • Fax: 016977 3396 • e-mail: info@blacksmithstalkin.co.uk
website: www.blacksmithstalkin.co.uk

The Blacksmith's Arms offers all the hospitality and comforts of a traditional country inn. Enjoy tasty meals served in the bar lounges, or linger over dinner in the well-appointed restaurant. The inn is personally managed by the proprietors, Anne and Donald Jackson, who guarantee the hospitality one would expect from a family concern. Guests are assured of a pleasant and comfortable stay. There are eight lovely bedrooms, all en suite. Peacefully situated in the beautiful village of Talkin, the inn is convenient for the Borders, Hadrian's Wall and the Lake District. There is a good golf course, walking and other country pursuits nearby. *See also Colour Advertisement.*

8 BEDROOMS, ALL WITH PRIVATE BATHROOM; FREE HOUSE; HISTORIC INTEREST; CHILDREN WELCOME; BAR AND RESTAURANT MEALS; NON-SMOKING AREAS; CARLISLE 9 MILES, BRAMPTON 3; S££, D££.

## GRAHAM ARMS HOTEL
Longtown, Near Carlisle, Cumbria CA6 5SE
Tel: 01228 791213 • Fax: 01228 792830 • website: www.cumbria.com/hotel

A warm welcome awaits you at this 180-year-old former coaching inn. Situated six miles from the M6 (Junction 44) and Gretna Green, the Graham Arms makes an ideal overnight stop or perfect touring base for the Scottish Borders, English Lakes, Hadrian's Wall and much more. There are 15 comfortable en suite bedrooms, including four-poster and family rooms, with television and radio. Meals and snacks are served throughout the day, and there is a friendly locals' bar serving real ale and a fine selection of malt whiskies, and a new 'Sports Bar'. There is secure courtyard parking for cars, cycles and motorcycles. Pets are welcome with well-behaved owners. Special breaks on request. *RAC* ★★

15 BEDROOMS ALL WITH PRIVATE BATHROOM; FREE HOUSE WITH REAL ALE; CHILDREN AND PETS WELCOME; BAR MEALS; NON-SMOKING AREAS; CARLISLE 8 MILES; S££/£££, D££/£££.

## BLACK BULL INN AND HOTEL
**1 Yewdale Road, Coniston, Cumbria LA21 8DU**
**Tel: 015394 41335 • Fax: 015394 41168**

A traditional wayside inn, the Black Bull was built about 400 years ago as a coaching inn accommodating travellers, coachmen and horses. In the shadow of Coniston's lofty 'Old Man", its position is picturesque, with the beck burbling by. Many famous people have lodged at this historic inn, their names synonymous with the Lake District – Turner the artist, Coleridge and, more recently, Donald Campbell when attempting his water speed records. Despite impressive modern improvements, the character of the inn remains, and the beamed bar with its open fire is cosy and inviting. First-rate accommodation is available, all rooms having bath or shower en suite, colour television, tea and coffee making facilities and central heating. Award-winning real ale is brewed on the premises. *Les Routiers*.

16 BEDROOMS, ALL WITH PRIVATE BATHROOM; FREE HOUSE WITH REAL ALE; HISTORIC INTEREST; CHILDREN AND PETS WELCOME; BAR MEALS, RESTAURANT EVENINGS ONLY; NON-SMOKING AREAS; AMBLESIDE 6 MILES; S£££ £, D£££.

## THE BRITANNIA INN
**Elterwater, Ambleside, Cumbria LA22 9HP**
**Tel: 015394 37210 • Fax: 015394 37311 • e-mail: info@britinn.net**
**website: www.britinn.net**

A quintessential English Lakeland inn nestled in the centre of the picturesque village of Elterwater amidst the imposing mountains of the Langdale Valley. The Britannia Inn offers sanctuary from hectic daily life with ales and foods to satisfy all tastes - the dining room is much in demand, lunch and evening menus provide an eclectic dining experience, from popular favourites to the more unusual, with local produce used wherever possible. For a more informal setting, meals and refreshments are also available in the bar and on the patio. Comfortable twin and double rooms are available with en suite facilities. Each room has tea and coffee facilities, colour television, telephone and hairdryer. Lounge and car park solely for residents use. Guests are free to take advantage of Langdale Estate Country Club adjacent to the Britannia, providing a health and beauty salon, exercise studio, luxury pool, sanarium, spa and squash courts. *ETC* ★★★, *AA/RAC* ★★

9 BEDROOMS, 8 WITH PRIVATE SHOWER; FREE HOUSE WITH REAL ALE; HISTORIC INTEREST; CHILDREN AND PETS WELCOME; BAR MEALS, RESTAURANT EVENINGS ONLY; NON-SMOKING AREAS; S££££, D£££.

## SHEPHERD'S ARMS HOTEL
**Ennerdale Bridge, Lake District National Park, Cumbria CA23 3AR**
**Tel & Fax: 01946 861249 • e-mail: enquiries@shepherdsarmshotel.co.uk**

Although one of the smaller lakes, Ennerdale can fairly claim to be the most beautiful. From here, valley paths, forest tracks and lake shores offer a variety of rewarding walks suitable for all ages and capabilities. Other activities available include fishing, canoeing, bird watching and pony trekking. With an informal and relaxed atmosphere on one of the most attractive stretches of Wainwright's Coast to Coast footpath, this splendid small hotel presents first-rate food and accommodation. Several real ales are served and there is an extensive bar menu including daily 'specials'. Traditional comforts are very much in evidence and bedrooms have central heating, remote-control colour television, direct-dial telephone and tea and coffee-makers.

8 BEDROOMS, 6 EN SUITE, 2 WITH PRIVATE BATHROOM; FREE HOUSE WITH REAL ALE; CHILDREN AND PETS WELCOME; BAR MEALS, RESTAURANT EVENINGS ONLY; NON-SMOKING AREAS; WHITEHAVEN 8 MILES; S£££, D££.

## THE GILPIN BRIDGE INN & HOTEL
Bridge End, Levens, Near Kendal, Cumbria LA8 8EP
Tel: 015395 52206 • Fax: 015395 52444 • e-mail: info@gilpinbridgeinn.co.uk
website: www.gilpinbridgeinn.co.uk

Beautifully furnished and of immense character, this family-run establishment lies on the A590, just 10 minutes from Junction 36 of the M6. At the gateway to the lakes and on the edge of the National Parks, the inn is steeped in history and legend. It is said that it is named after a Norman knight, Richard de Gylpin, who, returning from the Crusades, delivered the local populace from the ravages of a blood-thirsty wild boar. Peace reigns today at this hospitable retreat which provides first-class refreshment in the most attractive surroundings. A memorable break amidst awe-inspiring scenery is further assured by superbly appointed en suite accommodation with a hearty Lakeland breakfast to start the day's activities. Additional attractions are a children's outdoor play area and a beer garden.

9 BEDROOMS, ALL WITH PRIVATE BATHROOM; ROBINSONS HOUSE WITH REAL ALE; HISTORIC INTEREST; CHILDREN WELCOME, PETS BY ARRANGEMENT; BAR AND RESTAURANT MEALS; NON-SMOKING AREAS; KENDAL 5 MILES; S£££, D££.

## WHITE LION INN
Patterdale, Penrith, Cumbria CA11 0NW
Tel: 01768 482214

This old world country inn with a friendly atmosphere is situated near Lake Ullswater and Helvellyn, an ideal centre for walking, fishing and sailing. The seven cosy letting bedrooms are mostly en suite with all facilities. Traditional beers and good food are served. Whatever the reason for visiting the White Lion, you will always leave with the memory of a good time. Open all year. *ETC* ◆◆◆

7 BEDROOMS, ALL WITH PRIVATE BATHROOM; REAL ALES; CHILDREN AND DOGS WELCOME; BAR MEALS; WINDERMERE 12 MILES; S££, D££.

## THE TROUTBECK INN
Troutbeck, Penrith, Cumbria CA11 0SJ
Tel: 017684 83635 • Fax: 017684 83928 • e-mail: enquires@troutbeck-inn.com
website: www.troutbeck-inn.com

A peaceful Lakeland touring centre between Keswick and Penrith and close to the shores of lovely Ullswater, this friendly and well-appointed inn enjoys sweeping fell views and is a haven for a variety of outdoor pursuits, especially walking, rock climbing, fishing and pony trekking. The inn is known for its excellent varied food and real ales, meals being taken in either an attractive dining room or cosy lounge where a blazing fire combats winter chill. Tastefully furnished bedrooms have en suite facilities, colour television and tea and coffee-makers and there are three self-catering cottages, recently converted from the former barn and stables, which are centrally heated and furnished to the highest standards. *ETC* ★★★★

7 BEDROOMS, ALL WITH PRIVATE BATHROOM; FREE HOUSE WITH REAL ALE; CHILDREN AND PETS WELCOME; BAR AND RESTAURANT MEALS; NON-SMOKING AREAS; KESWICK 8 MILES; S££, D£/££.

## BRACKENRIGG INN
Watermillock, Ullswater, Penrith, Cumbria CA11 0LP
Tel: 01768 486206 • Fax: 01768 486945 • website: www.brackenrigginn.co.uk
e-mail: enquiries@brackenrigginn.co.uk

With breathtaking views across Ullswater, this 18th century coaching inn is an informal port of call with a cheerful bar warmed by an open fire and a reputation for excellent food. A bar menu is available for lunch and dinner, with a table d'hôte menu added in the evenings; the chef-inspired fare can be enjoyed in the bar, lounge or restaurant. With so much to see and do in the area as nature intended, this is a rewarding place in which to stay. With the benefit of a fabulous panorama of lake and fells, the comfortable guest rooms have en suite facilities, colour television and tea and coffee-makers; all are centrally heated, including spacious suites and superior rooms. There is wheelchair access and a suite suitable for disabled guests is available. *AA* ◆◆◆, *Les Routiers*. *See also Colour Advertisement.*

17 BEDROOMS, ALL WITH PRIVATE BATHROOM; FREE HOUSE WITH REAL ALE; HISTORIC INTEREST; CHILDREN WELCOME, DOGS BY ARRANGEMENT; BAR AND RESTAURANT MEALS; NON-SMOKING AREAS; POOLEY BRIDGE 3 MILES; S££/£££, D££/£££.

# Derbyshire

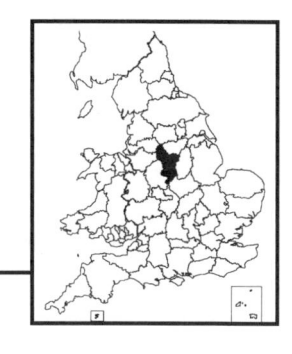

## LEATHERBRITCHES' BENTLEY BROOK INN
Fenny Bentley, Ashbourne, Derbyshire DE6 1LF
Tel: 01335 350278 • Fax: 01335 350422 • e-mail: all@bentleybrookinn.co.uk
website: www.bentleybrookinn.co.uk

One of the most attractive hostelries in the Peak District National Park, this is the home of the Leatherbritches Brewery, brewers of CAMRA award-winning, cask-conditioned ales which attract connoisseurs from far and wide. This is an interesting port of call just two miles from Dovedale, with a bar arranged around a central log fire. From noon to 9.00pm, informal, home-cooked meals are served to eat in the bar or garden whilst, in the restaurant, the chef and his dedicated team prepare dishes of the highest quality in both traditional and exotic style. A lively venue in which to find good company and refreshment (maybe at the garden barbecue), the inn has splendidly appointed en suite accommodation. *ETC* ★★, *AA*.

9 BEDROOMS, ALL WITH PRIVATE BATHROOM; FREE HOUSE WITH REAL ALE; CHILDREN AND PETS WELCOME;
BAR AND RESTAURANT MEALS; NON-SMOKING AREAS; ASHBOURNE 2 MILES; S£££, D££.

## THE WALTZING WEASEL
New Mills Road, Birch Vale, High Peak, Derbyshire SK22 1BT
Tel & Fax: 01663 743402 • e-mail: w-weasel@zen.co.uk
website: www.w-weasel.co.uk

There are pub names of infinite variety but this one must take the biscuit for originality. This is, in fact, a dyed-in-the-wool traditional country inn that is without the need of gimmicks to attract lovers of good food and drink. Bang in the heart of the Peak District, the inn possesses a restful ambience induced by subdued lighting, antiques and mullioned windows through which there are fine views of Kinder Scout. Wholesome fare is served in a cosy restaurant and those seeking first rate accommodation in this lovely area have handsome en suite bedrooms at their disposal, all with colour television, direct-dial telephone and tea and coffee making facilities.

8 BEDROOMS, ALL WITH PRIVATE BATHROOM; FREE HOUSE WITH REAL ALE; HISTORIC INTEREST; CHILDREN AND PETS WELCOME; BAR AND RESTAURANT MEALS; NON-SMOKING AREAS; HAYFIELD 1 MILE; S££££, D££££.

## THE DEVONSHIRE ARMS
Peak Forest, Near Buxton, Derbyshire SK17 8EJ
Tel: 01298 23875 • Fax: 01298 23598
e-mail: fionaclough@virgin.net • website: www.devarms.com

Traditional inn situated in a village location in the heart of the Peak District. Close to all main attractions and in excellent walking country. All rooms are en suite and have been furbished to a high standard, with television and tea and coffee making facilities. Excellent meals and traditional ales available every day. A warm welcome to all. Dogs and children free. *ETC* ◆◆◆

6 BEDROOMS, ALL WITH PRIVATE BATHROOM; FREE HOUSE WITH REAL ALE; HISTORIC INTEREST; CHILDREN AND PETS WELCOME; BAR AND RESTAURANT MEALS; NON-SMOKING AREAS; CHAPEL-EN-LE-FRITH 4 MILES; S££, D£.

# YE OLDE CHESHIRE CHEESE INN
How Lane, Castleton, Hope Valley, Derbyshire S33 8WJ
Tel: 01433 620330 • Fax: 01433 621847 • e-mail: kslack@btconnect.com
website: www.cheshirecheeseinn.co.uk

This delightful 17th century free house is situated in the heart of the Peak District and is an ideal base for walkers and climbers; other local attractions include cycling, swimming, gliding, horse riding and fishing. All bedrooms are en suite with colour television and tea/coffee making facilities. A "Village Fayre" menu is available all day, all dishes home-cooked in the traditional manner; there is also a selection of daily specials. Large car park. Full Fire Certificate. All credit cards accepted. Special golf packages arranged. Personal training instructor and gym available on premises. *ETC* ◆◆◆ *See also Colour Advertisement.*

10 BEDROOMS, ALL WITH PRIVATE BATHROOM; FREE HOUSE WITH REAL ALE; HISTORIC INTEREST; CHILDREN WELCOME; BAR AND RESTAURANT MEALS; HATHERSAGE 5 MILES; ££££ (PER ROOM).

# THE MANIFOLD INN
Hulme End, Hartington, Derbyshire SK17 0EX
Tel: 01298 84537

The Manifold Inn is a 200-year-old coaching inn offering warm hospitality and good pub food at sensible prices. This lovely mellow stone inn nestles on the banks of the River Manifold opposite the old toll house that used to serve the turnpike and river ford. All guest accommodation is in the old stone blacksmith's shop in the secluded rear courtyard of the inn. The bedrooms have en suite showers, colour television, tea/coffee making facilities and telephone. *ETC* ◆◆◆

5 BEDROOMS, ALL WITH PRIVATE SHOWER/TOILET; FREE HOUSE WITH REAL ALE; BAR MEALS AND DINING ROOM; NON-SMOKING AREAS; CHILDREN WELCOME, BUXTON 10 MILES, ASHBOURNE 10, BAKEWELL 10, LEEK 8; S£££, D££.

---

The £ symbol when appearing at the end of the italic section of an entry shows the anticipated price, during 2005, for full Bed and Breakfast.

| *Normal Bed & Breakfast rate per person* (in single room) | | *Normal Bed & Breakfast rate per person* (sharing double/twin room) | |
| --- | --- | --- | --- |
| PRICE RANGE | CATEGORY | PRICE RANGE | CATEGORY |
| **Under £25** | S£ | **Under £25** | D£ |
| **£26-£35** | S££ | **£26-£35** | D££ |
| **£36-£45** | S£££ | **£36-£45** | D£££ |
| **Over £45** | S££££ | **Over £45** | D££££ |

This is meant as an indication only and does not show prices for Special Breaks, Weekends, etc. Guests are therefore advised to verify all prices on enquiring or booking.

## YORKSHIRE BRIDGE INN
Ashopton Road, Bamford in the High Peak, Hope Valley, Derbyshire S33 0AZ
Tel & Fax: 01433 651361 • e-mail: mr@ybridge.force9.co.uk
website: www.yorkshire-bridge.co.uk

One of the finest residential inns in the Peak District and one that has attracted awards for its food, hospitality and 'inn-ability', this charming free house lies amidst majestic scenery; the Ladybower Dam is only a short stroll away, beyond which stretch the Derwent and Howden Reservoirs, affording breathtaking views and lovely walks through woods, over rolling hills and alongside tinkling streams. A neat and well-stocked bar and restaurant await visitors to promote the qualities of real ale and reasonably-priced, chef-prepared cuisine. The 14 en suite cottage-style bedrooms will make your stay complete. *ETC* ★★ *and Silver Award, AA* ★★

14 BEDROOMS, ALL WITH PRIVATE BATHROOM; FREE HOUSE WITH REAL ALE; HISTORIC INTEREST; CHILDREN WELCOME, PETS BY ARRANGEMENT; BAR AND RESTAURANT MEALS; NON-SMOKING AREAS; HATHERSAGE 2 MILES; S££££, D£££.

## LITTLE MILL INN
Rowarth, High Peak, Derbyshire SK22 1EB
Tel: 01663 746305/743275 • Fax: 01663 742686
website: www.littlemillrowarth.co.uk

Those nostalgic for the great days of railway travel will enjoy a visit to the Little Mill for there, in the delightful garden, is a Pullman dining car, once an integral part of the famous Brighton Belle. Resplendent with all its original wood panelling and brass fittings, it has been skilfully converted into luxurious en suite bedrooms. This is a fascinating experience amidst colourful surroundings with the millstream running nearby and with swings for the children. The inn has a relaxed and informal atmosphere; real ale is served and each evening the Carvery presents meals of high quality; bar meals and snacks are also available daily. There are also two self-contained holiday cottages equipped with all modern amenities.

7 BEDROOMS, ALL WITH PRIVATE BATHROOM; FREE HOUSE WITH REAL ALE; HISTORIC INTEREST; CHILDREN AND PETS WELCOME; BAR MEALS, RESTAURANT EVENINGS ONLY; NON-SMOKING AREAS; HAYFIELD 2 MILES; S££, D£.

---

# FHG
## Other specialised
## FHG PUBLICATIONS
Published annually: available in all good bookshops or direct from the publisher (post-free to addresses in the UK)

- • PETS WELCOME! £8.99
- • Recommended COUNTRY HOTELS of Britain £7.99
- • Recommended SHORT BREAK HOLIDAYS in Britain £7.99
- • THE GOLF GUIDE Where to Play/Where to Stay £9.99

### FHG PUBLICATIONS LTD,
Abbey Mill Business Centre,
Seedhill, Paisley, Renfrewshire PA1 1TJ
Tel: 0141-887 0428 • Fax: 0141-889 7204
e-mail: fhg@ipcmedia.com
website: www.holidayguides.com

# Devon

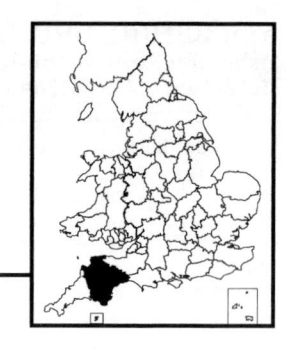

## THE RISING SUN INN
Woodland, Ashburton, Devon TQ13 7JT
Tel: 01364 652544 • Fax: 01364 653628 • e-mail: mail@risingsunwoodland.co.uk
website: www.risingsunwoodland.co.uk

In the shadow of the rolling expanses of Dartmoor and within easy reach of the Torbay resorts, this countryfied inn is well recommended by leading guides. In the matter of refreshment, it is renowned for its succulent home-made pies, West Country cheeses, Princetown Jail ale, local Luscombe cider and an extensive wine list. Families are most welcome; cosy log fires combat winter chill and, in summer, the lovely garden with its children's play area, is in popular demand. Splendidly appointed accommodation is available in four double and two twin-bedded rooms, all with en suite facilities, television and tea and coffee-makers. Ideal for an informal combined sea and country holiday. *AA Four Red Diamonds.*

6 BEDROOMS, ALL WITH PRIVATE BATHROOM; FREE HOUSE WITH REAL ALE; CHILDREN AND PETS WELCOME;
BAR AND RESTAURANT MEALS; NON-SMOKING AREAS; ASHBURTON 2 MILES; S£££, D££.

## THE DURANT ARMS
Ashprington, Totnes, Devon TQ9 7UP
Tel: 01803 732240/732471 • Fax: 01803 732471
e-mail: info@thedurantarms.com • website: www.thedurantarms.com

Nestling amidst the verdant beauty of the Dart Valley in a picturesque and well-preserved South Hams village, this attractive inn has all the virtues of a traditional English country inn with the comforts of the contemporary holiday-maker in mind. With many footpaths and bridleways nearby leading to the leafy shores of the River Dart, this lovely hostelry will repay a casual or even longer visit. The cuisine is worthy of special mention with a wide range of main courses catering for all tastes plus an interesting selection of imaginative desserts. Just three miles past the Elizabethan town of Totnes, this is a fine overnight stop and several beautifully appointed bedrooms suit the purpose admirably. AA ◆◆◆◆. *See also Colour Advertisement.*

7 BEDROOMS, ALL EN SUITE; FREE HOUSE WITH REAL ALE; HISTORIC INTEREST; PETS WELCOME;
BAR AND RESTAURANT MEALS; NON-SMOKING AREAS; TOTNES 3 MILES; S£££, D£££.

---

## PLEASE NOTE

All the information in this book is given in good faith in the belief that it is correct. However, the publishers cannot guarantee the facts given in these pages, neither are they responsible for changes in policy, ownership or terms that may take place after the date of going to press. Readers should always satisfy themselves that the facilities they require are available and that the terms, if quoted, still apply.

## THE POACHER'S POCKET
Burlescombe, Near Tiverton, Devon EX16 7JY
Tel: 01823 672286 • e-mail: poachers.pocket@virgin.net
website: www.poacherspocket.co.uk

Retaining all the character of yesteryear, this tidy little hostelry dates from the 17th century. Whether your visit be long and lingering or short and sweet, you may be sure of a warm welcome from hosts, Graeme and Gill Yeo, aided in practical terms by a real log fire in the bar. A delicious variety of home-cooked meals is served daily, and can be enjoyed either in the restaurant, or, more informally, in the lounge bar. Direct on the A38 between Junctions 26 and 27 of the M5 and within easy reach of Exmoor and several areas of outstanding beauty, this former coaching inn provides excellent accommodation at very reasonable rates in double, twin or family rooms, all with private facilities.

8 BEDROOMS, ALL WITH PRIVATE BATHROOM; FREE HOUSE WITH REAL ALE; HISTORIC INTEREST; CHILDREN WELCOME; BAR AND RESTAURANT MEALS; TIVERTON 7 MILES; S£££, D££.

## THREE CROWNS HOTEL
High Street, Chagford, Devon TQ13 8AJ
Tel: 01647 433444 • Fax: 01647 433117 • e-mail: threecrowns@msn.com
website: www.chagford-accom.co.uk

Fine mullioned windows, massive oak beams and a huge open fireplace are features that give salient evidence of this superb inn's origins in the 13th century. Granite-built, the mellow aura of unhurried days gone by makes an immediate impression, and one can almost feel the character of this remarkable hostelry when bringing to mind all those who have enjoyed good refreshment and company over the centuries. Fine modern amenities have been skilfully introduced, primarily in respect of the accommodation, all the centrally heated rooms now having bath or shower en suite, colour television and tea and coffee-making facilities. But still the time-honoured ambience remains. The lovely old bar (and skittle alley) encourages friendly chit-chat (and rivalry) in which locals are likely to join, and musical evenings, known as 'chimney corners', are held regularly. Sunny days will find the beer gardens well-patronised. And so to dine; an attractive dining room presents a titillating choice between the tempting table d'hôte menu and the comprehensive à la carte selection, augmented by an interesting wine list. Whatever one's fancy, the result – superb. At lunchtime, the daily 'specials' are much in demand. Within easy reach are all the pleasures of Dartmoor and the coast; Chagford, an old stannary town, and this splendid hotel in particular, makes the perfect base for a memorable break. *ETC/AA/RAC* ★★

17 BEDROOMS, ALL WITH PRIVATE BATHROOM; FREE HOUSE WITH REAL ALE; HISTORIC INTEREST; CHILDREN AND PETS WELCOME; BAR MEALS, RESTAURANT EVENINGS ONLY; MORETONHAMPSTEAD 4 MILES; S£££££, D£££££.

**FHG** Free or reduced rate entry to Holiday Visits and Attractions - see our **READERS' OFFER VOUCHERS** on pages 21-40

## THE ROYAL OAK INN
**Dunsford, Near Exeter, Devon EX6 7DA**
**Tel: 01647 252256**

Enjoy a friendly welcome in our traditional Country Pub in the picturesque thatched village of Dunsford. Quiet en suite bedrooms are available in the tastefully converted cob barn. An ideal base for touring Dartmoor, Exeter and the coast, and the beautiful Teign Valley. Real ale and home-made meals are served. Well behaved children and dogs are welcome. Please ring Mark or Judy Harrison for further details. *CAMRA, Good Pub Guide.*

8 BEDROOMS, 5 WITH PRIVATE BATHROOM; FREE HOUSE WITH REAL ALE; CHILDREN WELCOME; BAR FOOD; NON-SMOKING AREAS; EXETER 6 MILES, MORETONHAMPSTEAD 4; s££,D£.

## THE FOREST INN
**Hexworthy, Dartmoor, Devon PL20 6SD**
**Tel: 01364 631211 • Fax: 01364 631515 • e-mail: info@theforestinn.co.uk**
**website: www.theforestinn.co.uk**

A haven for walkers, riders, fishermen, canoeists, or anyone just looking for an opportunity to enjoy the natural beauty of Dartmoor – muddy paws and boots welcome! The restaurant specialises in home-cooked foods using local produce wherever possible. As an alternative, there is an extensive range of snacks which can be enjoyed in the more informal setting of the Huccaby Room. With the emphasis on Devon beers and cider, you have the opportunity to quench your thirst after the efforts of the day with a drink in the bar or relaxing on the chesterfields in the lounge area, which is complete with a log fire for winter evenings. *ETC* ◆◆◆◆

10 BEDROOMS, ALL WITH PRIVATE BATHROOM; FREE HOUSE WITH REAL ALE; HISTORIC INTEREST; CHILDREN AND PETS WELCOME; BAR MEALS, RESTAURANT EVENINGS ONLY; NON-SMOKING AREAS; ASHBURTON 7 MILES; s£££, D£££.

## MILDMAY COLOURS INN
**Holbeton, Plymouth, Devon PL8 1NA**
**Tel: 01752 830248 • Fax: 01752 830432 • website: www.mildmay-colours.co.uk**

A magnet for real ale buffs and racing enthusiasts, this old inn was built in 1617 and is set in a beautiful village near superb beaches and with Dartmoor and the fine city of Plymouth within easy reach. Golf, fishing, horse riding, sailing and walking the Devon Coastal Path are local activities to be enjoyed. Renamed in memory of the steeplechasing legend, the late Anthony Mildmay, it offers a choice of locally brewed beers. There is a large bar with an extensive menu, and a popular à la carte restaurant known for its delicious home cooking. Excellent en suite accommodation is available in tastefully decorated bedrooms.

6 BEDROOMS, ALL WITH PRIVATE BATHROOM; FREE HOUSE WITH REAL ALE; HISTORIC INTEREST;
CHILDREN AND PETS WELCOME; BAR AND RESTAURANT MEALS; NON-SMOKING AREAS; PLYMOUTH 10 MILES; s££, D££.

## THE TWISTED OAK PUBLIC HOUSE & RESTAURANT
Little John's Cross Hill, Ide, Exeter, Devon EX2 9RG
Tel: 01392 273666

With new owners and a fresh new image, the Twisted Oak at Ide is the place to be seen. With the best locally sourced produce at the right price, each dish is cooked to order by head chef, Michael Balbi, and his team, whilst the front of house staff provide a friendly, professional service. A great deal of time has been spent on devising the menu, which caters for all tastes, incorporating classic pub favourites and more imaginative dishes with influences from around the globe, as well as the blackboard with seasonal specials and fresh, locally caught fish. The wine list is well balanced and complements the menu, with a good selection by the glass, and they will always serve local real ale. *See also Colour Advertisement.*

NO ACCOMMODATION; REAL ALE; CHILDREN WELCOME; BAR AND RESTAURANT MEALS; EXETER 2 MILES.

## THE CASTLE INN, HOTEL & RESTAURANT
Lydford, Okehampton, Devon EX20 4BH
Tel: 01822 820241 • Fax: 01822 820454 • e-mail: info@castleinnlydford.co.uk
website: www.castleinnlydford.co.uk

One of the finest traditional wayside inns in the West Country, this romantic Elizabethan, family-run hotel simply oozes character. Featured in Conan Doyle's 'The Hound of the Baskervilles', it nestles on the western slopes of Dartmoor, offering first-class food in a bar and restaurant with slate floors, bowed ceilings, low, lamp-lit beams and fascinating antiques; dining by candlelight from imaginative à la carte menus is a memorable experience. Close by is Lydford Castle, built in 1195, and picturesque Lydford Gorge. Guest rooms, decorated in individual style, are beautifully furnished and equipped. This is a wonderful place to shake off the cobwebs of urban existence and appreciate the really worthwhile things of life. *See also Colour Advertisement.*

8 BEDROOMS, ALL WITH PRIVATE BATHROOM; HEAVITREE HOUSE WITH REAL ALE; HISTORIC INTEREST; CHILDREN AND PETS WELCOME; BAR AND RESTAURANT MEALS; NON-SMOKING AREAS; OKEHAMPTON 8 MILES; s£££, D££.

---

## *The* FHG GOLF GUIDE
*Where to Play*
*Where to Stay*

Available from most bookshops, **THE GOLF GUIDE** (published annually) covers details of every UK golf course – well over 2800 entries – for holiday or business golf. Hundreds of hotel entries offer convenient accommodation, accompanying details of the courses – the 'pro', par score, length etc.

*In association with 'Golf Monthly' and including Holiday Golf in Ireland, France, Portugal, Spain, The USA, South Africa and Thailand*

£9.99 from bookshops or from the publishers (postage charged outside UK) • FHG Publications, Abbey Mill Business Centre, Paisley PA1 1TJ

## RISING SUN HOTEL & RESTAURANT
Harbourside, Lynmouth, Devon EX35 6EG
Tel: 01598 753223 • Fax: 01598 753480 • website: www.specialplace.co.uk
e-mail: reception@risingsunlynmouth.co.uk

Dating back to the 14th century, the Rising Sun Hotel is an historic smugglers' Inn nestled in the picturesque harbour of Lynmouth. Over the years it has been gently transformed into an elegant harbourside hotel, whilst retaining its character and charm, with oak panelled dining room and bar, crooked corridors and delightful rooms. Boasting superior service, comfortable surroundings and fine cuisine, combined with truly magnificent views of the harbour and Exmoor coastline, the Rising Sun offers warmth, friendliness and a personal touch whilst providing the highest standards. All our individually furnished bedrooms are comfortably appointed and possess a charm and individuality seldom found in modern hotels. Most have views over the harbour, assuring guests of an unforgettable experience. Our restaurant provides an intimate and relaxed ambience. Incorporating the season's produce, maintaining quality and freshness, your meal will reach the highest standards of presentation, taste and creativity. *See also Inside Front Cover.*

ALL BEDROOMS WITH EN SUITE SHOWER/BATHROOM; BAR AND RESTAURANT MEALS;
BARNSTAPLE 20 MILES, MINEHEAD 17.

---

## BLACKCOCK INN
Molland, South Molton, Devon EX36 3NW
Tel: 01769 550297 • Fax: 01769 550101 • e-mail: info@blackcockinn.com
website: www.blackcockinn.com

On the southern fringe of Exmoor and romantically remote, this homely, stone-built inn, set in a picturesque valley, extends a real Devon welcome to families. Excellent real ales and home-cooked bar and restaurant meals are served seven days a week. Children are welcome and there is a beer garden, an indoor heated swimming pool and a family and games room; free live entertainment is provided on Saturday evenings. Accommodation is provided in delightfully equipped cottages situated just behind the pub where there is a caravan and camping site. An idyllic retreat with coarse fishing available nearby.

SELF-CATERING ACCOMMODATION AVAILABLE; FREE HOUSE WITH REAL ALE; HISTORIC INTEREST;
CHILDREN AND PETS WELCOME; BAR AND RESTAURANT MEALS; NON-SMOKING AREAS; SOUTH MOLTON 6 MILES.

## THE SMUGGLERS
North Morte Road, Mortehoe, North Devon EX34 7DR
Tel: 01271 870891 • Fax: 01271 871288
e-mail: smugglers@barbox.net

Situated in the pretty village of Mortehoe, The Smugglers offers luxury accommodation from twin rooms to family suites. Treat yourselves and your pets to beautiful coastal walks and golden beaches, before you sample our delicious home-cooked meals, real ales and warm, year-round hospitality.

8 BEDROOMS, ALL WITH PRIVATE BATHROOM; FREE HOUSE WITH REAL ALE; HISTORIC INTEREST; CHILDREN AND PETS WELCOME; BAR AND RESTAURANT MEALS; NON-SMOKING AREAS; ILFRACOMBE 4 MILES. S£/££.

## THE RING OF BELLS INN
North Bovey, Devon TQ13 8RB
Tel: 01647 440375 • Fax: 01647 440746 • e-mail: info@ringofbellsinn.com
website: www.ringofbellsinn.com

For a real taste of Dartmoor, stay at the 13th century thatched Ring of Bells Inn in the delightfully unspoilt village of North Bovey. The Ring of Bells is surrounded by beautiful countryside, and is ideal as a base for exploring Dartmoor. The recently refurbished accommodation consists of five charming double/twin bedrooms, all with en suite bathrooms, tea and coffee facilities, and colour TV. Low beams and real fires add to the ambience, and as well as a variety of home-cooked bar meals, there is a cosy dining room where the chefs provide excellent fixed price and à la carte menus, which include local loin of venison, tender North Bovey steaks, Devon duckling, fresh Brixham fish, and some inspired vegetarian dishes. There is an interesting wine list, and a selection of well-kept local ales on tap. Featured as one of 'Devon's Finest', and awarded the 'Gold Seal' of excellence for quality and service, The Ring of Bells is simply enchanting. *ETC* ♦♦♦♦. *See also Colour Advertisement.*

5 BEDROOMS, ALL WITH PRIVATE BATHROOM; FREE HOUSE WITH REAL ALE; HISTORIC INTEREST; CHILDREN AND PETS WELCOME; BAR AND RESTAURANT MEALS; NON-SMOKING AREAS; MORETONHAMPSTEAD 2 MILES; S£££, D£££.

## THE OXENHAM ARMS HOTEL
South Zeal, Okehampton, Devon EX20 2JT
Tel: 01837 840244 • Fax: 01837 840791 • e-mail: theoxenhamarms@aol.com
website: www.oxenhamarms.co.uk

The fascinating history of this ancient inn dates back even further than 1477, when it was first licensed. Intriguing architectural features are to be found at every turn, among them a prehistoric monolith set in the wall of one of the smaller lounges: this is believed to be part of the original site with the inn actually constructed around it by the lay monks who were the original builders. In the main lounge is a large granite fireplace and a granite pillar supporting the beam in the old dining room is of interest. In this setting and also in the bar, a wide variety of traditional and international dishes of quality may be savoured. Unobtrusively modernised, the inn provides excellent en suite accommodation. *ETC* ★★, *AA*.

8 BEDROOMS, ALL WITH PRIVATE BATHROOM; FREE HOUSE WITH REAL ALE; HISTORIC INTEREST; CHILDREN AND PETS WELCOME; BAR MEALS, RESTAURANT EVENINGS ONLY; OKEHAMPTON 4 MILES; S£££, D££££

## THE WATERMAN'S ARMS
Bow Bridge, Ashprington, Near Totnes, Devon TQ9 7EG
Tel: 01803 732214 • Fax: 01803 732314 • website: www.roomattheinn.info
e-mail: watermansarms.ashprington@eldridge-pope.co.uk

Over the years, this famous old residential inn has been a smithy and brewhouse, a prison during the Napoleonic Wars and a haunt of the dreaded press gangs. Now tranquillity rules. The attractive hostelry lies peacefully on the banks of the River Harbourne, an ideal location for the holidaymaker seeking good food and drink among the byways of rural Devon or the businessman in need of temporary escape from routine. One can eat memorably in a cosy restaurant with a wide choice of tasty dishes available or al fresco in the beautiful riverside garden. Children are very welcome and have their own menu. This is a rewarding area for birdwatching and fishing can be arranged. A delightful place in which to stay, the inn has excellent en suite accommodation. *RAC* ♦♦♦♦

15 BEDROOMS, ALL WITH PRIVATE BATHROOM; ELDRIDGE POPE HOUSE WITH REAL ALE; HISTORIC INTEREST; CHILDREN AND PETS WELCOME; BAR AND RESTAURANT MEALS; NON-SMOKING AREAS; TOTNES 2 MILES; S£££££, D££

## KING'S ARMS INN
Tedburn St Mary, Near Exeter, Devon EX6 6EG
Tel: 01647 61224 • Fax: 01647 61324 • e-mail: reception@kingsarmsinn.co.uk
website: www.kingsarmsinn.co.uk

Just off the A30 and well placed for close acquaintance with the myriad pleasures of Devon's homely towns and incomparable countryside and with Exeter and the south coast not far distant, this historic and visually appealing hostelry dates back to the early 17th century. Originally known as the 'Taphouse Inn', it is said that King Charles II and his entourage stayed here whilst journeying to Cornwall in the mid-1600s and in recognition of his patronage, the King granted permission for the inn's name to be changed and accordingly to display his coat of arms. A right royal welcome is still extended to visitors with initiative enough to divert from the busy A30 to enjoy good food, drink and, if need be, accommodation in a typical Devon pub. *ETC* ◆◆, *AA, RAC*.

10 BEDROOMS, ALL WITH PRIVATE BATHROOM; FREE HOUSE WITH REAL ALE; HISTORIC INTEREST; CHILDREN AND PETS WELCOME; BAR AND RESTAURANT MEALS; NON-SMOKING AREAS; EXETER 7 MILES; S££, D££.

## SEA TROUT INN
Staverton, Near Totnes, Devon TQ9 6PA
Tel: 01803 762274 • Fax: 01803 762506 • website: www.seatroutinn.com

Over the years, this old friend, so conveniently placed for Dartmoor and the pleasures of Torbay and the South Devon coast, has served countless happy holidaymakers. Hidden away in the tranquil Dart Valley, the inn dates back to to the 15th century, and until thirty or so years ago was known as the Church House, an inn name that abounds in the county. Visually the archetypal traditional English inn, the Sea Trout has two attractive bars with oak beams, log fires, brasses and prize specimens of fish in showcases. With an excellent selection of bar meals, cask-conditioned ales and a wide range of wines, spirits and especially, malt whiskies, relaxation is easy, and the friendly locals in the adjoining Village Bar will be happy to accept challenges at pool and darts. The conservatory restaurant is an elegant place in which to enjoy an imaginative and intriguing choice from the set dinner menus in the evenings, with vegetarian dishes always available. Delightful bedrooms in cottage style await the overnight guest; all are delectably furnished and appointed with private bathroom, individually controlled central heating, colour television, and direct-dial telephone. Permits for trout, sea trout and salmon fishing are available from the Inn, the unofficial headquarters of the Dart Angling Association. For a real taste of rural Devon in the heart of an Area of Outstanding Natural Beauty, the Sea Trout has it all! *ETC* ★★, *AA Two Rosettes*.

10 BEDROOMS, ALL WITH PRIVATE BATHROOM; FREE HOUSE WITH REAL ALE; CHILDREN AND PETS WELCOME; BAR AND RESTAURANT MEALS; NON-SMOKING AREAS; TOTNES 2 MILES; S£££, D££.

---

Visit the FHG website **www.holidayguides.com**
for details of the wide choice of accommodation featured in
the full range of FHG titles

# Dorset

## ACORN INN
**28 Fore Street, Evershot, Dorchester, Dorset DT2 0JW**
**Tel: 01935 83228 • Fax: 01935 83707 • e-mail: stay@acorn-inn.co.uk**
**website: www.acorn-inn.co.uk**

This splendid 16th century village inn has remained true to its origins and although now blessed with the finest modern practicalities, the atmosphere and charm of its beamed bars remain to beguile guests to this idyllic Dorset village. Evershot is in fact "Evershead" in Hardy's Tess of the D'Urbervilles and the individually decorated and exceptionally well equipped bedrooms take their names from the novel. Dining by candlelight, having chosen from an imaginative and reasonably-priced à la carte menu and an extensive wine list, is a special pleasure. There is a well equipped games room for the young and young-in-heart, and a choice of cosy lounge and bar areas. *ETC/RAC/AA* ◆◆◆◆, *AA Rosette, RAC Blue Ribbon*.

9 BEDROOMS, ALL WITH PRIVATE BATHROOM; FREE HOUSE WITH REAL ALE; HISTORIC INTEREST; CHILDREN AND PETS WELCOME; BAR AND RESTAURANT MEALS; NON-SMOKING AREAS; DORCHESTER 13 MILES; S££££, D£££.

---

The **£** symbol when appearing at the end of the italic section of an entry shows the anticipated price, during 2005, for full Bed and Breakfast.

*Normal Bed & Breakfast rate per person (in single room)*

| PRICE RANGE | CATEGORY |
|---|---|
| Under £25 | S£ |
| £26-£35 | S££ |
| £36-£45 | S£££ |
| Over £45 | S££££ |

*Normal Bed & Breakfast rate per person (sharing double/twin room)*

| PRICE RANGE | CATEGORY |
|---|---|
| Under £25 | D£ |
| £26-£35 | D££ |
| £36-£45 | D£££ |
| Over £45 | D££££ |

This is meant as an indication only and does not show prices for Special Breaks, Weekends, etc. Guests are therefore advised to verify all prices on enquiring or booking.

## THE POACHERS INN
**Piddletrenthide, Dorchester, Dorset DT2 7QX**
**Tel: 01300 348358 • Fax: 01300 348153 • website: www.thepoachersinn.co.uk**
This delightful Country Inn is set in the heart of the lovely Piddle Valley, within easy reach of all Dorset's attractions. All rooms are en suite and have colour television, tea/coffee making facilities and telephone. For relaxation there is an outdoor swimming pool and a riverside garden. Half board guests choose from our à la carte menu at no extra cost. Brochure with full details on request. *ETC/AA* ◆◆◆◆. *See also Colour Advertisement.*

18 BEDROOMS, ALL WITH PRIVATE FACILITIES; CHILDREN AND PETS WELCOME; NON-SMOKING AREAS; DORCHESTER 8 MILES; S££, D££.

## THE ALBION HOTEL
**19 High Street, Wimborne, Dorset BH21 1HR**
**Tel: 01202 882492 • Fax: 01202 639333**
This attractively attired former coaching inn dates from the 17th century, and merits close consideration for a variety of reasons. Quite apart from the appeal of the bar where a selection of Badger real ales and appetising lunchtime 'daily specials' are served, the 'Albion' claims to be the haunt of a friendly ghost invested with the earthy name of 'Reg' by the locals. Also invoking the supernatural epithet is a millstream at the foot of the sizeable beer garden, where guests may relax, feed the ducks and catch glimpses of darting trout. With free parking in the hotel grounds, this is a fine touring base providing comfortable Bed and Breakfast accommodation at remarkably reasonable rates. *ETC* ◆◆

4 BEDROOMS, 1 WITH PRIVATE BATHROOM; HALL & WOODHOUSE HOUSE WITH REAL ALE; HISTORIC INTEREST; CHILDREN AND PETS WELCOME; BAR AND RESTAURANT MEALS; BOURNEMOUTH 7 MILES; D£.

---

## • • *Some Useful Guidance for Guests and Hosts* • •

Every year literally thousands of holidays, short breaks and overnight stops are arranged through our guides, the vast majority without any problems at all. In a handful of cases, however, difficulties do arise about bookings, which often could have been prevented from the outset.

*It is important to remember that when accommodation has been booked, both parties – guests and hosts – have entered into a form of contract. We hope that the following points will provide helpful guidance.*

### GUESTS:
- When enquiring about accommodation, be as precise as possible. Give exact dates, numbers in your party and the ages of any children.
- State the number and type of rooms wanted and also what catering you require – bed and breakfast, full board etc. Make sure that the position about evening meals is clear – and about pets, reductions for children or any other special points.
- Read our reviews carefully to ensure that the proprietors you are going to contact can supply what you want. Ask for a letter confirming all arrangements, if possible.
- If you have to cancel, do so as soon as possible. Proprietors do have the right to retain deposits and under certain circumstances to charge for cancelled holidays if adequate notice is not given and they cannot re-let the accommodation.

### HOSTS:
- Give details about your facilities and about any special conditions. Explain your deposit system clearly and arrangements for cancellations, charges etc. and whether or not your terms include VAT.
- If for any reason you are unable to fulfil an agreed booking without adequate notice, you may be under an obligation to arrange suitable alternative accommodation or to make some form of compensation.

*While every effort is made to ensure accuracy, we regret that FHG Publications cannot accept responsibility for errors, omissions or misrepresentations in our entries or any consequences thereof. Prices in particular should be checked because we go to press early. We will follow up complaints but cannot act as arbiters or agents for either party.*

# Durham

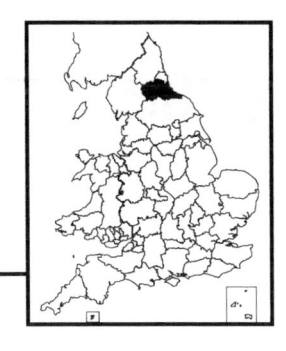

## THREE HORSESHOES INN
**Running Waters, Sherburn House, Durham DH1 2SR**
**Tel: 0191 372 0286 • Fax: 0191 372 3386 • website: www.activehotels.com**

A comfortable old country inn a short distance south-east of Durham City and just two miles from the A1(M), the 'Shoes' is the place to visit for a vast range of tempting fare from reasonably-priced 'daily specials' to salads and traditional favourites, including enormous steaks – remember to leave room for one of the delicious desserts. Children have their own menu and the Sunday lunch is a popular family feature. Several immaculately appointed double, twin and single bedrooms await overnight guests, each room having en suite facilities, colour television, hairdryer, tea and coffee-makers and lovely views across the Durham countryside. A function room is available for social and business gatherings. *ETC* ◆◆◆

6 BEDROOMS, ALL WITH PRIVATE BATHROOOM; FREE HOUSE WITH REAL ALE; HISTORIC INTEREST; CHILDREN AND PETS WELCOME; BAR AND RESTAURANT MEALS; NON-SMOKING AREAS; DURHAM 4 MILES; S£££££, D££.

## PUBLISHER'S NOTE

**FHG**

While every effort is made to ensure accuracy, we regret that FHG Publications cannot accept responsibility for errors, misrepresentations or omissions in our entries or any consequences thereof. Prices in particular should be checked because we go to press early. We will follow up complaints but cannot act as arbiters or agents for either party.

# Essex

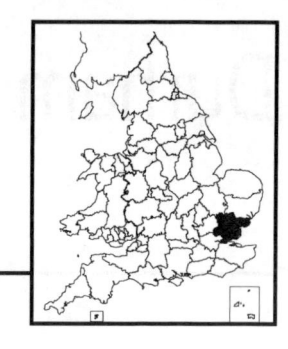

### FERRY BOAT INN
**North Fambridge, Essex CM3 6LR**
**Tel: 01621 740208 • website: www.ferryboatinn.net**
**enquiries@ferryboatinn.net**

Full of character, this weather-boarded riverside pub holds multiple appeal: as a tranquil retreat in which to unwind after a busy day; as a safe haven for those who like messing about in boats; and as an unspoilt base for the naturalist, far from the madding crowd and yet so near the great urban jungle. Good food and drink may be enjoyed in a bar with an open fire, in a sunny conservatory or in the low-beamed dining room which is said to date from the 1400s. Recently, several elegantly furnished suites have been added to the attractions of this centuries-old pub, each one having a private bathroom, colour television and coffee-making facilities. *ETC* ◆◆◆

6 BEDROOMS, ALL WITH PRIVATE BATHROOM; FREE HOUSE WITH REAL ALE; HISTORIC INTEREST; CHILDREN AND PETS WELCOME; BAR AND RESTAURANT MEALS; NON-SMOKING AREAS; BURNHAM-ON-CROUCH 6 MILES; S£€, D£££

---

Visit the **FHG** website
**www.holidayguides.com**
for details of the wide choice of accommodation
featured in the full range of FHG titles

# Gloucestershire

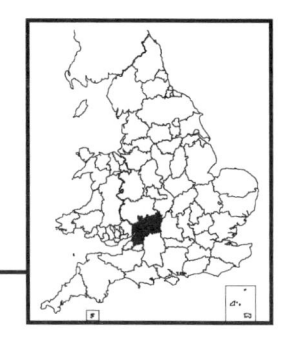

## BECKFORD INN HOTEL
Cheltenham Road, Beckford, Near Tewkesbury, Gloucestershire GL20 7AN
Tel: 01386 881532 • Fax: 01386 882021 • website: www.beckfordinn.co.uk

This splendid 18th century free house, built of warm Cotswold stone, is an imposing edifice. It stands on the A46 between Evesham and Cheltenham amidst glorious rolling countryside, a position that renders it an ideal touring base or for attending Cheltenham's National Hunt racecourse. Exhibiting the care and attention of a well-organised family-run establishment that itself welcomes families, the hotel has great character, especially apparent in the lounge bar with its oak beams and original fireplaces. Several cask ales are served and one may sit or eat out in the attractive gardens in fair weather, where there is plenty of play space for children. Bar meals cover a wide variety of dishes from the traditional to Chinese and Thai specialities and most dishes are cooked to order. There is a choice of vegetarian dishes and an appetising selection of desserts. The à la carte fare on offer in the Garden Restaurant is imaginative, and that 'family favourite', the Sunday lunch, is always a well-attended feature. Service is excellent and everywhere one is conscious of attention to detail. The comfortable accommodation takes the form of twin and double bedrooms, all of which have an en suite shower/wc, remote-control television and clock radio alarm. The hotel is also an experienced and popular venue for business and social functions, the facilities for which are of the highest order.

8 BEDROOMS, ALL WITH PRIVATE SHOWER/WC; FREE HOUSE WITH REAL ALE; HISTORIC INTEREST; CHILDREN WELCOME; BAR AND RESTAURANT MEALS; NON-SMOKING AREAS; TEWKESBURY 6 MILES; S£££, D££.

## THE KING'S ARMS HOTEL
The Square, Chipping Campden, Gloucestershire GL55 6AW
Tel: 01386 840256 • Fax: 01386 841598 • e-mail: info@thekingsarmshotel.com
website: www.thekingsarmshotel.com

In the very centre of a charming Cotswold town, the King's Arms is a fine 18th century Grade II Listed town house that offers great rewards in the matter of food, service and accommodation, enhanced by an atmosphere of subtle style. Representing remarkably good value for money, the fare served in both brasserie and restaurant is worthy of an accolade in its own right; dining before a roaring log fire in winter or al fresco in the garden in summer. But then, the newly renovated en suite guest rooms have equal claim to excellence. Very much to be recommended for a memorable Cotswold holiday, the hotel is also a popular and friendly venue for mini-conferences and social functions. *ETC/AA* ◆◆◆◆

12 BEDROOMS, ALL WITH PRIVATE BATHROOM; FREE HOUSE WITH REAL ALE; HISTORIC INTEREST; CHILDREN AND SMALL DOGS WELCOME; BAR LUNCHES AND RESTAURANT MEALS; NON-SMOKING AREAS; EVESHAM 8 MILES; S££££, D££££.

---

**FHG** **FHG PUBLICATIONS** publish a large range of well-known accommodation guides. We will be happy to send you details or you can use the order form at the back of this book.

## CROWN INN AND HOTEL
High Street, Blockley, Moreton-in-Marsh, Gloucestershire GL56 9EX
Tel: 01386 700245 • Fax: 01386 700247 • www.crown-inn-blockley.co.uk
e-mail: info@crown-inn-blockley.co.uk

Radiating warmth from the very stones of its honey-coloured facade, this lovely, 16th century inn on Blockley's High Street seems to have grown in stature and appeal over the years we have known it. A traditional hostelry in one of the most picturesque and unspoilt of all Cotswold villages, it is now very much in the hotel class without losing its intimate ambience, as may be witnessed in the convivial bars where real ale and light meals may be appreciated in company with friendly concourse with the locals before a blazing log fire. For first-rate dining, the informal brasserie is one of the finest in the area, whilst the very best in English and French cuisine will titillate the palate when dining by candlelight in Rafters Restaurant, so attractively furnished in contemporary style. For visits to Cheltenham and touring the Cotswolds, there are few better places in which to stay and Stratford-upon-Avon, Warwick, Worcester, Kenilworth and Oxford are also within easy reach. Modern conveniences of the highest calibre blend perfectly with old beams and mellow stone walls in the en suite guest rooms, all of which have colour television, radio, hair dryer and tea and coffee-making facilities. Several charming suites are also available, some resplendent with beautiful four-poster beds. Special breaks in co-ordination with Naunton Downs Golf Club are organised at reasonable rates with starting times guaranteed. *ETC/AA/RAC* ★★★, *Best Loved Hotels of the World.*

24 BEDROOMS, ALL WITH PRIVATE BATHROOM; FREE HOUSE WITH REAL ALE; HISTORIC INTERST; CHILDREN AND PETS WELCOME; BAR AND RESTAURANT MEALS; NON-SMOKING AREAS; MORETON-IN-MARSH 3 MILES; S££££, D£££.

---

*The* **FHG**
**GOLF**
**GUIDE**
*Where to Play*
*Where to Stay*

Available from most bookshops, **THE GOLF GUIDE** (published annually) covers details of every UK golf course – well over 2800 entries – for holiday or business golf. Hundreds of hotel entries offer convenient accommodation, accompanying details of the courses – the 'pro', par score, length etc.

*In association with 'Golf Monthly' and including Holiday Golf in Ireland, France, Portugal, Spain, The USA, South Africa and Thailand*

**£9.99 from bookshops or from the publishers (postage charged outside UK) • FHG Publications, Abbey Mill Business Centre, Paisley PA1 ITJ**

# THE WYNDHAM ARMS HOTEL
Clearwell, Near Coleford, Gloucestershire GL16 8JT
Tel: 01594 833666 • Fax: 01594 836450 • e-mail: res@thewyndhamhotel.co.uk
website: www.thewyndhamhotel.co.uk

The Wyndham Arms is situated in the heart of the picturesque village of Clearwell on the edge of the Royal Forest of Dean, near the beautiful Wye Valley. The building dates back to the 13th century, when it was a manor house, and today there are 18 en suite bedrooms (family, double, twin and single), with a large oak-beamed suite in the main building for that extra touch of luxury. Local beer, cider and country wines accompany the fresh local and seasonal produce used to create the ever-changing menus on offer. In summer there is outdoor seating, and in cooler seasons a log fire will warm you after a day's walking or exploring. The area offers much to see and do, including cycling, fishing and canoeing. *AA* ♦♦♦

18 BEDROOMS, ALL WITH PRIVATE BATHROOM, FAMILY SUITE; FREE HOUSE WITH REAL ALE; HISTORIC INTEREST; CHILDREN AND PETS WELCOME; BAR AND RESTAURANT MEALS; NON-SMOKING AREAS; COLEFORD 2 MILES; S£££, D£££.

# KING'S ARMS INN
The Street, Didmarton, Near Badminton, Gloucestershire GL9 1DT
Tel : 01454 238245 • Fax: 01454 238249
e-mail: bookings@kingsarmsdidmarton.co.uk

With the traditional ambience of a 17th century coaching inn, the 'King's Arms' has been lovingly refurbished throughout. Two attractive bars serve a wide selection of beers, wines and light meals, whilst the popular restaurant is already renowned for its imaginative menu. Facilities that would do credit to a many-starred hotel have been put in place without diminution of the character of the building. Delightfully furnished bedrooms all have en suite amenities and are equipped with television, radio alarm, direct-dial telephone, hairdryer and tea and coffee-makers. Open fire in the winter. Beautiful garden with boules pitch. A fine touring headquarters for the beautiful Cotswold countryside, Bath and Bristol, the inn also provides three excellent self-catering units in a converted stable block. *AA* ♦♦♦♦, *Taste of the West*, *CAMRA*.

4 BEDROOMS, ALL WITH PRIVATE BATHROOM; FREE HOUSE WITH REAL ALE; HISTORIC INTEREST; CHILDREN WELCOME, PETS IN BAR ONLY; BAR AND RESTAURANT MEALS; NON-SMOKING AREAS; TETBURY 6 MILES; S£££, D££.

# THE HOLLOW BOTTOM
Guiting Power, Cheltenham, Gloucestershire GL54 5UX
Tel: 01451 850392 • Fax: 01451 850945 • e-mail: hello@hollowbottom.com
website: www.hollowbottom.com

With the inn's long tradition of association with National Hunt racing at nearby Cheltenham, this is really one for jumping enthusiasts. Bars, interspersed with interesting nooks and crannies, buzz with animated conversation discussing the performances and projected promise of four-legged favourites (and dark horses!) and there are tables at front and back when the going is firm. Hugh and Charlie take benevolent charge of the welfare of visitors, the former front of house, the latter responsible for the superb fare. In the verdant heart of the Cotswolds, this attractive 'theme' pub is of great character. Excellent Bed and Breakfast accommodation is available too – but book early. And those breakfasts! *ETC/AA* ♦♦♦♦

4 BEDROOMS, ALL WITH PRIVATE BATHROOM; FREE HOUSE WITH REAL ALE; HISTORIC INTEREST; CHILDREN AND PETS WELCOME; BAR AND RESTAURANT MEALS; STOW-ON-THE-WOLD 6 MILES; S£££, D££.

## THE BELL INN
**High Street, Moreton-in-Marsh, Gloucestershire GL56 0AF**
**Tel: 01608 651688 • Fax: 01608 652195 • e-mail: keith.pendry@virgin.net**

An integral part of a handsome Cotswold town, the golden stone facade of this splendid 200-year-old beamed coaching house conveys a warm invitation to experience delights within. The invitation should be accepted with alacrity, for the rewards are outstanding food and drink and an ambience that charms both young and young-in-heart. A large selection of real ales feature in the bar and the restaurant's home-cooked fare offers excellent value. Meals may be enjoyed in an attractive courtyard and there is also a flower-bedecked beer garden. Several guest rooms of old-world character have been delightfully updated to include en suite facilities and tea and coffee-makers; two of them have disabled access. *ETC* ◆◆◆

5 BEDROOMS, ALL WITH PRIVATE BATHROOM; ENTERPRISE INNS HOUSE WITH REAL ALE; HISTORIC INTEREST;
CHILDREN AND PETS WELCOME; BAR MEALS; NON-SMOKING AREAS; CHIPPING NORTON 8 MILES; S£££££, D£££££.

## FALCON INN
**Painswick, Gloucestershire GL6 6UN**
**Tel: 01452 814222 • Fax: 01452 813377 • e-mail: bleninns@clara.net**
**website: www.falconinn.com**

Being situated right on the popular Cotswold Way, this fine 16th century coaching inn and posting house is a particular favourite with walkers and touring parties who appreciate the ambience of the bars with their stone floors, wood panelling and log fires; there is even a special drying room for ramblers should the weather disappoint. The inn has a fascinating history, having, in its time, served as a courthouse, the venue for cockfights and as an important coaching inn with stage coaches leaving regularly for destinations throughout the country. It also claims the world's oldest bowling green in the grounds. Excellent accommodation awaits guests, facilities being on a par with those offered by the restaurant which is renowned for its superb fare. There is a large car park. *ETC* ★★, *CAMRA, AA, Good Pub Guide; Les Routiers, Excellence Awards – Accommodation Inn of the Year.* ***See also Colour Advertisement.***

12 BEDROOMS, ALL WITH PRIVATE BATHROOM; FREE HOUSE WITH REAL ALE; HISTORIC INTEREST;
CHILDREN AND PETS WELCOME; BAR AND RESTAURANT MEALS; NON-SMOKING AREAS; STROUD 3 MILES; S£££, D££.

---

The **£** symbol when appearing at the end of the italic section of an entry shows the anticipated price, during 2005, for full Bed and Breakfast.

*Normal Bed & Breakfast rate per person*
*(in single room)*

| PRICE RANGE | CATEGORY |
|---|---|
| Under £25 | S£ |
| £26-£35 | S££ |
| £36-£45 | S£££ |
| Over £45 | S££££ |

*Normal Bed & Breakfast rate per person*
*(sharing double/twin room)*

| PRICE RANGE | CATEGORY |
|---|---|
| Under £25 | D£ |
| £26-£35 | D££ |
| £36-£45 | D£££ |
| Over £45 | D££££ |

This is meant as an indication only and does not show prices for Special Breaks, Weekends, etc. Guests are therefore advised to verify all prices on enquiring or booking.

---

See the ***Family-Friendly Pubs & Inns***
Supplement on pages 163-171 for establishments
which really welcome children

## THE FOUNTAIN INN
Parkend, Royal Forest of Dean, Gloucestershire GL15 4JD
Tel: 01594 562189 • Fax: 01594 564438 • e-mail: TheFountainInn@aol.com
website: www.thefountaininnandlodge.com

A traditional village inn, well known locally for its excellent meals and real ales. An extensive menu offers such delicious main courses as Lamb Steak in Woodland Berry Sauce and Gloucester Sausage in Onion Gravy, together with a large selection of curries, vegetarian dishes and snacks. Centrally situated in one of England's foremost wooded areas, the inn makes an ideal base for sightseeing, or for exploring some of the many peaceful forest walks nearby. All bedrooms (including one especially adapted for the less able) are en suite, decorated and furnished to an excellent standard, and have television and tea/coffee making facilities. Various half-board breaks are available throughout the year. *ETC* ◆◆◆. *See also Colour Advertisement.*

8 BEDROOMS, ALL WITH PRIVATE BATHROOM; HISTORIC INTEREST; FREE HOUSE WITH REAL ALE;
BAR AND RESTAURANT MEALS; CHILDREN AND PETS WELCOME; LYDNEY 4 MILES; S£££, D££

## UNICORN HOTEL
Sheep Street, Stow-on-the-Wold, Gloucestershire GL54 1HQ
Tel: 01451 830257 • Fax: 01451 831090 • e-mail: reception@birchhotels.co.uk
website: www.birchhotels.co.uk

The Unicorn Hotel is a 17th century coaching inn with honey stone walls and flower boxes. Set in the beautiful rolling Cotswold countryside, the Unicorn is located on the Roman Fosseway which runs between Cirencester and Warwick. Surrounded by some of the country's finest historic houses and gardens, and the cultural attractions of Stratford and Cheltenham, the hotel's central location is ideal. The dining room offers modern British cooking using seasonal local produce, created by our head chef, Michael Carr, while the oak-panelled bar serves appetising lighter meals reflecting the same high standards and imaginative flair. Afternoon tea can be taken in the relaxed atmosphere of the snug, whilst soaking up the history of our rare 'Spit Jack' fire. *ETC/AA/RAC* ★★★, *RAC Dining Award.*

20 BEDROOMS, ALL WITH PRIVATE BATHROOM; REAL ALE; HISTORIC INTEREST; CHILDREN WELCOME;
BAR MEALS, RESTAURANT EVENINGS ONLY; NON-SMOKING AREAS; CHIPPING NORTON 8 MILES; S££££, D£££/££££

---

**FHG** — Free or reduced rate entry to Holiday Visits and Attractions - see our **READERS' OFFER VOUCHERS** on pages 21-40

---

## PUBLISHER'S NOTE

While every effort is made to ensure accuracy, we regret that FHG Publications cannot accept responsibility for errors, misrepresentations or omissions in our entries or any consequences thereof. Prices in particular should be checked because we go to press early. We will follow up complaints but cannot act as arbiters or agents for either party.

# Hampshire

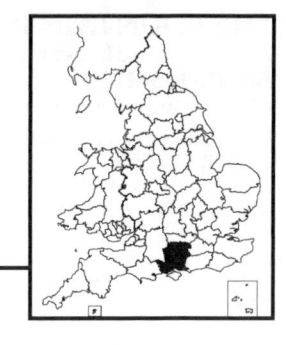

## THE COMPASSES INN
**Damerham, Near Fordingbridge, Hampshire SP6 3HQ**
**Tel: 01725 518231 • Fax: 01725 518880 • e-mail: info@compassesinn.net**
**website: www.compassesinn.net**

A perfect example of the traditional English country inn, The Compasses offers excellent value for money and a really warm welcome. Superb accommodation is available, with a choice of single, double and family rooms and a four-poster room. All are en suite, with television and tea and coffee making facilities. Great pride is taken in both the quality and variety of food and drink, with freshly produced food, an extensive wine list, a selection of over 100 malt whiskies and several real ales. The Compasses is situated in the heart of rural Wessex and offers excellent opportunities for exploring the New Forest, South Coast and many other local attractions. *ETC/AA* ◆◆◆◆

6 BEDROOMS, ALL WITH PRIVATE BATHROOM; FREE HOUSE WITH REAL ALE; HISTORIC INTEREST; CHILDREN AND PETS WELCOME; BAR AND RESTAURANT MEALS; NON-SMOKING AREAS; FORDINGBRIDGE 3 MILES; S£££, D££.

## THE TROOPER INN
**Alton Road, Froxfield, Petersfield, Hampshire GU32 1BD**
**Tel: 01730 827293 • Fax: 01730 827103 • e-mail: info@trooperinn.com**
**website: www.trooperinn.com**

High above the Hampshire Downs and backing on to the beautiful Ashford Hangers Nature Reserve, stands this distinguished 17th century country inn. A spacious bar, warmed by a log fire in winter, is a convivial gathering place flanked by discreet dining areas, whilst country cooking of the highest order is exhibited in a most attractive restaurant. In addition to the imaginative regular menu are appetising and constantly updated 'daily blackboard specials'. Just the place for a quiet country break, the inn has tastefully decorated guest rooms available with en suite facilities, television, telephone, hairdryer and trouser press. *ETC* ◆◆◆◆

8 BEDROOMS, ALL WITH PRIVATE BATHROOM; FREE HOUSE WITH REAL ALE; HISTORIC INTEREST; CHILDREN WELCOME; PETS IN BAR ONLY; BAR LUNCHES AND RESTAURANT MEALS; NON-SMOKING AREAS; PETERSFIELD 3 MILES; S££££, D£££.

## THE BELL INN HOTEL
**Brook, Lyndhurst, Hampshire SO43 7HE**
**Tel: 023 8081 2214 • Fax: 023 8081 3958 • e-mail: bell@bramshaw.co.uk**
**website: www.bramshaw.co.uk**

With delightful period pieces betraying its late 18th century origins, this handsome Listed building in the heart of the New Forest presents amenities well in keeping with a multi-starred establishment. The bar with its inglenook fireplace is a convivial meeting place and the cuisine is a gastronome's delight; traditional and imaginative dishes complemented by well-chosen wines. This fine inn-cum-hotel is of paramount interest to golfers with both the nearby Bramshaw and Dunwood Manor courses under the same ownership as the 'Bell'. Guests are offered temporary membership during their stay with reserved tee times. Double, twin and single bedrooms adhere to the highest modern standards of comfort, having en suite facilities, colour (teletext) television, direct-dial telephone and hospitality tray. *ETC* ★★★, *AA Rosette*.

26 BEDROOMS, ALL WITH PRIVATE BATHROOM; FREE HOUSE WITH REAL ALE; HISTORIC INTEREST; CHILDREN WELCOME; BAR AND RESTAURANT MEALS; NON-SMOKING AREAS; LYNDHURST 4 MILES; S£££££, D£££££.

## THE GEORGE HOTEL
**High Street, Odiham, Hook, Hampshire RG29 1LP**
**Tel: 01256 702081 • e-mail: reception@georgehotelodiham.com**
**website: www.georgehotelodiham.com**

To step over the threshold of The George is like entering a living history lesson - at every turn one's gaze meets a reminder of its noble past. Here, an Elizabethan wall painting; there, wattle and daub walls and original timber framing; in the oak-panelled Cromwell's Seafood Restaurant superbly preserved stone flags and an intricately carved fire surround. Rest assured, however, that all modern amenities are available in the individually styled bedrooms (some with four-posters). Dining here is a particular pleasure, candlelight and attentive service complementing the imaginative menus and excellent wine list. And afterwards, relax in the friendly bars, whose popularity with locals bears testimony to the fine quality of their ales! *ETC* ★★, *AA*.

28 BEDROOMS, ALL WITH PRIVATE BATHROOM; FREE HOUSE WITH REAL ALE; HISTORIC INTEREST; CHILDREN AND PETS WELCOME; BAR AND RESTAURANT MEALS; NON-SMOKING AREAS; BASINGSTOKE 7 MILES; S££££, D££££.

**FHG** FHG PUBLICATIONS publish a large range of well-known accommodation guides. We will be happy to send you details or you can use the order form at the back of this book.

## THE HIGH CORNER INN
Near Linwood, Ringwood, Hampshire BH24 3QY
Tel: 01425 473973 • website: www.highcornerinn.com

Nestled deep in the heart of the New Forest, the High Corner Inn is set in seven beautiful acres of woodland. Both oak-beamed bars have open fireplaces and views across the patio and gardens. Children are welcome, and will delight in playing in the outdoor adventure playground. A full range of Wadworth cask-conditioned ales is available, as well as an excellent selection of wines and spirits. We serve a wide range of quality home-cooked meals, bar snacks, plus a Sunday carvery. Accommodation is available in seven en suite double bedrooms, all with colour television and tea/coffee facilities. Dogs and horses are welcome – stables and paddocks are available for DIY livery. *See also Colour Advertisement.*

7 BEDROOMS, ALL WITH PRIVATE BATHROOM; REAL ALE; CHILDREN AND PETS WELCOME; BAR MEALS; BOURNEMOUTH 10 MILES; S££££, D££££.

## THE FOUNTAIN INN
34 The Green, Rowlands Castle, Hampshire PO9 6AB
Tel & Fax: 023 9241 2291 • e-mail: fountaininn@amserve.com

This elegantly furnished former 18th century coaching inn presents a plethora of pleasures in the hands of Herbie Armstrong, one-time member of Van Morrison's band, and his charming, Swedish-born wife, Elizabeth. In the most convivial surroundings, one may eat, drink and relax in style; in winter, a log fire extends a welcome in company with real ales and tasty meals in the traditional bar, whilst the award-winning Thai Bistro gives the opportunity to savour authentic Thai cuisine. Within easy reach of Chichester and Portsmouth and surrounded by lush countryside, this is a highly recommended place for a rewarding break, and several delightfully designed en suite bedrooms are available at very reasonable rates. *ETC/AA* ◆◆◆◆

4 BEDROOMS, ALL WITH PRIVATE BATHROOM; FREE HOUSE WITH REAL ALE; HISTORIC INTEREST; CHILDREN AND PETS WELCOME; RESTAURANT WED-SAT EVENINGS + SUN LUNCH; NON-SMOKING AREAS; HAVANT 3 MILES; S££/£££, D£/££.

## FHG

### Other specialised
## FHG PUBLICATIONS

Published annually: available in all good bookshops or direct from the publisher (post-free to addresses in the UK)

- PETS WELCOME!   £8.99
- Recommended COUNTRY HOTELS of Britain   £7.99
- Recommended SHORT BREAK HOLIDAYS in Britain   £7.99
- THE GOLF GUIDE Where to Play/Where to Stay   £9.99

**FHG PUBLICATIONS LTD,**
Abbey Mill Business Centre,
Seedhill, Paisley, Renfrewshire PA1 1TJ
Tel: 0141-887 0428 • Fax: 0141-889 7204
e-mail: fhg@ipcmedia.com
website: www.holidayguides.com

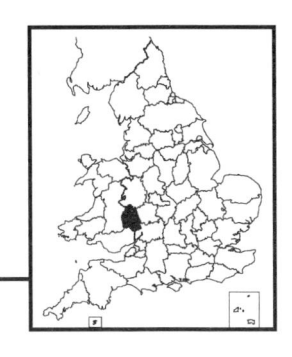

# Herefordshire

## THE TALBOT
**New Street, Ledbury, Herefordshire HR8 2DX**
Tel: 01531 632963 • Fax: 01531 633796 • www.visitledbury.co.uk/talbot
e-mail: talbot.ledbury@wadworth.co.uk

Take a step back in time to this owner-run historic inn which offers a warm and friendly welcome. It has an original oak-panelled restaurant and an old world bar with log fire, where guests can enjoy an excellent choice of refreshments, including well-kept ales. A regularly changing menu available lunchtimes and evenings will satisfy most tastes and budgets. Ideally placed for visiting historic Malvern and the Wye Valley, the Talbot makes a good base whether on business or touring, and however long or short your stay you will be assured of warm hospitality and first-class service. Good value accommodation is offered in double and twin bedrooms, all en suite. *ETC* ★★, *CAMRA, Good Beer Guide.*

7 BEDROOMS, 6 WITH PRIVATE BATHROOM; WADWORTH & CO HOUSE WITH REAL ALE; HISTORIC INTEREST;
BAR AND RESTAURANT MEALS; HEREFORD 12 MILES; S£££, D££££.

## THE INN ON THE WYE
**Kerne Bridge, Goodrich, Near Ross-on-Wye, Herefordshire HR9 5QS**
Tel: 01600 890872 • Fax: 01600 890594 • website: www.theinnonthewye.co.uk

This beautifully restored 18th century coaching inn with views of Goodrich Castle sits on the banks of the River Wye. The en suite bedrooms, some with four-poster beds, have colour television, telephone and the usual facilities. As well as the à la carte and bar snack menus offering home-cooked food, the inn also serves a traditional roast on Sundays. Peaceful country walks, idyllic scenery, close to local attractions - the ideal base for touring, walking, fishing, canoeing, golfing, etc. Families are welcome, pets by arrangement, and there is a children's play area, beer garden and large car park. *RAC* ◆◆◆

9 BEDROOMS, ALL WITH PRIVATE BATHROOM; FREE HOUSE WITH REAL ALE; HISTORIC INTEREST; CHILDREN AND PETS WELCOME;
BAR MEALS, RESTAURANT EVENINGS ONLY + SUN LUNCH; NON-SMOKING AREAS; ROSS-ON-WYE 4 MILES; S£££, D££.

## THE NEW INN
St Owen's Cross, Near Ross-on-Wye, Herefordshire HR2 8LQ
Tel: 01989 730274 • website: www.newinn.net

With its black and white timbered facade decorated with colourful hanging baskets, this one-time coaching inn dates from around 1540 and its time-hallowed character is epitomised by its many beams and huge inglenook fireplaces. The New Inn has a fine reputation for supplying outstanding food and drink; the majority of the dishes on the extensive menu being home-made and prepared from fresh local produce. On fine days, there are few better places in which to relax with a glass of one's fancy than in the spacious beer garden with views stretching across undulating countryside towards the Black Mountains. For a revivifying break away from so-called civilization, the inn has two well-appointed four-poster bedrooms.

2 BEDROOMS, BOTH WITH PRIVATE BATHROOM; BANKS HOUSE WITH REAL ALE; HISTORIC INTEREST; CHILDREN AND PETS WELCOME; BAR MEALS, RESTAURANT EVENINGS ONLY; NON-SMOKING AREAS; ROSS-ON-WYE 4 MILES; S£££££, D£££££.

## THE MARSHPOOLS COUNTRY INN
Ledgemoor, Near Weobley, Herefordshire HR4 8RN
Tel & Fax: 01544 318215 • e-mail: enquiries@country-inn.co.uk
website: www.country-inn.co.uk

This well-run inn was, we are told, originally an old thatched cottage, and stands now in a glorious rural situation a stone's throw from the picturesque black and white village of Weobley. All is neat, tidy, spacious and impeccably decorated within; real ales and Herefordshire cider are popular orders in the bar, in company with freshly prepared snacks and three-course meals. Fine opportunities exist locally for pony trekking, salmon and coarse fishing. The perfect location for a relaxing country holiday, the inn boasts delightfully appointed guest rooms (non-smoking), all en suite and with colour television, radio alarm, toiletries and tea and coffee-making facilities. *ETC* ◆◆◆

3 BEDROOMS, ALL WITH PRIVATE BATHROOM; FREE HOUSE WITH REAL ALE; CHILDREN AND PETS WELCOME; BAR AND RESTAURANT MEALS; NON-SMOKING AREAS; HEREFORD 9 MILES; S£££, D££.

# PLEASE NOTE

All the information in this book is given in good faith in the belief that it is correct. However, the publishers cannot guarantee the facts given in these pages, neither are they responsible for changes in policy, ownership or terms that may take place after the date of going to press. Readers should always satisfy themselves that the facilities they require are available and that the terms, if quoted, still apply.

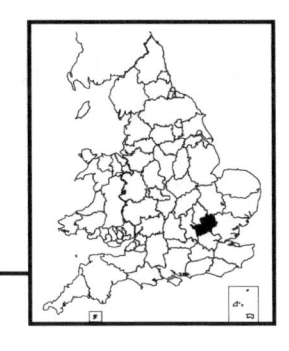

# Hertfordshire

## SALISBURY ARMS HOTEL
Fore Street, Hertford, Hertfordshire SG14 1BZ
Tel: 01992 583091 • Fax: 01992 552510 • www.salisbury-arms-hotel.co.uk
e-mail: reception@salisbury-arms-hotel.co.uk

Hertford's oldest hostelry offers guests excellent food, traditional local ales and an extensive list of wines available by the glass and bottle in surroundings that have character and charm. This is complemented by great service by the team. The two bars and the lounge are excellent for winding down and putting the world to rights. The wood panelled, air-conditioned restaurant has an excellent value table d'hôte and à la carte menu that offers a combination of traditional and contemporary dishes and is well known for its superb food in the surrounding areas. The rooms are all en suite with satellite TV. There are two rooms that have been specially designed for those guests who require disabled facilities. The meeting room is air conditioned and can accommodate up to 40 people for conferences/company dinners or celebration parties. The surrounding area has much to offer in terms of places of interest. Green fee discounts are available to guests with booked tee times at many of the surrounding golf clubs. There are two main line railway stations in the Hertford area, central London is 35 minutes away.
*ETC/AA* ★★★ *See also Colour Advertisement.*

31 BEDROOMS, ALL WITH PRIVATE BATHROOM; MCMULLENS OF HERTFORD HOUSE WITH REAL ALE; HISTORIC INTEREST; CHILDREN WELCOME; BAR AND RESTAURANT MEALS; NON-SMOKING AREAS; LONDON 20 MILES; S£££££, D£££££.

---

The £ symbol when appearing at the end of the italic section of an entry shows the anticipated price, during 2005, for full Bed and Breakfast.

*Normal Bed & Breakfast rate per person (in single room)*

| PRICE RANGE | CATEGORY |
|---|---|
| Under £25 | S£ |
| £26-£35 | S££ |
| £36-£45 | S£££ |
| Over £45 | S££££ |

*Normal Bed & Breakfast rate per person (sharing double/twin room)*

| PRICE RANGE | CATEGORY |
|---|---|
| Under £25 | D£ |
| £26-£35 | D££ |
| £36-£45 | D£££ |
| Over £45 | D££££ |

This is meant as an indication only and does not show prices for Special Breaks, Weekends, etc. Guests are therefore advised to verify all prices on enquiring or booking.

# Isle of Wight

## FOUNTAIN HOTEL
**High Street, Cowes, Isle of Wight PO31 7AW**
Tel: 01983 292397 • Fax: 01983 299554 • website: www.oldenglish.co.uk
e-mail: fountain.cowes@oldenglishinns.co.uk

Popular with visitors to the enchanted isle and the yachting fraternity in particular, this homely and well-run hotel has the twin advantages of superb maritime views and a situation adjacent to the Red-Jet passenger ferry. Recently refurbished, the 'Fountain' is well known for the first-class fare that is served throughout the day in its convivial bars and also for the excellent guest accommodation which is available at realistic rates. One does not have to be a 'wet bob' to appreciate the facilities here and the multifarious attractions of the island are all within easy travelling distance. This is a recommended base for a memorable holiday 'across the water'.

20 BEDROOMS, ALL WITH PRIVATE BATHROOM; FREE HOUSE WITH REAL ALE; HISTORIC INTEREST; CHILDREN WELCOME; BAR AND RESTAURANT MEALS; NON-SMOKING AREAS; NEWPORT 4 MILES; S££££, D££££.

## NEW INN
**Mill Road, Shalfleet, Isle of Wight PO30 4NS**
Tel & Fax: 01983 531314
e-mail: info@thenew-inn.co.uk • website: www.thenew-inn.co.uk

A charming little inn close by Shalfleet Creek and the National Trust protected Newtown estuary, the New Inn is full of traditional, old-world charm epitomised by snug bars with real fires burning in the inglenooks, just the place in which to relax with a glass of one's fancy on cool days, whilst on sunny days the garden beckons. However, come rain or shine, visitors are recommended to study a menu featuring mouth-watering dishes which are available at lunchtime and in the evening, fish dishes being a speciality of the house. A small inn with a big heart. *I.O.W. Dining Pub of the Year 2002 & 2003.*

NO ACCOMMODATION; REAL ALE; HISTORIC INTEREST; CHILDREN AND PETS WELCOME; BAR AND RESTAURANT MEALS; NON-SMOKING AREAS; YARMOUTH 4 MILES.

# Kent

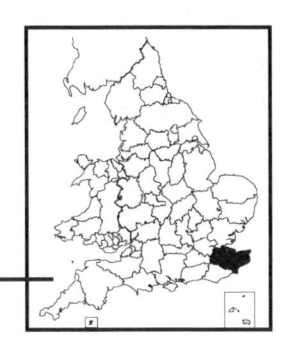

## THE OLD COACH HOUSE
Dover Road (A2), Barham, Kent CT4 6SA
Tel: 01227 831218 • Fax: 01227 831932

Halfway between the historic city of Canterbury and the Channel port of Dover, here is a first-class opportunity to enjoy the flavour of France without recourse to ferry or tunnel. Under the expert care of chef/patron, Jean-Claude Rozard, this early 17th century coaching inn is the venue for the happy marriage of fine Continental cuisine and English rural charm. Run on the relaxed lines of a French country auberge, the Old Coach House is widely acknowledged by bon viveurs and specialised feature writers for its outstanding fare, dishes featuring, in particular, local game in season and fresh turbot, bass, grilled lobster and Dover sole. Accommodation includes two large family rooms, each suitable for up to five people. *ETC* ★★

7 BEDROOMS, ALL WITH PRIVATE BATHROOM; FREE HOUSE; HISTORIC INTEREST; CHILDREN WELCOME;
RESTAURANT BOOKINGS ONLY, EVENINGS; NON-SMOKING; CANTERBURY 7 MILES, CHANNEL TUNNEL 10 MINUTES,
MANSTON AIRPORT 15 MINUTES; S£££, D££.

## THE SWINGATE INN & HOTEL
Deal Road, Dover, Kent CT15 5DP
Tel & Fax: 01304 204043 • e-mail: info@swingate.com
website: www.swingate.com

Well worth patronising as a touring centre or as an excellent stop-over venue for onward travel, this well-organised free house is conveniently situated within three minutes of the ferry ports and it is but ten minutes by car to the Euro Tunnel. First-class overnight accommodation is available in comfortable en suite rooms appointed with colour television, radio, clock alarm, hairdryer and tea and coffee-making facilities. Convivial bar areas and an à la carte restaurant specialising in seafood are other reasons for the inn's popularity. Children have their own menu and will appreciate a play area in the lovely garden with a bouncy castle and pets' corner. *ETC/AA* ♦♦♦

11 BEDROOMS, ALL WITH PRIVATE BATHROOM; FREE HOUSE WITH REAL ALE; CHILDREN WELCOME;
BAR AND RESTAURANT MEALS; NON-SMOKING AREAS; CANTERBURY 15 MILES; S£££, D££

## THE RINGLESTONE INN & FARMHOUSE HOTEL
Near Harrietsham, Maidstone, Kent ME17 1NX
Tel: 01622 859900 • Fax: 01622 859966 • e-mail: bookings@ringlestone.com
website: www.ringlestone.com

Since the early 1600s this unique inn has offered a "ryghte joyouse and welcome greetynge to ye all", and still today its original brick and flint walls, sturdy oak beams, inglenooks and traditional wooden furniture reflect the relaxed atmosphere of less hurried times. The Ringlestone offers superb lunches and interesting evening menus, featuring the best of local produce. Those in search of refreshment will savour the selection of well-kept real ales and the interesting range of English country fruit wines – something really different! Set in five acres of peaceful gardens deep in the lush Kent countryside, this truly welcoming inn upholds the finest traditions of English inn-keeping. *ETC/AA/RAC* ♦♦♦♦♦ and Gold Award.

3 BEDROOMS, ALL WITH PRIVATE BATHROOM; FREE HOUSE WITH REAL ALE; HISTORIC INTEREST; CHILDREN WELCOME;
BAR AND RESTAURANT MEALS; NON-SMOKING AREAS; MAIDSTONE 7 MILES; S£££££, D££££.

# Lancashire

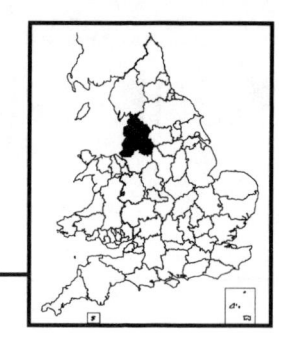

## OWD NELL'S CANALSIDE TAVERN

Guy's Thatched Hamlet, St Michael's Road, Bilsborrow, Lancashire PR3 0RS
Tel: 01995 640010 • Fax: 01995 640141 • e-mail: info@guysthatchedhamlet.com
website: www.guysthatchedhamlet.com

Here's one for collectors of the unusual and the idyllic – a thatched oldtime refreshment house tucked away by the side of the Lancaster Canal. Open all day dispensing the best of home made country tavern fayre, Owd Nell's is renowned for its range of tempting bar dishes designed to serve all palates and pockets, as well as its great selection of cask-conditioned ales. This gem is just one unit in the complex that is Guy's Thatched Hamlet, where guests can step back in time and enjoy the good things in life in a relaxed and unfussy atmosphere. Superb overnight accommodation with the highest modern standards is provided in Guy's Lodge, comprising en suite rooms with colour television with SKY channels, telephone and tea and coffee making facilities; some with spas. Some accommodation is suitable for disabled guests. For dining "par excellence", guests just have to follow their noses to the adjacent Guy's Eating Establishment, where the emphasis is on tasteful informality, the variety of dishes ranging from freshly made pizza to a succulent sirloin steak. Without venturing beyond this quaint and attractive complex one may confirm the time warp illusion by strolling through the old world elegance of Spout Lane and School House Square to visit the craft shops. Golf can be arranged; canal walks. Our own cricket ground with thatched pavilion can be hired, and there is crown green bowling. Other amenities include conference rooms and a licensed pavilion. Short breaks are available – ring for further information. All major credit cards accepted. *ETC* ★★★

65 BEDROOMS, ALL EN SUITE; FREE HOUSE WITH REAL ALE; CHILDREN WELCOME; BAR AND RESTAURANT MEALS; PRESTON 6 MILES, M6/M55 3, GARSTANG 3; S££, D£.

---

*The* **FHG**
*GOLF GUIDE*
**Where to Play Where to Stay**

Available from most bookshops, THE GOLF GUIDE (published annually) covers details of every UK golf course – well over 2800 entries – for holiday or business golf. Hundreds of hotel entries offer convenient accommodation, accompanying details of the courses – the 'pro', par score, length etc.

*In association with 'Golf Monthly' and including Holiday Golf in Ireland, France, Portugal, Spain, The USA, South Africa and Thailand*

£9.99 from bookshops or from the publishers (postage charged outside UK) • FHG Publications, Abbey Mill Business Centre, Paisley PAI ITJ

## THE FARMERS' ARMS
Wood Lane, Heskin, Near Chorley, Lancashire PR7 5NP
Tel: 01257 451276 • Fax: 01257 453958 • website: www.farmersarms.co.uk

Way back in the 17th century, weary travellers called this fine old pub the 'Pleasant Retreat', a name that applies in essence today, although the inn was renamed in 1902. Very much a Rothwell family concern, this attractive country hostelry retains its old-world charm and continues to provide good wholesome fare accompanied by traditional, hand-pulled cask ales. Here is all the warmth and appeal of a typical English wayside inn. However, perceptively aware of the needs of the modern era, superb overnight accommodation has been installed and quality en suite four-poster, double, twin and single rooms are available, all with showers, colour television and tea and coffee-makers. *ETC* ◆◆◆

5 BEDROOMS, ALL WITH PRIVATE BATHROOM; ENTERPRISE INNS HOUSE WITH REAL ALE; HISTORIC INTEREST; CHILDREN WELCOME, PETS BY ARRANGEMENT; BAR AND RESTAURANT MEALS; NON-SMOKING AREAS; CHORLEY 4 MILES; S££, D£.

## THE INN AT WHITEWELL
Forest of Bowland, Near Clitheroe, Lancashire BB7 3AT
Tel: 01200 448222 • Fax: 01200 448298

With seven miles of salmon and trout fishing available to guests, this is very much a country-lovers' delight in the wide, wild (and some say magic) Forest of Bowland. The inn stands perched on the bank of the River Hodder, the oldest parts of the building dating back to the 14th century. In contrast to those far-off days, the bedrooms that provide guest accommodation have en suite facilities, television and other thoughtful extras. This is good place to sample wholesome food in the 'mother-used-to-make' category thanks to a team of dedicated cooks. Bar food is available at lunchtime, and bar suppers and restaurant meals in the evening. With a wine merchant sharing the premises, diners are assured of an interesting choice of bins. *ETC* ◆◆◆◆, *AA*.

17 BEDROOMS, ALL WITH PRIVATE BATHROOM; FREE HOUSE WITH REAL ALE; HISTORIC INTEREST; CHILDREN AND PETS WELCOME; BAR MEALS, RESTAURANT EVENINGS ONLY; CLITHEROE 6 MILES; S££££, D££££.

## HARK TO BOUNTY INN
Slaidburn, Near Clitheroe, Lancashire BB7 3EP
Tel: 01200 446246 • Fax: 01200 446361 • e-mail: manager@harktobounty.co.uk
website: www.harktobounty.co.uk

Dating back to the 13th century, this old inn was known as 'The Dog' until 1875. Entertaining the local hunt, the entertainment was interrupted by the persistent baying of the favourite dog of the local squire who was heard to exclaim 'Hark to Bounty' and the name has stuck ever since. In the heart of the scenic Forest of Bowland, the inn was once the seat of the Bowland Forest Court and anyone giving it a trial today will pronounce a most favourable verdict in respect of accommodation, cuisine and service. A popular haunt of locals and tourists alike, the oak beamed bar provides excellent bar meals and real ale with more substantial fare served in a highly commended restaurant.

9 BEDROOMS, ALL WITH PRIVATE BATHROOM; REAL ALE; HISTORIC INTEREST; CHILDREN WELCOME, PETS NOT ALLOWED IN EATING AREAS; BAR MEALS, RESTAURANT WED-SAT +SUN LUNCH; NON-SMOKING AREAS; CLITHEROE 7 MILES; S££, D££.

# Leicestershire & Rutland

## RAM JAM INN
**The Great North Road, Stretton, Oakham, Rutland LE15 7QX**
**Tel: 01780 410776 • Fax: 01780 410361 • rji@rutnet.co.uk**
**website: www.ramjaminn.co.uk**

A well-known port of call on the A1 between Grantham and Stamford, the 'Ram Jam' has amenities which demand more than temporary acquaintance. It lies in the heart of hunting country where the counties of Leicestershire, Rutland and Lincolnshire meet. Whether for business or pleasure, the inn offers outstanding food, drink and accommodation and serves as a perfect touring base. There is a notable restaurant and bistro where an extensive range of wholesome, home-cooked fare can be savoured, including the legendary Rutland Sausage. Handsomely appointed double, twin and single bedrooms have en suite bathrooms with power shower, colour television, direct-dial telephone, modem socket and tea and coffee-makers. The inn also caters expertly for business meetings and private parties. *AA* ★★ *and Rosette, RAC* ★★

7 BEDROOMS, ALL WITH PRIVATE BATHROOM; FREE HOUSE WITH REAL ALE; HISTORIC INTEREST; CHILDREN WELCOME; PETS IN BEDROOMS ONLY; BAR AND RESTAURANT MEALS; NON-SMOKING AREAS; STAMFORD 8 MILES; S£££££, D£££££.

## KING'S ARMS INN
**Top Street, Wing, Rutland LE15 8SE**
**Tel: 01572 737634 • Fax: 01572 737255 • www.thekingsarms-wing.co.uk**
**e-mail: info@thekingsarms-wing.co.uk**

Recognised for the high quality of its food, service and accommodation, The King's Arms has considerable old-world appeal in its beamed bar and hidey-hole nooks and crannies and where a log fire thwarts winter chill. Locally brewed real ales prove justly popular and one may eat informally in the bar or in the restaurant. Accommodation is delightfully furnished and appointed, with en suite bath and shower, colour television, radio alarm clock, telephone, hairdryer and tea and coffee hospitality tray. Located just one mile from the A47, the inn is convenient for visits to nearby historic towns and for the wide range of sporting and leisure activities at Rutland Water. *ETC/AA* ♦♦♦♦

8 BEDROOMS, ALL WITH PRIVATE BATHROOM; FREE HOUSE WITH REAL ALE; HISTORIC INTEREST; CHILDREN WELCOME; BAR AND RESTAURANT MEALS; NON-SMOKING AREAS; OAKHAM 4 MILES; S££££, D££.

---

**FHG**
Visit the website
**www.holidayguides.com**
for details of the wide choice of accommodation
featured in the full range of FHG titles

# Lincolnshire

## THE FINCH HATTON ARMS
**43 Main Street, Ewerby, Sleaford, Lincolnshire NG34 9PH**
**Tel: 01529 460363 • Fax: 01529 461703 • e-mail: paul@finchhatton.fsnet.co.uk**

This is something of a surprise – a fully equipped small hotel of some distinction in a picturesque little village, if not in the middle of nowhere, then precious near to it! Its success is due, in no small part, to its attractive Tudor-style bar and restaurant where traditional ales and an imaginative menu draw custom from nearby Sleaford and even Newark, Grantham, Boston and Lincoln to prove the proposition that value for money is a sure winner. The hotel wing provides first-class overnight accommodation, each room having a bath/shower en suite, remote-control colour television, direct-dial telephone and tea and coffee-making facilities and there is the promise of a hearty English breakfast in the morning. *ETC* ★★

8 BEDROOMS, ALL WITH PRIVATE BATHROOM; FREE HOUSE WITH REAL ALE; BAR AND RESTAURANT MEALS;
NON-SMOKING AREAS; SLEAFORD 4 MILES.

## THE POACHERS COUNTRY HOTEL
**Swineshead Road, Kirton Holme, Lincolnshire PE20 1SQ**
**Tel: 01205 290310 • Fax: 01205 290254**
**e-mail: poachers@kirtonholme.wanadoo.co.uk**

On the A52, close to the historic port of Boston, this spruce country hostelry presents the opportunity to wine and dine in style thanks to an imaginative selection of home-cooked, à la carte fare: the dining rooms are delightfully furnished with attractive panelling, antiques, pictures and books. Prior to dining, close acquaintance with a bar full of character and almost secret alcoves is recommended. Here, relaxation is easily acquired with a glass of one's favourite tipple in hand. It comes as no surprise to learn that this is a popular venue for social and business events. The accommodation would not be out of place in a multi-starred, fashionable establishment and rates are moderate in the extreme. The en suite bedrooms include two with four-posters and whirlpool baths. *ETC/AA* ★★

16 BEDROOMS, ALL WITH PRIVATE BATHROOM; FREE HOUSE WITH REAL ALE; CHILDREN AND PETS WELCOME;
BAR AND RESTAURANT MEALS; NON-SMOKING AREAS; BOSTON 4 MILES; S£££, D££.

## GEORGE HOTEL
**Leadenham, Lincolnshire LN5 0PN**
**Tel: 01400 272251 • Fax: 01400 272091**

A homely atmosphere and reputation for fine food served in the Tudor Restaurant makes this excellent little country hotel a haven for tourist and holidaymaker alike. It is situated on the A17 midway between Newark and Sleaford, just eight miles from the A1. Appetising bar food awaits at lunchtime and evening daily, and the aptly named Scotch Lounge features around 680 different whiskies from all over the world as well as numerous draught beers. Accommodation for overnight guests is housed in a quiet cottage behind the inn and the reasonable charge for a comfortably furnished room with television and tea-maker includes a substantial English breakfast. Some rooms with en suite facilities are available. *ETC* ◆◆◆

6 BEDROOMS, 4 WITH PRIVATE BATHROOM; FREE HOUSE WITH REAL ALE; HISTORIC INTEREST;
CHILDREN AND PETS WELCOME; BAR AND RESTAURANT MEALS; NON-SMOKING AREAS; SLEAFORD 8 MILES; S££, D£.

## THE BLUE COW INN AND BREWERY
High Street, South Witham, Grantham, Lincolnshire NG33 5QB
Tel & Fax: 01572 768288 • e-mail: richard@thirlwell.fslife.co.uk
website: www.thebluecowinn.co.uk

Activating a dream, inspired by the potential of a pub that almost died of neglect, Dick and Julia Thirlwell rolled up their sleeves and set about restoring the 'Blue Cow' back to conscious life. So successful were they in rescuing the inn from dereliction, that this is now one of the most popular hostelries in an area of pastoral beauty. Yet only a mile off the A1, on the borders of Lincolnshire, Leicestershire and Rutland, this is a charming place to visit on a short or long term basis. Today, exposed stone walls, beamed ceilings, slab-stone floors and log fires give atmosphere to the bar and, outside, is a beautiful garden with far-reaching views of the unspoilt countryside. An attractive feature of the inn is its own brewery, there being no limit apparently to Dick Thirlwell's ambitions. The various Thirlwell ales have already achieved widespread acclaim and have won CAMRA awards. Guided tours of the micro-brewery may be arranged. This is a rewarding place in which to stay: there are three golf courses within four miles and Rutland Water, Europe's largest man-made lake with its watersports facilities, is close by. Well-furnished rooms with en suite facilities provide excellent overnight accommodation. Another imaginative service to guests is a free mini-bus option for parties of eight or more, operating in a ten-mile radius, for restaurant diners. This re-birth of an inn is a revelation and Dick and Julia deserve every success with their endeavours. *ETC* ◆◆◆, *AA*.

6 BEDROOMS, ALL WITH PRIVATE BATHROOM; FREE HOUSE WITH REAL ALE; HISTORIC INTEREST; CHILDREN AND PETS WELCOME; BAR AND RESTAURANT MEALS; NON-SMOKING AREAS; GRANTHAM 9 MILES; S£££, D£/££.

## THE RED LION INN
Main Road, Partney, Spilsby, Lincolnshire PE23 4PG
Tel: 01790 752271 • Fax: 01790 753360
e-mail: redlionpartney@onetel.net.uk

Situated at the junction of the A16/A158 at Partney. Award-winning home-made food – over 20 dishes to choose from including vegetarian specials. Luxury en suite accommodation – three bedrooms, all with shower and toilet, radio, colour TV and beverage-making facilities. Ideally situated on the edge of the Lincolnshire Wolds. Great for walking and sightseeing in Lincoln, Grimsby, Boston, Skegness, Horncastle and much more.

3 BEDROOMS, ALL WITH PRIVATE BATHROOM; SKEGNESS 11 MILES.

## PUBLISHER'S NOTE

**FHG**

While every effort is made to ensure accuracy, we regret that FHG Publications cannot accept responsibility for errors, misrepresentations or omissions in our entries or any consequences thereof. Prices in particular should be checked because we go to press early. We will follow up complaints but cannot act as arbiters or agents for either party.

# Norfolk

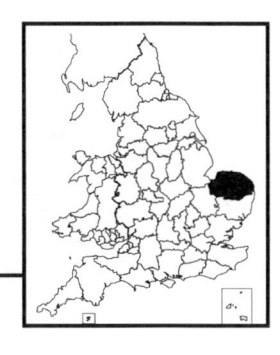

## THE JOHN H. STRACEY
**West End, Briston, Melton Constable, Norfolk NR24 2JA**
**Tel: 01263 860891 • Fax: 01263 862984 • e-mail: thejohnhstracey@btinternet.com**

Named after a famous boxer, this fine old inn, in fact, dates from the 16th century when it was a staging post on the Wells to Norwich road. Captivating indeed is the time-honoured ambience exuded by its low ceilings, oak beams and copper knick-knacks reflecting the glow of a welcoming log fire. The old hostelry used to be called the Three Horseshoes and synonymous with the change of name, the stables were converted into a splendid, well-patronised restaurant known for its wholesome, home-cooked fare. This is a place of infinite character in tranquil, rural Norfolk with the coast within easy reach. *AA* ◆◆◆

3 BEDROOMS, 1 WITH PRIVATE BATHROOM; FREE HOUSE WITH REAL ALE; CHILDREN WELCOME; BAR AND RESTAURANT MEALS; NON-SMOKING AREAS; HOLT 4 MILES; D££.

## THE ANGEL INN
**Larling, Norwich, Norfolk NR16 2QU**
**Tel: 01953 717963 • Fax : 01953 718561**

With lovely views across open country, this delightful, family-run country inn on the A11 Thetford to Norwich road dates from the 17th century and once performed the sterling duty of a coaching halt. Its mature character is much in evidence today, an attraction for modern-day visitors who appreciate the choice of real ales and the excellent, homely fare on the extensive menu. A charming place in which to stay, with friendly service assured, this little gem of a retreat provides really comfortable Bed and Breakfast accommodation in en suite bedrooms and at terms that represent very good value. There is a field adjoining with first-rate facilities for caravans and camping. *CAMRA*.

5 BEDROOMS, ALL WITH PRIVATE BATHROOM; FREE HOUSE WITH REAL ALE; HISTORIC INTEREST; CHILDREN WELCOME; BAR LUNCHES AND RESTAURANT MEALS; NON-SMOKING AREAS; THETFORD 7 MILES; S££, D££.

---

The £ symbol when appearing at the end of the italic section of an entry shows the anticipated price, during 2005, for full Bed and Breakfast.

*Normal Bed & Breakfast rate per person (in single room)*

| PRICE RANGE | CATEGORY |
|---|---|
| Under £25 | S£ |
| £26-£35 | S££ |
| £36-£45 | S£££ |
| Over £45 | S££££ |

*Normal Bed & Breakfast rate per person (sharing double/twin room)*

| PRICE RANGE | CATEGORY |
|---|---|
| Under £25 | D£ |
| £26-£35 | D££ |
| £36-£45 | D£££ |
| Over £45 | D££££ |

This is meant as an indication only and does not show prices for Special Breaks, Weekends, etc. Guests are therefore advised to verify all prices on enquiring or booking.

## THE PLOUGH INN
Norwich Road, Marsham, Norwich, Norfolk NR10 5PS
Tel: 01263 735000 • Fax: 01263 735407 • e-mail: enquiries@ploughinnmarsham.co.uk
website: www.ploughinnmarsham.co.uk

Within easy reach of the Broads, the resorts of Cromer and Sheringham and the city of Norwich, this well-appointed inn will appeal to the lover of outdoor pursuits and the tranquil way of life. This is good terrain for unexacting country walks and for the fishing enthusiast there are several lakes and rivers offering excellent sport. A ride on the Bure Valley Narrow Gauge Railway through the peaceful Norfolk countryside is another attraction. For a place to stay, one need look no further than this first-class hotel, free house and restaurant where proprietors, Damien and Eileen Beatty, extend the warmest of welcomes to guests. The cuisine is of the highest calibre and accommodation comprises well equipped en suite guest rooms. *ETC* ◆◆◆◆, *AA, RAC*.

11 BEDROOMS, ALL WITH PRIVATE BATHROOM; FREE HOUSE WITH REAL ALE; HISTORIC INTEREST; CHILDREN WELCOME; BAR AND RESTAURANT MEALS; NON-SMOKING AREAS; AYLSHAM 2 MILES; S£££, D££.

## THE LIFEBOAT INN
Ship Lane, Thornham, Norfolk PE36 6LT
Tel: 01485 512236 • Fax: 01485 512323 • website: www.lifeboatinn.co.uk
e-mail: reception@lifeboatinn.co.uk

A lovely sixteenth century traditional English inn, the Lifeboat, once the haunt of smugglers, has magnificent views over Thornham harbour to the sea beyond. The bar, with its low ceiling, pillars and uneven floor, conjured up visions of the unhurried life of years gone by as we sampled an excellent pint of real ale and tucked into our Fisherman's Pie. Daily specials increase the already excellent choice of freshly prepared dishes available in the bar; alternatively one may dine in the restaurant, where a frequently changing menu makes the best of local seasonal produce. All the comfortable bedrooms have en suite bathrooms and most enjoy views over the harbour to the sea. *See also Colour Advertisement*.

12 BEDROOMS, ALL WITH PRIVATE BATHROOM; FREE HOUSE WITH REAL ALE; HISTORIC INTEREST; CHILDREN AND PETS WELCOME; BAR MEALS, RESTAURANT EVENINGS ONLY; HUNSTANTON 4 MILES; S££££, D£££

## THE HALF MOON INN
The Street, Rushall, Near Diss, Norfolk IP21 4QD
Tel & Fax: 01379 740793 • website: www.rushallhalfmooninns.co.uk

This 16th century coaching inn offers a warm welcome to business guests and holidaymakers alike. Seven bedrooms are in modern chalet-style accommodation, and the remainder are in the inn which has a wealth of exposed beams. Bedrooms have colour television, central heating and tea and coffee making facilities. An excellent selection of home-cooked meals is available, complemented by our range of local cask-conditioned ales and keenly priced wine list. The friendly atmosphere, reasonably priced accommodation and delightful rural location combine to make this an excellent base for visiting East Anglia.

10 BEDROOMS, 8 WITH PRIVATE BATHROOM; FREE HOUSE WITH REAL ALE; HISTORIC INTEREST;
CHILDREN WELCOME; BAR AND RESTAURANT MEALS; NON-SMOKING AREAS; HARLESTON 2 MILES; S££, D£££.

## THE CROWN HOTEL
The Buttlands, Wells-next-the-Sea, Norfolk NR23 1EX
Tel: 01328 710209 • Fax: 01328 711432 • website: www.thecrownhotelwells.co.uk
e-mail: reception@thecrownhotelwells.co.uk

Lovely Wells with its bijou harbour and expansive sands and dunes is a wonderful place for carefree family holidays and, to this end, a visit to this well-run former coaching inn is well recommended. Elevated to hotel status by hosts, Chris and Jo Coubrough, it has an attractive beamed bar with an open fire and one may eat well here or in the adjoining conservatory. For formal dining, the restaurant offers imaginatively cooked dishes representing the best of modern British cuisine, accompanied by those with Pacific Rim influence. Superb wines complement the menus. The en suite guest rooms are light and airy; all have television, and the two family suites also have video players and baby-monitors. *AA Rosette.*

11 BEDROOMS, ALL WITH PRIVATE BATHROOM; FREE HOUSE WITH REAL ALE; HISTORIC INTEREST;
CHILDREN WELCOME, PETS IN BAR/GARDEN ONLY; BAR MEALS, RESTAURANT EVENINGS ONLY;
NON-SMOKING AREAS; FAKENHAM 9 MILES; S££££, D££££.

---

For our guide to
# Pet-Friendly Pubs, Inns & Hotels
see pages 149-162

---

# PUBLISHER'S NOTE

**FHG**

While every effort is made to ensure accuracy, we regret that FHG Publications cannot accept responsibility for errors, misrepresentations or omissions in our entries or any consequences thereof. Prices in particular should be checked because we go to press early. We will follow up complaints but cannot act as arbiters or agents for either party.

# Northamptonshire

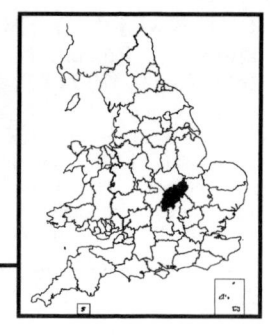

## THE RED LION HOTEL
East Haddon, Northamptonshire NN6 8BU
Tel: 01604 770223 • Fax: 01604 770767
website: www.redlionhoteleasthaddon.co.uk

This traditional, stone-built inn sits snugly in the charming village of East Haddon, just seven miles from Junction 18 on the M1 and eight miles from Northampton. Leisure facilities in the area are excellent – golf, fishing, squash, swimming and snooker are all available locally. Riding stables in village close to Althorp House. Those wishing to make the most of a relaxing weekend break will find comfortable, spick-and-span bedrooms with full en suite facilities, television, etc. Good English cooking is the basis of the carefully balanced à la carte menu and a comprehensive range of gourmet bar food is available at lunchtime and in the evening. Lighter appetites are well catered for in the brass and copper bedecked bars, with a tasty range of gourmet bar food, accompanied by one's choice from the well-kept ales, beers, wines and other refreshments. *Egon Ronay, Good Food Guide.* **See also Colour Advertisement.**

5 BEDROOMS; TRADITIONAL HOUSE WITH REAL ALE; HISTORIC INTEREST; CHILDREN WELCOME; BAR AND RESTAURANT MEALS; NON-SMOKING AREAS; NORTHAMPTON 8 MILES, M1 JUNCTION 16 7 MILES, CLOSE TO A14; S£££, D£££.

---

The £ symbol when appearing at the end of the italic section of an entry shows the anticipated price, during 2005, for full Bed and Breakfast.

*Normal Bed & Breakfast rate per person per person  (in single room)*

*Normal Bed & Breakfast rate (sharing double/twin room)*

| PRICE RANGE | CATEGORY | PRICE RANGE | CATEGORY |
|---|---|---|---|
| **Under £25** | S£ | **Under £25** | D£ |
| **£26-£35** | S££ | **£26-£35** | D££ |
| **£36-£45** | S£££ | **£36-£45** | D£££ |
| **Over £45** | S££££ | **Over £45** | D££££ |

This is meant as an indication only and does not show prices for Special Breaks, Weekends, etc. Guests are therefore advised to verify all prices on enquiring or booking.

# Northumberland

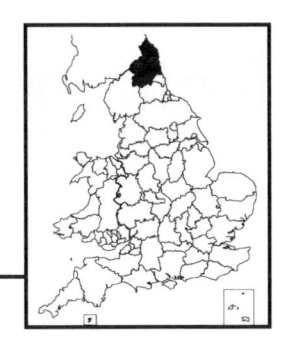

## QUEEN'S HEAD HOTEL
Townfoot, Rothbury, Northumberland NE65 7SR
Tel: 01669 620470 • Fax: 01669 621305 • enqs@queensheadrothbury.com
website: www.queensheadrothbury.com

The warmly traditional facade of this mature hotel graces the centre of a picturesque village in the heart of the Coquet Valley. Little wonder that this situation is such a magnet for artists, photographers and nature-lovers; what better place to seek refreshment and accommodation than this charismatic retreat with its convivial and relaxed atmosphere and jealously guarded reputation for the à la carte fare served in the Armstrong Suite Restaurant, lunches being available in a lovely old beamed bar. Sporting diversions in the area include fishing and golf and only one mile away is Cragside House and Country Park. Double, twin and family rooms all have en suite facilities, colour television and hospitality tray. *ETC* ◆◆◆

7 BEDROOMS, ALL WITH PRIVATE BATHROOM; PUNCH HOUSE WITH REAL ALE; HISTORIC INTEREST; CHILDREN WELCOME; BAR MEALS, RESTAURANT EVENINGS ONLY; NON-SMOKING AREAS; ALNWICK 11 MILES; S££, D££.

---

## FHG PUBLICATIONS
publish a large range of well-known accommodation guides. We will be happy to send you details or you can use the order form at the back of this book.

---

Visit the **FHG** website
**www.holidayguides.com**
for details of the wide choice of accommodation featured in the full range of FHG titles

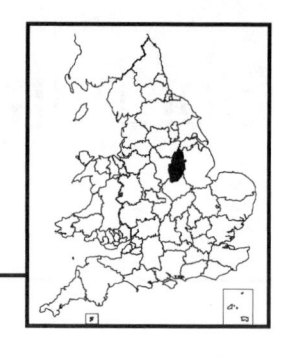

# Nottinghamshire

## WILLOW TREE INN
Front Street, Barnby in the Willows, Newark, Nottinghamshire NG24 2SA
Tel: 01636 626613 • Fax: 01636 626060 • website: www.willowtreeinn.co.uk
e-mail: howard@willowinn.f9.co.uk

A charming village inn built at the turn of the 18th century, the homely Willow Tree is well known for its quality food and the traditional ales served in its heavily beamed bar. Situated in a conservation area and within a short drive of Nottingham, Lincoln and Sherwood Forest, as well as nearby 12th/15th century Newark Castle, this is a gem of a place in which to stay, with recently refurbished bedrooms and new bathrooms. Sporting attractions locally include golf, horse riding and excellent fishing on the Trent and Witham. The 24-cover à la carte restaurant offers a wide choice of tempting dishes, including plenty of fresh fish such as lobster and whole sole. There is a daily specials board with venison, wild boar and T-bone steaks. All food is freshly prepared, with a selection of home-made sweets to follow. ETC/AA ◆◆◆

7 BEDROOMS, ALL WITH PRIVATE BATHROOM; FREE HOUSE WITH REAL ALE; HISTORIC INTEREST;
CHILDREN AND PETS WELCOME; BAR AND RESTAURANT MEALS EVENINGS, PLUS WEEKEND LUNCHTIMES;
NON-SMOKING AREAS; NEWARK 4 MILES; S£££, D££££.

---

# FHG
## Other specialised
## FHG PUBLICATIONS
Published annually: available in all good bookshops or direct from the publisher (post-free to addresses in the UK)

- PETS WELCOME!    £8.99
- Recommended COUNTRY HOTELS of Britain    £7.99
- Recommended SHORT BREAK HOLIDAYS in Britain    £7.99
- THE GOLF GUIDE Where to Play/Where to Stay    £9.99

FHG PUBLICATIONS LTD,
Abbey Mill Business Centre,
Seedhill, Paisley, Renfrewshire PA1 1TJ
Tel: 0141-887 0428 • Fax: 0141-889 7204
e-mail: fhg@ipcmedia.com
website: www.holidayguides.com

# Oxfordshire

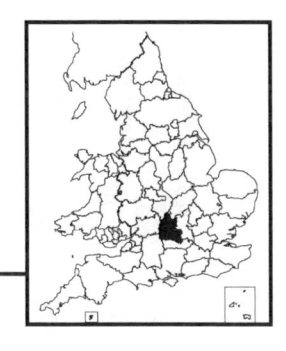

## THE DOG HOUSE HOTEL
Frilford Heath, Abingdon, Oxfordshire OX13 6QJ
Tel: 01865 390830 • Fax: 01865 390860

It is seldom that one would claim to be delighted to be 'in the dog house', but when the establishment in question is this sturdy stone-built inn, a stay here is a privilege, not a punishment! The attractively furnished bedrooms, all en suite, offer a full range of facilities, and special Friday and Saturday rates make a weekend break a particularly attractive proposition. The Hotel Restaurant offers an extensive choice of menu with the emphasis very firmly on quality and professional service; meals can be enjoyed in the light and airy conservatory or in the bar, where a range of blackboard specials prove excellent value for money. The golfing enthusiast will be delighted to find two 18-hole golf courses almost next door. *See also Colour Advertisement.*

20 BEDROOMS, ALL WITH PRIVATE BATHROOM; GREENE KING HOUSE WITH REAL ALE; HISTORIC INTEREST; CHILDREN WELCOME; BAR AND RESTAURANT MEALS; NON-SMOKING AREAS; OXFORD 6 MILES; S££££, D££££.

## THE KING'S HEAD INN AND RESTAURANT
Bledington, Near Kingham, Oxfordshire OX7 6XQ
Tel: 01608 658365 • Fax: 01608 658902 • e-mail: kingshead@orr-ewing.com
website: www.kingsheadinn.net

Facing Bledington's village green with its brook and ducks stands the 15th century King's Head Inn, an establishment which has echoed with the sounds of convivial hospitality for over four centuries. Bledington nestles in the heart of the Cotswolds and is within easy reach of all top tourist attractions. The charming accommodation is in keeping with the atmosphere, all bedrooms (en suite) having television, telephone and hot drinks facilities. High quality and inventive bar fare is served, with full à la carte and table d'hôte menus in the award-winning restaurant in the evenings. A selection of real ales and interesting whiskies is served in the bar which has original old beams and an inglenook fireplace. *AA* ♦♦♦♦, *Egon Ronay* ★, *Good Pub Guide Dining County Pub of the Year, Logis. See also Colour Advertisement.*

12 BEDROOMS, ALL WITH PRIVATE BATHROOM; FREE HOUSE WITH REAL ALE; HISTORIC INTEREST; CHILDREN WELCOME; BAR FOOD, RESTAURANT EVENINGS ONLY; NON-SMOKING AREAS; STOW-ON-THE-WOLD 4 MILES; S£££, D£££.

## THE LAMB AT BUCKLAND
Lamb Lane, Buckland, Faringdon, Oxfordshire SN7 8QN
Tel: 01367 870484 • Fax: 01367 870675 • www.thelambatbuckland.co.uk
e-mail: enquiries@thelambatbuckland.co.uk

When one thinks of the Lamb, one automatically thinks of food for its tempting range of bar meals and dinners are worth coming a long way to marvel at and enjoy. In a peaceful village on the edge of the Cotswolds, the 18th century Lamb is a welcoming port of call with a convivial bar serving real ale and a pleasant garden where refreshment may be taken in good weather. Rest assured, the food served in the restaurant and bar is calculated to suit all palates and purses. Excellent overnight en suite accommodation is available, also at moderate rates. *AA Rosette.*

1 BEDROOM, WITH PRIVATE BATHROOM; FREE HOUSE WITH REAL ALE; CHILDREN WELCOME; BAR AND RESTAURANT MEALS; NON-SMOKING AREAS; FARINGDON 4 MILES; S££££, D££££.

# Tell us about YOUR favourite inn or pub

If you have visited an inn, pub or hotel which you think deserves to feature in this publication, then write and tell us about it!

Perhaps the food is particularly good, the landlord especially friendly (or a bit of a character!), or the beers and ales kept in tip-top condition. If children are made especially welcome, or pets allowed in and made a fuss of, then we would like to hear about it.

If you send us details, using the form below, then we will send you a FREE copy of one of our Year 2005 holiday guides (please choose from the list at the back of the book).

------------------------------------------------------------

**TO: FHG PUBLICATIONS LTD,
ABBEY MILL BUSINESS CENTRE, SEEDHILL, PAISLEY PA1 1TJ**

Name & Address of Pub/Inn/Hotel .................................................................................
........................................................................................................................................
........................................................................................................................................

Telephone .......................................................................................................................

Name of Licensee (if known) ..........................................................................................

Why this establishment is special




Your name & adddress (please PRINT) ..........................................................................
........................................................................................................................................
........................................................................................................................................

Which one of our Year 2005 publications would you like? (totally free of charge) – see back of book for full list.

........................................................................................................................................

*94*

# Shropshire

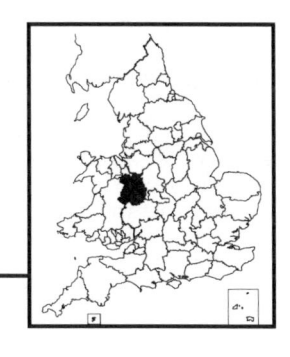

## BOAR'S HEAD HOTEL
Church Street, Bishop's Castle, Shropshire SY9 5AE
Tel: 01588 638521 • Fax: 01588 630126 • e-mail: sales@boarsheadhotel.co.uk
website: www.boarsheadhotel.co.uk

Close to the medieval towns of Ludlow and Shrewsbury and slumbering amidst delightful, unspoilt countryside, Bishop's Castle is the perfect location for a quiet, relaxing break away from the hustle and bustle of urban life. The Boar's Head, with its wealth of exposed beams and welcoming log fire, is just the place to choose as a base for such an escapade. It comfortably meets the challenge of contemporary times by providing excellent en suite accommodation, the rooms having colour television, telephone and tea and coffee making facilities. In the matter of refreshment, an extensive choice ranges from lunchtime bar meals to a full à la carte evening selection with a traditional roast on Sundays. *ETC* ♦♦♦, *AA*.

4 BEDROOMS, ALL WITH PRIVATE BATHROOM; FREE HOUSE WITH REAL ALE; HISTORIC INTEREST; CHILDREN WELCOME;
PETS IN GUEST ROOMS ONLY; BAR AND RESTAURANT MEALS; NON-SMOKING AREAS; CRAVEN ARMS 8 MILES; S£££, D££.

## THE ROEBUCK INN
Brimfield, Ludlow, Shropshire SY8 4NE
Tel: 01584 711230 • Fax: 01584 711654 • e-mail: peter@theroebuckinn.com
website: www.theroebuckinn.com

In a pretty village between Ludlow and Leominster, the Roebuck is widely renowned for its superb dining room which serves imaginative and interesting dishes based on the finest fresh local ingredients. This is an ideal venue for a rewarding break in tranquil surroundings, and excellent en suite accommodation is available in comfortable and cosy bedrooms. Three bars offer a choice of venues for relaxation and convivial conversation. Ludlow is a picturesque market town steeped in history with an impressive Norman castle, whilst Leominster, with its origins in the wool trade, has numerous antique shops. *ETC* ♦♦♦♦. *AA Two Rosettes.*

3 BEDROOMS, ALL WITH PRIVATE BATHROOM; FREE HOUSE WITH REAL ALE; CHILDREN AND PETS WELCOME;
BAR LUNCHES, RESTAURANT MEALS; NON-SMOKING AREAS; LUDLOW 4 MILES; S£££, D££.

## THE BRADFORD ARMS HOTEL
Llanymynech, Oswestry, Shropshire SY22 6EJ
Tel: 01691 830582 • Fax: 01691 830728 • e-mail: info@bradfordarmshotel.com
website: www.bradfordarmshotel.com

A peaceful retreat ideally suited to those with an interest in a variety of outdoor pursuits, the cosy little village of Llanymynech, on the English/Welsh border, is situated on a branch of the Shropshire Union canal system and nearby there are first-rate opportunities for indulging in fishing, canoeing, mountain biking, rock climbing, horse riding, and golf. As a handy base for all these diversions, the Bradford Arms, privately owned by Bud and Fiona Winter, presents a high standard of comfort, service and cuisine for their guests; all rooms have the best contemporary appointments and at terms that reflect excellent value. *AA Four Red Diamonds.*

5 BEDROOMS, ALL WITH PRIVATE BATHROOM; FREE HOUSE WITH REAL ALE; HISTORIC INTEREST; CHILDREN WELCOME;
BAR LUNCHES WED-SUN, RESTAURANT TUES-SAT EVENINGS; NON-SMOKING AREAS; OSWESTRY 6 MILES; S£££, D££

## THE CHURCH INN
**Buttercross, Ludlow, Shropshire SY8 1AW**
**Tel: 01584 872174 • Fax: 01584 877146 • website: www.thechurchinn.com**

This historic inn has undergone several changes of name over the centuries – it was originally called the "Cross Keys" – but retains the fine old-fashioned traditions of good ale and good food which have ensured its lasting popularity through the ages. Nine cosy en suite bedrooms, all with telephone and modem point, provide first-rate overnight accommodation, and a full range of catering, from freshly cut sandwiches to succulent steaks, ensures that appetites large and small will be amply satisfied. Regularly changing guest beers supplement the already extensive range of wines, spirits and ales on offer. The ancient town of Ludlow is an ideal base for exploring the Border counties and the Welsh Marches, and is conveniently located for road and rail links to the Midlands. Single discount midweek. *ETC/AA/RAC* ♦♦♦, *CAMRA*.

9 BEDROOMS, ALL WITH PRIVATE BATHROOM; FREE HOUSE WITH REAL ALE; HISTORIC INTEREST; CHILDREN WELCOME; BAR LUNCHES, RESTAURANT EVENINGS ONLY; NON-SMOKING AREAS; SHREWSBURY 24 MILES; D£££.

## THE FOUR ALLS INN & HOTEL
**Newport Road, Woodseaves, Market Drayton, Shropshire TF9 2AG**
**Tel: 01630 652995 • Fax: 01630 653930 • e-mail: inn@thefouralls**
**website: www.thefouralls.com**

Window boxes and bright red shutters enhance the clear-cut lines of this attractive free house, a welcome sight on the A529 just north of Market Drayton. Delightfully decorated throughout with a tutored eye for colour harmony, the inn has a spruce, oak-beamed bar and a comfortable and visually striking restaurant where the varied à la carte menu places due emphasis on wholesome home cooking. There is also a selective bar menu and the lunchtime carvery is a popular innovation. A well-planned chalet-style unit provides first-rate accommodation, the centrally heated rooms having en suite facilities, radio alarm clocks and refreshment trays. Social functions and business meetings are splendidly catered for in a spacious functions room. *AA* ♦♦♦

9 BEDROOMS, ALL WITH PRIVATE BATHROOM; FREE HOUSE WITH REAL ALE; CHILDREN WELCOME; BAR AND RESTAURANT MEALS; NON-SMOKING AREAS; MARKET DRAYTON 2 MILES; S££, D£££.

## THE CROWN COUNTRY INN
**Munslow, Near Craven Arms, Shropshire SY7 9ET**
**Tel: 01584 841205 • Fax: 01584 841255 •website: www.crowncountryinn.co.uk**
**e-mail: info@crowncountryinn.co.uk**

Set below the rolling hills of Wenlock Edge, the Crown Country Inn is an ideal place to stay and explore the area. This Grade II Listed Tudor inn retains many historic features, including oak beams and flagstone floors. Here you can sample traditional ales, fine food and a warm welcome from hosts, Richard and Jane Arnold. The menu offers a tempting variety of traditional and more exotic dishes, plus daily 'specials', all freshly prepared using the finest ingredients. Accommodation is available in three large bedrooms, all en suite, with television and tea/coffee making facilities. All rooms are non-smoking. *AA* ♦♦♦♦, *CAMRA*, Shropshire Good Eating Awards - Restaurant of the Year 2001/2002 and 2003/2004. *See also Colour Advertisement.*

3 BEDROOMS, ALL WITH PRIVATE BATHROOM; FREE HOUSE; HISTORIC INTEREST; CHILDREN AND PETS WELCOME; BAR MEALS; NON-SMOKING AREAS; LUDLOW 8 MILES; S££, D££.

---

**For our guide to**
**Pet-Friendly**
**Pubs, Inns & Hotels**
**see pages 149-162**

# Somerset

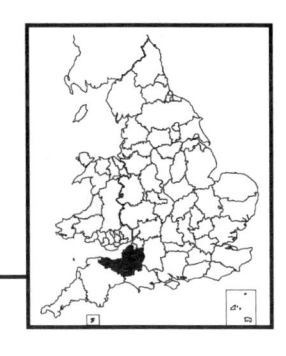

## HORSE POND INN & MOTEL
**The Triangle, Castle Cary, Somerset BA7 7BD**
**Tel: 01963 350318 • Fax: 01963 351762**

Nestling at the foot of Castle Cary, an attractive 12th century country town, the Horse Pond Inn is centrally located for either business or pleasure, and is close to the Bath and West Showground. Accommodation is available in very comfortable, spacious rooms, all en suite, with telephone, tea and coffee making facilities, trouser press and hairdryer. Fresh, home-cooked meals are available in the non-smoking restaurant. Pets are welcome.

5 BEDROOMS, ALL WITH PRIVATE BATHROOM; YOUNGS HOUSE WITH REAL ALE; HISTORIC INTEREST; CHILDREN AND PETS WELCOME; BAR LUNCHES, RESTAURANT EVENINGS ONLY; NON-SMOKING AREAS; BRUTON 3 MILES; S£££.

## LION HOTEL
**Bank Square, Dulverton, Somerset TA22 9BU**
**Tel: 01398 323444 • Fax: 01398 323980**

The perfect headquarters for exploring the magic land of heather-clad moors, leafy lanes, nature trails, red deer and wild ponies of Exmoor, the attractive and comfortable Lion Hotel is set in the heart of the delightful little town of Dulverton, on Exmoor's southern fringe. Warm and friendly, the hotel takes great pride in the delicious home-cooked cuisine on offer in the charming restaurant. Alternatively, there is an extensive selection of meals available in the lounge bar. Full of character, guest rooms are fully en suite and have colour television, direct-dial telephone and beverage makers. Sporting activities available locally include riding, river and reservoir fishing, and golf. *AA* ★★

13 BEDROOMS, ALL WITH PRIVATE BATHROOMS; FREE HOUSE WITH REAL ALE; HISTORIC INTEREST; CHILDREN AND PETS WELCOME; BAR AND RESUTARANT MEALS; NON-SMOKING AREAS; TIVERTON 10 MILES; S££, D££.

## THE LION AT PENNARD
**Glastonbury Road, West Pennard, Glastonbury, Somerset BA6 8NH**
**Tel: 01458 832941 • Fax: 01458 830660 • e-mail: thelion@pennard.fsbusiness.co.uk**

The Lion at Pennard is a 15th century coaching inn, complete with deep inglenook fireplaces, flagstone floors and oak beams. Accommodation is available in seven comfortable en suite bedrooms, making this an ideal base for visiting the many places of interest in the area, including the historic towns of Wells and Glastonbury. Delicious bar and restaurant meals can be enjoyed each lunchtime and evening. Children are welcome, and have their own menu; high chairs are available if required. The lounge bar offers an excellent range of refreshments, and visitors will receive a warm welcome from the friendly staff – and perhaps from the resident ghost who is believed to sit there! Bed and breakfast rates are most reasonable, with bargain break terms and reductions for longer stays. *ETC* ◆◆◆

7 BEDROOMS, ALL WITH PRIVATE BATHROOM; USHERS OF TROWBRIDGE HOUSE WITH REAL ALE; HISTORIC INTEREST; CHILDREN WELCOME; BAR MEALS, RESTAURANT EVENINGS ONLY; NON-SMOKING AREAS; GLASTONBURY 3 MILES; S£££, D££.

## OLD POUND INN
**Aller, Langport, Somerset TA10 0RA**
**Tel & Fax: 01458 250469**

With all the credentials of a classic wayside inn, the 'Old Pound' changed its name from the 'White Lion' as recently as 1980 as it stands on the site of the old village pound. Starting life as a cider house in 1571, it has pursued its purpose of providing sustenance to the inhabitants of an idyllic Somerset village ever since, quite unmoved by the ravages of the Civil War which raged nearby. Peace reigns today with standards of refreshment and accommodation upgraded to a level somewhat higher than the surrounding fen-like countryside – a rich land of imposing sunsets. Two resident chefs hold sway over a splendid à la carte restaurant and the excellent accommodation comprises rooms with en suite facilities, colour television and tea and coffee-makers. *ETC* ◆◆◆, *Winner of JPC National Award for Best Pub of the Year 1999 and 2000.*

6 BEDROOMS, FREE HOUSE WITH REAL ALE; HISTORIC INTEREST; CHILDREN WELCOME; BAR AND RESTAURANT MEALS; NON-SMOKING AREAS; LANGPORT 2 MILES; S£££, D£££.

---

## THE TALBOT 15TH CENTURY COACHING INN AT MELLS
**Near Bath, Somerset BA11 3PN**
**Tel: 01373 812254 • Fax: 01373 813599**
**website: www.talbotinn.com**

This lovely old coaching inn, dating in part from the 15th century, is many visitors ideal of a rustic haven, offering the traditional warmth of the public bar with its real ales and real fires, and the culinary delights of the oak-beamed restaurant. Here one can enjoy either a quick snack or a superb à la carte meal expertly cooked by a resident chef. Set in a picturesque Mendip village, this homeliest of hostelries has a cobbled courtyard and a delightful cottage garden where refreshments may be taken in fine weather. A haven of rural tranquillity, the Talbot has accommodation reflecting its origins but with fine modern facilities skilfully introduced; the elegant Manor Suite offers that extra touch of pure luxury. *ETC/AA* ◆◆◆◆, *AA Rosette.*

8 BEDROOMS, ALL WITH PRIVATE BATHROOM; FREE HOUSE WITH REAL ALE; HISTORIC INTEREST; CHILDREN AND PETS WELCOME; BAR AND RESTAURANT MEALS; NON-SMOKING AREAS; BATH 18 MILES; S£££££, D£££.

## THE WHEELWRIGHTS ARMS
Monkton Combe, Near Bath, Somerset BA2 7HB
Tel: 01225 722287 • Fax: 01225 723029 • website: www.wheelwrightsarms.co.uk

With excellent accommodation housed in the converted barn and stables, this is a lovely base from which to visit the numerous houses, gardens and places of interest which lie within a few miles, including of course the city of Bath itself. The hostelry stands in the peace and quiet of the lovely Midford valley. A large selection of home cooked food is served, with the addition of a grill menu in the evening. In addition there is a choice of three real ales. The bedrooms (mostly beamed) are equipped with shower, toilet, washbasin, colour television, central heating, tea and coffee making facilities and hairdryers. The inn is also a lovely base for walking, fishing, riding or just relaxing. In the summer guests are free to use the pleasant garden and patio, and in winter cosy log fires warm the bar. *ETC* ◆◆

8 BEDROOMS, ALL WITH PRIVATE BATHROOM; FREE HOUSE WITH REAL ALE; HISTORIC INTEREST; PETS WELCOME; BAR AND RESTAURANT MEALS; BATH 2 MILES; S£££, D££.

## PHELIPS ARMS
The Borough, Montacute, Somerset TA15 6XB
Tel: 01935 822557 • website: www.phelipsarms.co.uk

First and foremost a traditional village pub, the 'Phelips Arms' is named after the family who built the Elizabethan mansion we now know as Montacute House and which is a short walk away. In a friendly and relaxed atmosphere, the bar serves well-kept real ales and a carefully selected list of over 70 wines. Under the expert supervision of Chef, Jim Smith, lunch and dinner menus are of the highest calibre and make use of the freshest ingredients. There is a lovely walled garden, a favourite venue for summer lunchtime diners, and a skittle alley. The verdant acres of 'Smiling Somerset' invite closer acquaintance and comfortable and recently refurbished accommodation is available with en suite facilities.

4 BEDROOMS, ALL WITH PRIVATE BATHROOMS; PALMERS HOUSE WITH REAL ALE; HISTORIC INTEREST; CHILDREN AND PETS WELCOME; BAR LUNCHES, RESTAURANT TUES-SAT EVENINGS; NON-SMOKING AREAS; YEOVIL 4 MILES; S£££, D££.

## KING'S ARMS INN & RESTAURANT
Bishopton, Montacute, Somerset TA15 6UU
Tel: 01935 822513 • Fax: 01935 826549 • e-mail: kingsarms@realemail.co.uk
website: www.greeneking-inns.co.uk

The first acquaintance many people make with this welcoming and charismatic 16th century hamstone inn is after visiting nearby Elizabethan Montacute House. The atmosphere of the Pickwick Bar is typically that of the traditional English inn of one's imaginings and, in such a setting, lunches and evening à la carte and table d'hôte menus are offered. For more formal dining, the Abbey Room Restaurant presents a splendid selection of à la carte meals. Blessed with impressive hotel amenities, the Kings Arms has a number of beautifully decorated guest rooms, including a half-tester room and one with a four-poster bed, and all have a private bathroom, colour television, radio and tea and coffee-making facilities. *ETC* ◆◆◆◆

15 BEDROOMS, ALL WITH PRIVATE BATHROOM; GREENE KING LEASED HOUSE WITH REAL ALE; HISTORIC INTEREST; CHILDREN AND PETS WELCOME; BAR LUNCHES AND RESTAURANT MEALS; NON-SMOKING AREAS; YEOVIL 4 MILES; S££££, D££££.

---

**FHG**
Visit the FHG website
**www.holidayguides.com**
for details of the wide choice of accommodation featured in the full range of FHG titles

*Somerset* 99

## THE GEORGE AT NUNNEY
Church Street, Nunney, Near Frome, Somerset BA11 4LW
Tel: 01373 836458 • Fax: 01373 836565 • www.georgenunneyhotel.co.uk
e-mail: enquiries@georgeatnunneyhotel.wanadoo.co.uk

This lovely old coaching inn nestles in a village of picturesque cottages dominated by an imposing 13th century castle. And what a charming place this is, with cask-conditioned ales, wines and over 100 speciality whiskies available in the friendly bars. Alongside is an attractive restaurant which features a palate-tingling menu. Nearby, the Mendips await exploration, as do Cheddar, Wookey Hole and the historic pleasures of Glastonbury, Wells and Bath. We can aver that this warmly recommended retreat is a difficult place to leave, so give in, and take advantage of the excellent and reasonably-priced accommodation, all rooms having en suite facilities, colour television with movie channel, direct-dial telephone and tea and coffee-makers. You'll not regret it.

10 BEDROOMS, ALL WITH PRIVATE BATHROOM; FREE HOUSE WITH REAL ALE; CHILDREN WELCOME;
BAR AND RESTAURANT MEALS; NON-SMOKING AREAS; FROME 3 MILES; S££££.

---

## SPARKFORD INN
Sparkford, Yeovil, Somerset BA22 7JN
Tel: 01963 440218 • e-mail: sparkfordinn@sparkford.fsbusiness.co.uk

Handy for the A303, the Sparkford Inn is a homely and welcoming old coaching inn with en suite accommodation, a rambling series of beamed bars and carvery restaurant, all with a mix of antique furniture and interesting old prints and photographs. No pool table or juke box. There is a log fire in the lounge bar and restaurant. The inn has a large car park, beer garden and children's adventure play area. At the Sunday luncheon with speciality choice of roasts, the two-course carvery is very reasonably priced; there is also a specials board in the bars. The pub is a free house and there are always four real ales available. Children are welcome in the restaurant and in some areas in the bar. *ETC* ◆◆◆

10 BEDROOMS, ALL WITH PRIVATE BATHROOM; FREE HOUSE WITH REAL ALE; CHILDREN AND PETS WELCOME;
BAR AND RESTAURANT MEALS; CASTLE CARY 4 MILES; S£££, D££££.

## THE GREYHOUND INN
**Staple Fitzpaine, Taunton, Somerset TA3 5SP**
Tel: 01823 480227 • Fax: 01823 481117 • www.thegreyhoundinn.fsbusiness.co.uk
e-mail: ivor_lucy@the-greyhoundinn.fsbusiness.co.uk

Nestled at the foot of the Blackdown Hills (Area of Outstanding Natural Beauty), this 16th century coaching inn offers so much warmth and hospitality. Fresh fish daily from Brixham in Devon, and other ingredients bought locally, bring fantastic flavours and variety to cater for everyone's palate. Carefully selected wines, from both the old and new world complement whatever dish you choose. The busy, traditional, flagstoned locals' bar offers cask marque real ales and Somerset ciders on pump. After enjoying such good fare, served on old wooden tables, worn nicely from frequent use, why not extend your stay in one of the superior en suite rooms offering fantastic facilities. The inn is set in a quiet yet central location between the A303 and the M5. Worth a visit or longer stay! *AA Four Red Diamonds.*

4 BEDROOMS, ALL WITH PRIVATE BATHROOM; FREE HOUSE WITH REAL ALE; HISTORIC INTEREST;
CHILDREN AND PETS WELCOME; BAR AND RESTAURANT MEALS; NON-SMOKING AREAS; TAUNTON 5 MILES; S£££££, D£££.

## THE CROSSWAYS INN
**West Huntspill, Near Highbridge, Somerset TA9 3DQ**
Tel: 01278 783756 • Fax: 01278 781899 • e-mail: crossways.inn@virgin.net
website: www.crossways-inn.com

Conveniently located on the A38 (Exits 22 and 23 from the M5), this spacious 17th century inn is very popular with families, whether on a day out or staying overnight. Children sharing a room with their parents are accommodated free and there is a special family room for meals and refreshments. In fine weather meals can be taken on picnic tables under the trees in the spacious garden. A good range of real ales is available, including a weekly-changing guest beer, and service is cheerful and efficient. The Crossways is ideally situated for exploring the West Country and is just a short drive from the lively holiday resort of Weston-super-Mare.

4 BEDROOMS, ALL WITH PRIVATE BATHROOM; FREE HOUSE WITH REAL ALE; HISTORIC INTEREST;
CHILDREN AND PETS WELCOME; BAR AND RESTAURANT MEALS; NON-SMOKING AREAS; BURNHAM-ON-SEA 3 MILES; S££, D£.

## THE HALFWAY HOUSE INN COUNTRY LODGE
**Chilthorne Domer, Near Yeovil, Somerset BA22 8RE**
Tel: 01935 840350 • Fax: 01935 849005 • e-mail: paul@halfwayhouseinn.com
website: www.halfwayhouseinn.com

In a sleepy little village with one of those evocative names that is 'forever England', this delightful discovery is to be found on the A37, halfway between Yeovil and Ilchester with the thrumming A303 another world away, all of two miles distant. It is well worth the detour to escape, even temporarily, to this pleasant village inn and enjoy good wholesome fare, convivial company and maybe the challenge of the skittle alley. It is quite possible that the thought of moving on will invoke a certain lack of enthusiasm. Worry not, for excellent en suite accommodation is available at the most reasonable rates. We know what we would do! *ETC/AA* ◆◆◆

15 BEDROOMS, ALL WITH PRIVATE BATHROOM; FREE HOUSE WITH REAL ALE; CHILDREN AND PETS WELCOME;
BAR AND RESTAURANT MEALS; NON-SMOKING AREAS; YEOVIL 3 MILES; S£££££, D££.

# Staffordshire

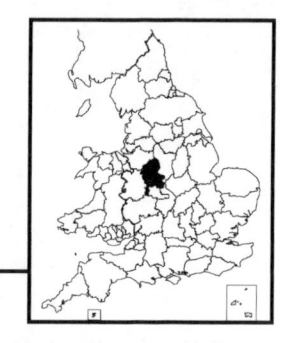

## THREE HORSESHOES INN & RESTAURANT
Blackshaw Moor, Leek, Staffordshire ST13 8TW
Tel: 01538 300296 • Fax: 01538 300320 • website: www.threeshoesinn.co.uk

This family-run inn is situated on the A53, approximately seven miles from Buxton and on the edge of the Peak District National Park, with breathtaking views of the Staffordshire moorlands and the bizarre stone formation of The Roaches. Slate floors, oak beams and log fires give an olde worlde atmosphere. The inn offers three styles of dining. The Bar Carvery offers traditionally cooked roast meats and home-cooked dishes in a bar atmosphere; the Brasserie has a relaxed and informal atmosphere to suit today's casual style of dining, serving traditional and speciality dishes with influences from around the world; and, for a more formal style of dining, the award-winning Kirks Restaurant (AA Rosette) offers all the tastes of the Brasserie, but with more elegance and style for that special occasion. At weekends there is a well-attended dinner dance. Accommodation is available in six cottage-style bedrooms, with shower, telephone, television and tea-making facilities. For relaxation in fine weather there are large gardens with patios, terraces and a children's play area. *ETC/AA* ★★, *AA Rosette*.

6 BEDROOMS, ALL WITH PRIVATE SHOWER; FREE HOUSE WITH REAL ALE; CHILDREN WELCOME; BAR AND RESTAURANT MEALS; NON-SMOKING AREAS; DERBY 28 MILES, STAFFORD 24, STOKE-ON-TRENT 11, S£££users£, D££.

## THE OLDE CORNER HOUSE HOTEL
Walsall Road, Muckley Corner, Lichfield, Staffordshire WS14 0BG
Tel: 01543 372182 • Fax: 01543 372211

An interesting old coaching inn, parts of which date back to 1683. It has 23 en suite bedrooms, a restaurant to seat 45 covers, and an adjoining pub with its own restaurant. Under new ownership, it has developed a reputation for excellent food, good service and a friendly atmosphere. Located on the A5/A461 intersection at Muckley Corner, it is ideally positioned for access to Birmingham and the NEC, The Belfry Golf Club, and the motorway network. Weekend Break rates for a two-night stay available by arrangement. *AA* ★★

23 BEDROOMS, ALL EN SUITE; FREE HOUSE WITH REAL ALE; CHILDREN WELCOME; BAR AND RESTAURANT MEALS; BIRMINGHAM 15 MILES; S££££, D££££.

# Suffolk

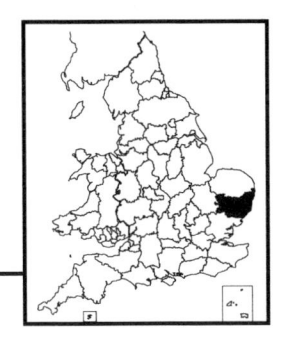

## THE CROWN HOTEL
**104 High Street, Bildeston, Suffolk IP7 7EB**
**Tel: 01449 740510 • Fax: 01449 741843**

Built in 1495 and probably a wealthy merchant's house for some time after, there is later proof of the Crown's existence as an inn in the mid-17th century. Over the past 20 years or so this former coaching inn has been restored to former glory. The timbered facade and a wealth of old beams in the bar still take the eye although first-rate modern amenities have been introduced. The restaurant boasts an extensive à la carte menu featuring some intriguing speciality dishes and an extensive range of lighter meals and snacks may be enjoyed in the bar. Bedrooms are individually decorated in romantic style and all have private facilities and colour television. Sheltered gardens to the rear provide a tranquil setting for relaxation and for the more energetic, there are opportunities for tennis, golf and swimming nearby.

9 BEDROOMS, ALL WITH PRIVATE BATHROOM; FREE HOUSE WITH REAL ALE; HISTORIC INTEREST; CHILDREN AND PETS WELCOME; BAR AND RESTAURANT MEALS; NON-SMOKING AREAS; HADLEIGH 5 MILES; S££££, D££££.

## THE SHIP INN
**St James Street, Dunwich, Near Saxmundham, Suffolk IP17 3DT**
**Tel: 01728 648219 • Fax: 01728 648675 • e-mail: shipinn@tiscali.co.uk**

On a grey, stormy day, Dunwich can be a melancholy place, especially if one pays heed to the legend of the old town inundated by the relentless sea. Stand on the shore and listen to the ghostly sound of the Bells of Dunwich tolling sadly beneath the waves. A far better place to be is the cosy main bar of this hospitable inn, itself a one-time haunt of smugglers. A cheerful fire adds to the warmth of welcome in chilly weather but on bright days enjoy the delightful garden, the focal point of which is a wonderful old fig tree. One may reflect over good refreshment here that Dunwich is a fascinating and historic place of great charm. The famous Bird Reserve of Minsmere is only a short walk along the coast.

3 BEDROOMS, ALL WITH PRIVATE BATHROOM; FREE HOUSE WITH REAL ALE; HISTORIC INTEREST; CHILDREN AND PETS WELCOME; BAR MEALS, RESTAURANT EVENINGS ONLY (SEASONAL); NON-SMOKING AREAS; SOUTHWOLD 4 MILES; S£££, D££.

## DOLPHIN INN
**Thorpeness, Aldeburgh, Suffolk IP16 4NA**
**Tel: 01728 454994 • Fax: 01728 453868 • e-mail: sales@thorpenessdolphin.com**
**website: www.thorpenessdolphin.com**

Rising like a phoenix from the ashes of the original inn which was burnt down in 1994, the new 'Dolphin' proudly resumes its place on Suffolk's Heritage Coast in the picturesque village of Thorpeness, created early in the 20th century as the brainchild of the dramatist, Glencairn Stuart Ogilvie, with a superb Meare studded with islets, the habitat of many interesting birds. The sprucely furnished inn has two attractive bars and a dining room, the setting for satisfying luncheons and dinners with a lovely garden and barbecue providing the opportunity to enjoy refreshment al fresco in summer months. Nearby is a safe bathing beach and golf may be played at adjacent Thorpeness Golf Club at a 20% discount to residents. *ETC* ★★★

3 BEDROOMS, ALL WITH PRIVATE BATHROOM; FREE HOUSE WITH REAL ALE; CHILDREN AND PETS WELCOME; BAR AND RESTAURANT MEALS; NON-SMOKING AREAS; ALDEBURGH 2 MILES; S££££, D£££.

# Surrey

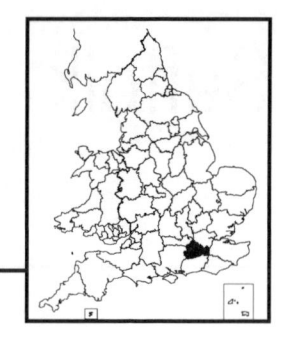

## WHEATSHEAF INN
**Grayswood Road, Grayswood, Haslemere, Surrey GU27 2DE**
**Tel: 01428 644440 • Fax: 01428 641285 • e-mail: thewheatsheef@aol.com**

Snug amidst the verdant countryside that stretches from Surrey across the border into West Sussex, this neat free house, just north of Haslemere, sets a high standard in relation to its refreshment and accommodation facilities. The hub of the inn is the attractive lounge bar which presents a good range of real ales and wines, the latter complementing the excellent meals which are served here or in the elegant adjacent dining room. The surrounding area is popular with walkers and visitors to the picturesque towns of Petworth and Midhurst. First-class accommodation is available in en suite bedrooms appointed with colour television, direct-dial telephone and hospitality tray. *AA* ◆◆◆, *RAC* ◆◆◆ *and Fine Dining Award.*

7 BEDROOMS, ALL WITH PRIVATE BATHROOM; FREE HOUSE WITH REAL ALE; PETS WELCOME;
BAR AND RESTAURANT MEALS LUNCHTIMES; NON-SMOKING AREAS; HASLEMERE 1 MILE; S£££££, D£££££.

---

The £ symbol when appearing at the end of the italic section of an entry shows the anticipated price, during 2005, for full Bed and Breakfast.

*Normal Bed & Breakfast rate per person*
*(in single room)*

| PRICE RANGE | CATEGORY |
|---|---|
| **Under £25** | *S£* |
| **£26-£35** | *S££* |
| **£36-£45** | *S£££* |
| **Over £45** | *S££££* |

*Normal Bed & Breakfast rate per person*
*(sharing double/twin room)*

| PRICE RANGE | CATEGORY |
|---|---|
| **Under £25** | *D£* |
| **£26-£35** | *D££* |
| **£36-£45** | *D£££* |
| **Over £45** | *D££££* |

This is meant as an indication only and does not show prices for Special Breaks, Weekends, etc. Guests are therefore advised to verify all prices on enquiring or booking.

## CHASE LODGE HOTEL
10 Park Road, Hampton Wick, Kingston-upon-Thames, Surrey KT1 4AS
Tel: 020 8943 1862 • Fax: 020 8943 9393 • e-mail: info@chaselodgehotel.com
websites: www.chaselodgehotel.com • www.surreyhotels.com

An award-winning hotel with style and elegance set in tranquil surroundings at affordable prices. Quality en suite bedrooms; some with jacuzzi and steam area. Full English breakfast and à la carte menu. Licensed bar. Easy access to Kingston town centre and all major transport links; 20 minutes from Heathrow Airport. All major credit cards accepted. *LTB* ★★★, *AA* ★★★ *and Two Rosettes, RAC Highly Acclaimed, Les Routiers.*

13 BEDROOMS, ALL WITH PRIVATE BATHROOM; HISTORIC INTEREST; CHILDREN AND PETS WELCOME;
LONDON 10 MILES; S££, D££.

## THE RUNNING HORSES
Old London Road, Mickleham, Surrey RH5 6DU
Tel: 01372 372279 • Fax: 01372 363004 • e-mail: info@therunninghorses.co.uk
website: www.therunninghorses.co.uk

Set amidst beautiful National Trust countryside with the vantage point of Box Hill a mere half-a-mile away, this lovely 400-year-old inn has welcomed a wide spectrum of society over the years. The main bar, even today, features a highwayman's hideaway and a cosy bar with an impressive inglenook fireplace. Owners, Josie and Steve Slayford, dispense good cheer and the present day visitor will find a restaurant offering a high standard of cuisine and accommodation facilities that would do credit to many a multi-starred establishment; en suite bedrooms, named after local racecourses, are appointed with colour television, direct-dial telephone and tea and coffee-makers. A function room is available for meetings and private parties.

5 BEDROOMS, ALL WITH PRIVATE BATHROOM; PUNCH TAVERNS HOUSE WITH REAL ALE; HISTORIC INTEREST;
PETS ALLOWED IN BAR ONLY; BAR LUNCHES; RESTAURANT MEALS; LEATHERHEAD 2 MILES; S££££, D££££.

# East Sussex

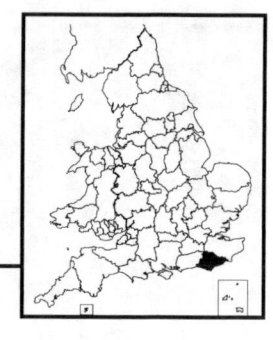

### THE ANCHOR INN
**Anchor Lane, Barcombe, Near Lewes, East Sussex BN8 5BS**
**Tel: 01273 400414 • Fax: 01273 401029 • www.anchorinnandboating.co.uk**

This delectable retreat hidden away on the west bank of the River Ouse is a great favourite. Peacefully situated in a beautiful part of leafy Sussex, the inn has an interesting history. It was built in 1790 and catered primarily for bargees whose horse-drawn barges plied between Newhaven and nearby Slaugham. After the decline of river traffic, locals continued to use the inn until the innkeeper was unwary enough to be caught smuggling in 1895: the licence was rescinded and not regained until 1963. At one with the unspoilt daily life of the river, this is a lovely place to escape to and boating can be arranged. The inn itself has great character and offers comfortable accommodation at reasonable rates. *ETC* ◆◆◆, *Les Routiers*.

3 BEDROOMS, ALL WITH PRIVATE BATHROOM; FREE HOUSE WITH REAL ALE; HISTORIC INTEREST;
CHILDREN AND PETS WELCOME; BAR AND RESTAURANT MEALS; NON-SMOKING AREAS; LEWES 3 MILES; S££££.

## PUBLISHER'S NOTE

**FHG**

While every effort is made to ensure accuracy, we regret that FHG Publications cannot accept responsibility for errors, misrepresentations or omissions in our entries or any consequences thereof. Prices in particular should be checked because we go to press early. We will follow up complaints but cannot act as arbiters or agents for either party.

# Warwickshire

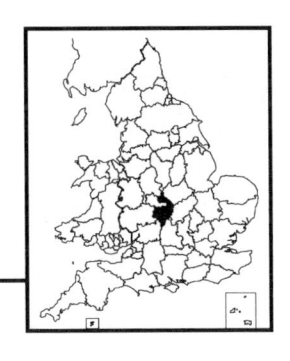

## THE BELL ALDERMINSTER
Shipston Road, Stratford-upon-Avon, Warwickshire CV37 8NY
Tel: 01789 450414 • Fax: 01789 450998 • e-mail: thebellald@aol.com
website: www.thebellald.co.uk

A refreshing sight on the A3400 Oxford to Stratford-upon-Avon road, this attractive wayside hostelry backs on to lovely, secluded gardens. In this tranquil and delightful situation, a programme of special events is organised by go-ahead hosts, Keith and Vanessa Brewer, and the restaurant is a popular rendezvous. Good facilities also exist for social functions. A recommended touring base, the inn has six handsomely furnished and decorated bedrooms with double or twin beds; each one has colour television and tea and coffee-makers. A typically English breakfast is served in the conservatory overlooking the Stour Valley and hills beyond. *ETC* ◆◆◆◆

6 BEDROOMS, 4 WITH PRIVATE BATHROOM; FREE HOUSE WITH REAL ALE; HISTORIC INTEREST; CHILDREN AND PETS WELCOME; BAR AND RESTAURANT MEALS; NON-SMOKING AREAS; STRATFORD-UPON-AVON 4 MILES; S££/£££, D££.

## WHITE BEAR HOTEL
High Street, Shipston-on-Stour, Warwickshire CV36 4AJ
Tel: 01608 661558 • Fax: 01608 662612 • e-mail: whitebearhot@hotmail.com
website: www.whitebearhotel.co.uk

A recommended port of call in a beautiful touring area, this charming hostelry offers simple and friendly bar service. A wide range of food is available daily in both the bars and the bistro-style restaurant, accompanied by an extensive range of refreshments including real ales and a thoughtfully selected wine list. The friendly staff will do everything possible to ensure that a stay here, however long or short, is a real pleasure. With ten well-appointed guest rooms, all with en suite bath or shower, colour television, telephone and tea/coffee making facilities, this is an ideal base for exploring the many places of interest within easy reach. *ETC* ◆◆

10 BEDROOMS, ALL WITH PRIVATE BATHROOM; PUNCH TAVERNS HOUSE WITH REAL ALE; HISTORIC INTEREST; CHILDREN AND PETS WELCOME; BAR AND RESTAURANT MEALS; NON-SMOKING AREAS; STRATFORD-UPON-AVON 8 MILES; S££,D£

## NEW INN
### Clifford Chambers, Stratford-upon-Avon, Warwickshire CV37 8HR
### Tel: 01789 293402 • e-mail: thenewinn65@aol.com
### website: www.thenewinnhotel.co.uk

In a picturesque village just two miles outside Stratford-upon-Avon, this handsome 400-year-old coaching inn offers tastefully furnished accommodation at very reasonable rates; all rooms have luxury bathrooms en suite, colour television and tea and coffee-making facilities. This is also a fine place to visit away from the tourist surge for freshly prepared food of the highest quality from either a comprehensive restaurant menu or the 'specials board' in an old-world bar warmed by an open log fire. The carvery which operates on Saturday evening and Sunday lunchtime is a popular feature. This is a tranquil venue from which to enjoy the many historic and cultural attractions of the area and there are several pleasant walks in the immediate vicinity. *ETC* ★★, *AA*.

12 BEDROOMS, ALL WITH PRIVATE BATHROOM; FREE HOUSE WITH REAL ALE; HISTORIC INTEREST; CHILDREN WELCOME; BAR AND RESTAURANT MEALS; NON-SMOKING AREAS; WARWICK 8 MILES; S£££, D££.

---

## THE BLUE BOAR INN
### Temple Grafton, Alcester, Warwickshire B49 6NR
### Tel: 01789 750010 • Fax: 01789 750635 • e-mail: blueboar@covlink.co.uk
### website: www.blueboarinn.co.uk

A real old English country tavern renowned for its traditional values, the 'Blue Boar' has a reputation for fine, cask-conditioned ales from the wood and a superb cuisine, the à la carte international menu and an extensive list of bar 'specials' calculated to suit all tastes and pockets. Attention is particularly drawn to the range of delicious desserts which are prepared daily. The oldest part of the inn dates from the early 17th century and an unusual feature is a glass-covered well which is some 35 feet deep and has been used in the brewing process for many years. Outside is a pleasant patio garden with far-reaching views towards the Cotswolds. *ETC* ◆◆◆

15 BEDROOMS, ALL WITH PRIVATE BATHROOM; FREE HOUSE WITH REAL ALE; HISTORIC INTEREST; CHILDREN AND PETS WELCOME; BAR LUNCHES, RESTAURANT EVENINGS ONLY; NON-SMOKING AREAS; STRATFORD-UPON-AVON 5 MILES; S££££, D££££.

---

## • • *Some Useful Guidance for Guests and Hosts* • •

Every year literally thousands of holidays, short breaks and overnight stops are arranged through our guides, the vast majority without any problems at all. In a handful of cases, however, difficulties do arise about bookings, which often could have been prevented from the outset.

*It is important to remember that when accommodation has been booked, both parties – guests and hosts – have entered into a form of contract. We hope that the following points will provide helpful guidance.*

**GUESTS:**
- When enquiring about accommodation, be as precise as possible. Give exact dates, numbers in your party and the ages of any children.
- State the number and type of rooms wanted and also what catering you require – bed and breakfast, full board etc. Make sure that the position about evening meals is clear – and about pets, reductions for children or any other special points.
- Read our reviews carefully to ensure that the proprietors you are going to contact can supply what you want. Ask for a letter confirming all arrangements, if possible.
- If you have to cancel, do so as soon as possible. Proprietors do have the right to retain deposits and under certain circumstances to charge for cancelled holidays if adequate notice is not given and they cannot re-let the accommodation.

**HOSTS:**
- Give details about your facilities and about any special conditions. Explain your deposit system clearly and arrangements for cancellations, charges etc. and whether or not your terms include VAT.
- If for any reason you are unable to fulfil an agreed booking without adequate notice, you may be under an obligation to arrange suitable alternative accommodation or to make some form of compensation.

*While every effort is made to ensure accuracy, we regret that FHG Publications cannot accept responsibility for errors, omissions or misrepresentations in our entries or any consequences thereof. Prices in particular should be checked because we go to press early. We will follow up complaints but cannot act as arbiters or agents for either party.*

# Wiltshire

## CASTLE INN HOTEL
**Castle Combe, Chippenham, Wiltshire SN14 7HN**
**Tel: 01249 783030 • Fax: 01249 782315**
**website: www.castle-inn.info**

Standing proudly in the market place of what is regarded by many as England's prettiest village, the Castle Inn typifies all that is finest in the hallowed traditions of English inn-keeping. Under the expert guidance of a talented and imaginative chef, it has gained an enviable reputation for its fine English cooking based on the freshest of ingredients, meals being taken in the elegant conservatory restaurant or in the informal surroundings of the bar. Needless to say, the range of refreshments on offer includes some excellent real ales, plus a good selection of lagers, spirits and wines. Accommodation is of the same superb standard, five of the eleven tastefully furnished bedrooms featuring whirlpool baths, and all having a full range of modern conveniences. *ETC* ★★, *AA, RAC*.

11 BEDROOMS, ALL WITH PRIVATE BATHROOM; FREE HOUSE WITH REAL ALE; HISTORIC INTEREST; CHILDREN AND PETS WELCOME; BAR AND RESTAURANT MEALS; NON-SMOKING AREAS; CHIPPENHAM 5 MILES; S££££, D££££.

## THE DOVE INN
**Corton, Near Warminster, Wiltshire BA12 0SZ**
**Tel: 01985 850109 • Fax: 01985 851041**

A traditional village inn in the verdant Wylye Valley, the 'Dove at Corton' is well worth the detour from the A36 Warminster-Salisbury road. Bars and dining areas are most attractively set out and good ale and outstanding food is assured, the à la carte fare and 'daily specials' being prepared under the supervision of a talented, award-winning chef. The restaurant is open at lunchtimes and in the evening every day of the week and, such is its popularity, that booking is advised and, indeed, essential at weekends. First-rate accommodation is available at the 'Dove'. Fine opportunities exist in the area for walking, cycling, horse-riding and golf, whilst the River Wylye is renowned for its excellent trout fishing. *ETC* ♦♦♦♦, *AA*.

6 BEDROOMS, ALL WITH PRIVATE BATHROOM; FREE HOUSE WITH REAL ALE; CHILDREN AND PETS WELCOME; BAR AND RESTAURANT MEALS; NON-SMOKING AREAS; WARMINSTER 6 MILES; S££££, D££.

## THE BLACK SWAN HOTEL
Market Place, Devizes, Wiltshire SN10 1JQ
Tel: 01380 723259 • Fax: 01380 729966 • www.blackswanhotel.fsnet.co.uk
e-mail: reservations@blackswanhotel.fsnet.co.uk

Overlooking the picturesque Market Place, this 18th century former coaching inn has traditional appeal in its spruce bar where visitors may enjoy excellent Wadworth ales as well as a range of tempting snacks; meals of high quality are served in the intimate restaurant. The service is friendly and helpful, the atmosphere relaxing and the cuisine varied and imaginative. Whether on holiday or on business, this is a rewarding place in which to stay; cosy, well-appointed rooms all have en suite bathroom/shower, colour television and beverage making facilities. Conferences and banquets are expertly catered for. *ETC* ★★

12 BEDROOMS, ALL WITH PRIVATE BATHROOM; WADWORTHS HOUSE WITH REAL ALE; HISTORIC INTEREST;
CHILDREN WELCOME; BAR AND RESTAURANT MEALS; NON-SMOKING AREAS; CHIPPENHAM 10 MILES; S££££, D£££.

---

## THE NEELD ARMS INN
The Street, Grittleton, Wiltshire SN14 6AP
Tel: 01249 782470 • Fax: 01249 782358 • e-mail: info@neeldarms.co.uk

This charming 17th century Cotswold-stone country inn in the unspoiled village of Grittleton offers comfortable accommodation and delicious home-cooked food. There are two twin bedrooms, a family room and three double rooms, one of which has a traditional four-poster bed; all are en suite (bath or shower) with colour television, tea and coffee making facilities, and radio alarm. The rooms are comfortable and cosy, in keeping with the rest of the inn, and each is individually decorated. In the bar, a fine range of wines, spirits and traditional ales is available, which you can enjoy in front of open log fires. The historic town of Bath is nearby, and many places of interest are within easy reach, such as Stonehenge, Avebury, Stow-on-the-Wold and other famous Cotswold towns. *ETC* ◆◆◆

6 BEDROOMS, ALL WITH PRIVATE BATHROOM; FREE HOUSE WITH REAL ALE; HISTORIC INTEREST;
CHILDREN AND PETS WELCOME; BAR AND RESTAURANT MEALS (EVENINGS); CHIPPENHAM 6 MILES; S£££, D££££.

---

## THE TOLLGATE INN
Ham Green, Holt, Near Bradford-on-Avon, Wiltshire BA14 6PX
Tel: 01225 782326 • Fax: 01225 782805 • website: www.tollgateholt.co.uk

This lovely old stone-built hostelry overlooking the village green rests snugly in 12 acres of land with a paddock beyond where goats and sheep browse contentedly. Inside, in bar and lounge, deep, comfortable sofas and log fires induce the same mood, as guests indulge their gastronomic fancies whilst considering the culinary creations of chef, Alexander Venables. Freshly produced and well balanced dishes are best described as modern English in style but with a Mediterranean influence, maximum use being made of high-quality local produce. Meals are served in two highly different and fascinating locations: an imaginatively decorated first-floor restaurant with a large open fire and wooden beams that has been created from what was once a chapel, and a cosy room downstairs with pews and cushions. Intriguing food, intriguing surroundings! There is an extensive wine list featuring vintages from all corners of the world and also a wide range of guest beers, some of them collectors' items. The atmosphere is warm and friendly, the staff quietly attentive and efficient, and all around this gem of a retreat is a tranquil and verdant countryside. The temptation to stay longer may be gratified by the availability of luxuriously-furnished en suite rooms, featuring oak beams, antiques and delightful views, including those of the famous Westbury White Horse. *AA Four Red Diamonds and Two Rosettes.*

4 BEDROOMS, ALL WITH PRIVATE BATHROOM; FREE HOUSE WITH REAL ALE; HISTORIC INTEREST; PETS WELCOME;
BAR AND RESTAURANT MEALS; NON-SMOKING AREAS; BRADFORD-ON-AVON 2 MILES; S££££, D£££.

---

Visit the FHG website **www.holidayguides.com**
for details of the wide choice of accommodation featured in
the full range of FHG titles

# Worcestershire

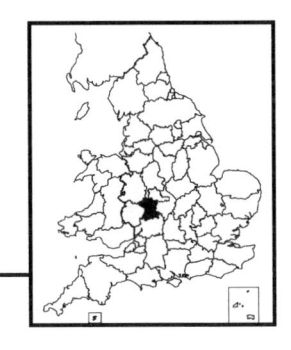

## THE MANOR ARMS COUNTRY INN
Abberley Village, Worcestershire WR6 6BN
Tel: 01299 896507 • Fax: 01299 896723 • e-mail: info@themanorarms.co.uk
website: www.themanorarms.co.uk

Of great charm and character and gracing a sleepy English village high in the Abberley Hills, the Manor Arms is over 300 years old and was originally owned by the Lord of the Manor. Whilst a number of changes have been made to the interior over the years, the inn retains much of its period ambience. The old oak beams in the walls and ceilings remain exposed and the imposing fireplace in the lounge bar was originally part of the private quarters. A huge beam supports the chimney breast which is decorated with brass ornaments and knick-knacks; a log fire ensures cosy warmth in cool weather. There is an excellent choice of Cask Marque award-winning traditional ales, along with a bar menu, grill menu, fresh fish menu, à la carte menu and sausage board. There are 11 individually furnished letting rooms, including a family suite (a double, twin and lounge area, accommodating up to six adults) and the Manor Suite which has a four-poster bed, luxury bathroom and sitting room. ETC/AA/RAC ♦♦♦, Cask Marque.
*See also Colour Advertisement.*

12 BEDROOMS, ALL WITH PRIVATE BATHROOM; FREE HOUSE WITH REAL ALE; HISTORIC INTEREST; CHILDREN WELCOME; BAR MEALS, RESTAURANT EVENINGS ONLY; NON-SMOKING AREAS; STOURPORT 5 MILES; S£££, D££.

## THE BOOT INN
Radford Road, Flyford Flavell, Worcestershire WR7 4BS
Tel: 01386 462658 • Fax: 01386 462547 • website: www.thebootinn.com

Gazing at its red brick exterior, it is hard to believe that parts of this family-run inn date back to the 13th century, but it soon apparent that the traditional values of hospitality and service remain, as fine real ales combine with wholesome fare to mark this obliging port of call as a venue well worth making a detour for. Situated just off the A422 Worcester to Stratford-upon-Avon road, it is, without doubt, a place for memorable dining. One may choose from the bar menu and extensive 'specials' board or the full à la carte option in a delightful restaurant. Why not stay the night? Beautifully appointed bedrooms await, all with en suite facilities, colour television, direct-dial telephone and beverage-makers. ETC ♦♦♦ *Silver Award, RAC Dining Award and Sparkling Diamond Award, AA Four Red Diamonds.*

5 BEDROOMS, ALL WITH PRIVATE BATHROOM; FREE HOUSE WITH REAL ALE; HISTORIC INTEREST; CHILDREN WELCOME; PETS IN BAR ONLY; BAR LUNCHES AND RESTAURANT MEALS; NON-SMOKING AREAS; WORCESTER 8 MILES; S££££, D£££.

---

**FHG** — Free or reduced rate entry to Holiday Visits and Attractions - see our **READERS' OFFER VOUCHERS** on pages 21-40

## ANCHOR INN AND RESTAURANT
Cotheridge Lane, Eckington, Near Pershore, Worcestershire WR10 3BA
Tel & Fax: 01386 750356 • e-mail: anchoreck@aol.com
website: www.anchoreckington.co.uk

In a tranquil village of traditional black and white cottages, idyllic is the most apt epithet for the situation of this lovely old inn, parts of which date from the 17th century, with the original timber ceiling beams and an exposed fireplace. Good boating facilities exist on the River Avon as it winds round the village and for walkers, footpaths lead to legendary Bredon Hill – a delightful setting. Excellent refreshment is obtainable here ranging from a bar snack to a splendid three-course dinner supported by fine wines. A peaceful haven in which to stay, the inn has en suite accommodation with the most up-to-date amenities including colour television and tea and coffee-makers. *ETC* ♦♦♦

5 BEDROOMS, ALL WITH PRIVATE BATHROOM; FREE HOUSE WITH REAL ALE; HISTORIC INTEREST; CHILDREN AND PETS WELCOME; BAR AND RESTAURANT MEALS; NON-SMOKING AREAS; PERSHORE 5 MILES; S££, D£.

## WALTER DE CANTELUPE INN
Main Road (A38), Kempsey, Worcestershire WR5 3NA
Tel: 01905 820572 • Fax: 01905 820873 • www.walterdecantelupeinn.com
e-mail: info@walterdecantelupeinn.com

The name of this fine inn immediately begs the question who was (or is) Walter de Cantelupe? This worthy was Bishop of Worcester way back in the 13th century, obviously a good man who deserved to have his name perpetuated to such a noble purpose. Very much as deserving, in a practical sense, is the inn's present owner/manager, Martin Lloyd Morris, FBII, who has put to telling effect all the tenets of good inn-keeping – wholesome food, satisfying drink, comfortable accommodation and warm hospitality. A strikingly decorated bar with its adjacent dining area is interestingly furnished, a large log-burning fire adding its cheer in cold weather. Outside is a pleasant walled garden where food and drink may be enjoyed, weather permitting. Quite apart from its individual attractions, this well-organised hostelry is in a superb location for sight-seeing. Worcester with its impressive cathedral, in the shadow of which is the county cricket ground and National Hunt racecourse, is only four miles distant and the diverse pleasures provided by the River Severn, with wonderful views of the Malvern Hills, is but a ten-minute stroll away. Hereford, Stratford-upon-Avon and the Cotswolds are all within easy reach. To this end, the inn possesses delightfully decorated guest rooms, all with private bath and shower, central heating, colour television, radio alarm clock and beverage-making facilities. A highly recommended place in which to stay; the Bishop himself would be highly impressed. *ETC* ♦♦♦, *AA*.

3 BEDROOMS, ALL WITH PRIVATE BATHROOM; FREE HOUSE WITH REAL ALE; HISTORIC INTEREST; DOGS WELCOME; BAR AND RESTAURANT MEALS (TUES-SAT, EVENINGS ONLY); NON-SMOKING AREAS; WORCESTER 4 MILES; S£££, D££.

---

**FHG PUBLICATIONS** publish a large range of well-known accommodation guides.
We will be happy to send you details or you can use the order form at the back of this book.

## THE ADMIRAL RODNEY
Berrow Green, Martley, Worcestershire WR6 6PL
Tel: 01886 821375 • Fax: 01886 822048 • e-mail: rodney@admiral.fslife.co.uk
website: www.admiral-rodney.co.uk

This homely and most attractive free house nestles in beautiful countryside within ten minutes' drive of Worcester and on the Worcester Way long-distance footpath. Recently refurbished throughout, the pub boasts two bars (one non-smoking) selling three guest real ales and Wye Valley bitter, and genuine scrumpy in the summer when the beer garden is in popular use. Good bar meals are served, and the à la carte restaurant is open every evening, a speciality of the house being fresh fish delivered direct from Fowey in Cornwall. Accommodation of character is in the form of handsomely decorated rooms, all appointed with en suite facilities, colour television, hairdryer, telephone and courtesy tray; a four-poster awaits that special occasion. *ETC* ◆◆◆, *AA Four Red Diamonds.*

3 BEDROOMS, ALL WITH PRIVATE BATHROOM; FREE HOUSE WITH REAL ALE; HISTORIC INTEREST; CHILDREN AND PETS WELCOME; BAR AND RESTAURANT MEALS (EVENINGS ONLY); NON-SMOKING AREAS; WORCESTER 7 MILES; S££££, D££££.

## THE BELL AT WILLERSEY
Willersey, Broadway, Worcestershire WR12 7PJ
Tel: 01386 858405 • Fax: 01386 853563 • website: www.the-bell-willersey.com
e-mail: reservations@bellatwillersey.fsnet.co.uk

Overlooking village green and duck pond, this is the archetypal Cotswold pub. Dating from the 17th century, it graces a village acclaimed as one of the most picturesque in the area. Here will be found good company, good ale and a tempting range of 'daily specials', and a restaurant renowned for its excellent home-cooked fare. The temptation to linger persists, so take note: the inn has several luxuriously furnished guest rooms, all with bath and shower en suite, king-size beds, television, radio alarm, hairdryer and tea and coffee-making facilities. And for that special occasion, there is a four-poster suite. So conveniently placed for countless places of historic and sporting interest, this is the perfect answer to the perfect holiday. *ETC* ◆◆◆◆

5 BEDROOMS, ALL WITH PRIVATE BATHROOM; ENTERPRISE INNS HOUSE WITH REAL ALE; HISTORIC INTEREST; CHILDREN WELCOME; BAR AND RESTAURANT MEALS; BROADWAY 2 MILES; S££££, D££££.

---

For our guide to
# Pet-Friendly
# Pubs, Inns & Hotels
see pages 149-162

---

*The* **FHG**
*GOLF*
*GUIDE*
**Where to Play**
**Where to Stay**

Available from most bookshops, **THE GOLF GUIDE** (published annually) covers details of every UK golf course – well over 2800 entries – for holiday or business golf. Hundreds of hotel entries offer convenient accommodation, accompanying details of the courses – the 'pro', par score, length etc.

*In association with 'Golf Monthly' and including Holiday Golf in Ireland, France, Portugal, Spain, The USA, South Africa and Thailand*

**£9.99 from bookshops or from the publishers (postage charged outside UK)** • FHG Publications, Abbey Mill Business Centre, Paisley PA1 ITJ

# North Yorkshire

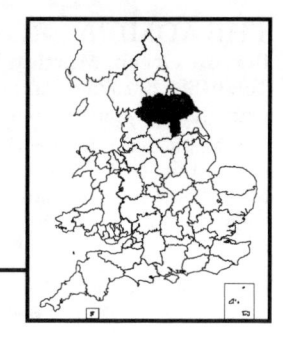

## THE CHARLES BATHURST INN
Arkengarthdale, Richmond, North Yorkshire DL11 6EN
Tel: 01748 884567 • Fax: 01748 884599 • e-mail: info@cbinn.co.uk
website: www.cbinn.co.uk

On the edge of the Pennine Way and hidden away in beautiful Arkengarthdale, this fine 18th century inn has one of the most evocative situations in the Yorkshire Dales National Park. Refurbished in 1996, open fires and antique pine in the bar and restaurant create a homely atmosphere in which to eat, drink and relax. Well-known cask-conditioned ales are served and the food is prepared to a very high standard. Dishes exhibit a sense of the adventurous, the daily menu displayed on an imposing mirror hanging at the end of the bar. There are interesting vegetarian dishes as well as a children's menu. A new wing was added recently, providing superb accommodation in individually designed en suite rooms with colour television and tea and coffee-making facilities. *ETC* ♦♦♦♦ *Silver Award, AA* ♦♦♦♦

18 BEDROOMS, ALL WITH PRIVATE BATHROOM; FREE HOUSE WITH REAL ALE; HISTORIC INTEREST; CHILDREN AND PETS WELCOME; BAR MEALS; NON-SMOKING AREAS; REETH 3 MILES; D£££.

## GEORGE AND DRAGON INN
Aysgarth, Leyburn, North Yorkshire DL8 3AD
Tel: 01969 663358 • Fax: 01969 663773 • www.georgeanddragonaysgarth.co.uk
e-mail: info@georgeanddragonaysgarth.co.uk

Surrounded by the stunning scenery of Upper Wensleydale, this attractive and well-tended inn has supplied travellers with rest and refreshment for nigh on 300 years. Today, tourists in the know flock here to relax in a cosy, beamed bar bedecked by interesting antiques and warmed by an open fire. True Dales hospitality is provided, and the accommodation is splendidly appointed. Locally brewed Black Sheep and Theakston's prove popular tipples amongst the cask-conditioned ales on offer, and lunch and dinner menus cover a wide spectrum of appetising dishes. Visitors to this lovely area are spoilt for sightseeing choice with picturesque falls, rivers, moorland, caves and castles to thrill the senses. *ETC/AA* ★★

7 BEDROOMS, ALL WITH PRIVATE BATHROOM; FREE HOUSE WITH REAL ALE; HISTORIC INTEREST; CHILDREN AND PETS WELCOME; BAR AND RESTAURANT MEALS; NON-SMOKING AREAS; LEYBURN 7 MILES; S£££/££££, D£££.

## THE BUCK INN
### Thornton Watlass, Near Bedale, Ripon, North Yorkshire HG4 4AH
### Tel: 01677 422461 • Fax: 01677 422447

Friendly country inn overlooking the delightful cricket green in a peaceful village just five minutes away from the A1. Refurbished bedrooms, most with en suite facilities, ensure that a stay at The Buck is both comfortable and relaxing. Delicious freshly cooked meals are served lunchtimes and evenings in the cosy bar and dining area. On Sundays a traditional roast with Yorkshire pudding is on the menu. Five excellent hand-pulled cask beers are always available, including Black Sheep, Theakstons, and at least one ale from a local independent. This is an ideal centre for exploring both the Yorkshire Dales and North York Moors. There is a children's playground in the secluded beer garden where quoits are also played. Private fly fishing available on River Ure and six golf courses within 20 minutes' drive. *ETC/AA* ★, *CAMRA Good Beer Guide, Room at the Inn, Good Pub Guide.*

7 BEDROOMS, 5 WITH PRIVATE FACILITIES; FREE HOUSE WITH REAL ALE; CHILDREN WELCOME;
BAR FOOD AND DINING AREA; NON-SMOKING AREAS; RIPON 11 MILES, NORTHALLERTON 9; S£££, D££.

## THE GREYHOUND COUNTRY INN
### Hackforth, Bedale, North Yorkshire DL8 1PB
### Tel & Fax: 01748 811415 • website: www.greyhoundinn.uk.com

This delightful country inn dates back to 1700 and offers a warm, personal welcome to all visitors. Situated in the peaceful village of Hackforth, it is overlooked by Hornby Castle, once the country estate of the Duke of Leeds. The Greyhound is ideally placed for exploring the Yorkshire Dales. The lovely market towns of Richmond, Bedale and Leyburn are just a few minutes' drive, and it is also convenient for Catterick, Ripon, Thirsk, Sedgefield, Wetherby and York races. The four comfortable bedrooms are all en suite, with tea/coffee making facilities, colour TV and antique furniture. In the cosy bar there is a choice of four cask-conditioned ales and an extensive range of malt whiskies. Chefs, Nicola and Andrea, are responsible for the inn's reputation for outstanding food. The no-smoking restaurant seats 42, and diners can now choose to eat in the new Courtyard Lounge. Outside there is a large beer garden and a delightful sheltered courtyard which creates a Mediterranean atmosphere.

4 BEDROOMS, ALL WITH PRIVATE BATHROOM; FREE HOUSE WITH REAL ALE; HISTORIC INTEREST;
CHILDREN AND PETS WELCOME; RESTAURANT MEALS; NON-SMOKING AREAS; CATTERICK 3 MILES; S£££, D££.

## THE BUCK INN
### Chop Gate, Bilsdale, Middlesbrough, North Yorkshire TS9 7JL
### Tel: 01642 778334

You are assured of a warm welcome at the Buck Inn, situated in a small, unspoilt village on the edge of the North York Moors, on the B1257 between Stokesley and Helmsley. The fully stocked bar offers well-kept ales and lagers, spirits and fine wines, and an excellent bar snack menu is served in a friendly atmosphere. An à la carte menu is available lunchtimes and evenings in the more formal, yet peaceful, surroundings of the dining area, and the freshly prepared dishes can be followed by a tempting choice of mouth-watering desserts. Bed and Breakfast accommodation is available in comfortably furnished double and twin en suite rooms, all with colour television and refreshment tray. *ETC* ◆◆◆

5 BEDROOMS, ALL WITH PRIVATE BATHROOM; FREE HOUSE WITH REAL ALE; CHILDREN AND PETS WELCOME;
BAR LUNCHES, RESTAURANT WED.-SAT. EVENINGS ONLY; NON-SMOKING AREAS; STOKESLEY 6 MILES; S££, D££.

## THE ROYAL OAK INN
Oak Lane, Dacre Banks, Harrogate, North Yorkshire HG3 4EN
Tel: 01423 780200 • Fax: 01423 781748 • e-mail: enquiries@theroyaloak.uk.com
website: www.theroyaloak.uk.com

An integral part of the historic village of Dacre, this Grade II Listed building is a free house with open fires and low timbered beams on which are painted quotations and old sayings about food and drink. Mouth-watering and imaginative dishes are served in both the non-smoking dining room, Eric's Pantry and Dale View, a ventilated smoking area, whilst an extensive range of lighter meals may be enjoyed in the cosy bar together with several interesting cask-conditioned ales. There is a games room and an attractive garden with lovely views over Nidderdale, and one may play boules. Ideal as a base for exploring the Dales, the inn has well-appointed en suite rooms available at reasonable terms. *ETC* ◆◆◆◆

3 BEDROOMS, ALL WITH PRIVATE BATHROOM; FREE HOUSE WITH REAL ALE; HISTORIC INTEREST; CHILDREN WELCOME; BAR AND RESTAURANT MEALS; NON-SMOKING AREAS; HARROGATE 10 MILES; S£response£, D£££.

## FOX AND HOUNDS INN
Ainthorpe, Danby, Whitby, North Yorkshire YO21 2LD
Tel & Fax: 01287 660218 • e-mail: ajbfox@globalnet.co.uk

With the unspoilt delights of the North York Moors beckoning wild and free, this attractive and welcoming hostelry is highly recommended as a base from which to commune with nature in all her glory, reviving both body and soul. Whether making a casual visit or planning a longer stay, refreshment of the highest order is the reward with good ale complementing the tempting range of 'blackboard specials', whilst an excellent à la carte selection is available every lunchtime and evening. Comforts, excellent fare and beautiful surroundings all conspire to make this a difficult place to leave; splendidly appointed guest rooms await and terms in all respects are moderate indeed. *ETC* ◆◆◆◆

7 BEDROOMS, ALL WITH PRIVATE BATHROOM; FREE HOUSE WITH REAL ALE; HISTORIC INTEREST; CHILDREN AND PETS WELCOME; NON-SMOKING AREAS; BAR AND RESTAURANT MEALS; WHITBY 12 MILES: S£££, D££.

## THE BLACK BULL INN
Main Street, Escrick, York, North Yorkshire YO19 6JP
Tel: 01904 728245 • Fax: 01904 728154 • e-mail: blackbullhotel@btconnect.com
website: www.yorkblackbullinn.co.uk

With all the traditional values of a much-loved English wayside inn, the 'Black Bull' nestles in a picturesque village amidst peaceful countryside just south of York. A log fire blazes a welcome in the cosy bar as several quality real ales and wines and a selection of tasty dishes merit close consideration, all representing excellent value for money. Families are very welcome; a prime example of Yorkshire hospitality at its very best. And what a rewarding place in which to stay. The recently refurbished guest rooms are delightful; all have en suite facilities, colour television and tea-makers – there is even a fancy four-poster! *ETC* ◆◆◆, *AA*.

10 BEDROOMS, ALL WITH PRIVATE BATHROOM; FREE HOUSE WITH REAL ALE; HISTORIC INTEREST; CHILDREN WELCOME; BAR MEALS; YORK 6 MILES; S£££, D££££.

## THE FORESTERS ARMS
Main Street, Grassington, Skipton, North Yorkshire BD23 5AA
Tel: 01756 752249 • Fax: 01756 753633

The Foresters Arms, Grassington, once an old coaching inn, is situated in the heart of the Yorkshire Dales. The inn, a family-run business for over 35 years, is an ideal centre for walking or touring. All bedrooms are en suite and have satellite TV and tea/coffee making facilities. Hand-pulled traditional ales are available in the bar, where meals are served at lunchtime and in the evening. *ETC* ◆◆◆ *See also Colour Advertisement.*

7 BEDROOMS, ALL WITH PRIVATE BATHROOM; FREE HOUSE WITH REAL ALE; CHILDREN AND PETS WELCOME; BAR AND DINING ROOM MEALS; SKIPTON 8 MILES; S££, D££.

# ROYAL OAK HOTEL
Great Ayton, North Yorkshire TS9 6BW
Tel: 01642 722361 • Fax: 01642 724047 • website: www.royaloak-hotel.co.uk

The extensive dinner menu at the Royal Oak is not one for the indecisive. Ditherers will find themselves at closing time still unable to choose from the delicious fillet dijon with its mustard and cream sauce, or perhaps pan-fried pork fillet with hot green peppers and cream. I would recommend speeding up the procedure by the tossing of coins - for whatever one selects one may be sure of the deepest satisfaction. Food is also available in the tastefully decorated, comfortably rustic bars, and guest bedrooms provide well appointed overnight accommodation, all being en suite, with central heating, colour television and tea-making facilities.

5 BEDROOMS, ALL WITH PRIVATE BATHROOM; REAL ALE; HISTORIC INTEREST; CHILDREN WELCOME;
BAR AND RESTAURANT MEALS; THIRSK 23 MILES, MIDDLESBROUGH 9; S££/D££

# THE BAY HORSE INN
York Road, Green Hammerton, York, North Yorkshire YO26 8BN
Tel: 01423 330338 • e-mail: info@thebayhorseinn.info
website: www.thebayhorseinn.info

Within easy reach of the varied attractions of York and Harrogate and a fine centre for exploration of the Yorkshire moors and dales, this cosy former coaching inn, just two miles off the A1(M), simply oozes character. Meals are served in either an intimate little restaurant or the traditional stone-clad bars, in company with a roaring log fire and a good range of liquid refreshment. For true Yorkshire hospitality, good accommodation and the homely, worthwhile things of life, this happy inn is well recommended for either a casual or longer stay. Well-furnished en suite bedrooms with remote-control television and tea and coffee-making facilities await overnight guests and rates represent excellent value.

10 BEDROOMS, ALL WITH PRIVATE BATHROOM; NEW CENTURY INNS HOUSE WITH REAL ALE; CHILDREN WELCOME;
BAR LUNCHES AND RESTAURANT MEALS; NON-SMOKING AREAS; BOROUGHBRIDGE 7 MILES; S£££, D££.

# COCKETT'S HOTEL
Market Place, Hawes, North Yorkshire DL8 3RD
Tel: 01969 667312 • Fax: 01969 667162 • e-mail: enquiries@cocketts.co.uk
website: www.cocketts.co.uk

Surrounded by the spectacular scenery of Upper Wensleydale, the delightful village of Hawes is the setting for this lovely, stone-built hostelry. Dating from the 17th century, it combines the relaxed ambience of days long gone with the fine modern amenities that have been introduced. En suite guest rooms, including two with four-poster beds, cater for overnight guests who are recommended to make this homely venue their base for touring the Dales. All rooms have central heating, colour television, shaver point, trouser press and tea-making facilities. The first-class catering is exemplified by worthy English and French fare with interesting wines provided at reasonable cost. Excellent value all round. *ETC* ♦♦♦♦

8 BEDROOMS, ALL WITH PRIVATE BATHROOM; FREE HOUSE; HISTORIC INTEREST; RESTAURANT EVENINGS ONLY;
NON-SMOKING AREAS; KIRKBY STEPHEN 14 MILES; D££/£££.

## GEORGE INN
**Kirk Gill, Hubberholme, Near Skipton, North Yorkshire BD23 5JE**
**Tel: 01756 760223**
**website: www.thegeorge-inn.co.uk**

A traditional Dales inn of flagstone floors, stone walls and mullioned windows, this homely, unpretentious retreat is a real jewel. It nestles beneath the fells in a seemingly remote hamlet alongside the River Wharfe; a picturesque and peaceful setting that will be of direct appeal to urban escapees. Here, in two cosy bars, one may revive body and spirit whilst enjoying an excellent range of no-nonsense, home-cooked meals and sweets as well as well-kept beers that include Black Sheep ale and a good selection of wines and spirits. Relax – there is no need to leave this tranquil paradise, for first-rate overnight accommodation is available in rooms with en suite facilities. *See also Colour Advertisement.*

6 BEDROOMS, ALL WITH PRIVATE BATHROOM; FREE HOUSE WITH REAL ALE; HISTORIC INTEREST; CHILDREN WELCOME; BAR MEALS; NON-SMOKING AREAS; KETTLEWELL 5 MILES; S£££, D££.

## THE COUNTRYMAN'S INN
**Hunton, Bedale, North Yorkshire DL8 1PY**
**Tel: 01677 450554 • e-mail: countrymans.inn@virgin.net**

In a charming little village between the market towns of Bedale and Leyburn, this is a homely inn to visit on a tour of the Yorkshire Dales, and with accommodation of quality to recommend it as a base. The attractive wide-fronted inn, now in the caring and efficient hands of Neil and Maureen Gardener, offers outstanding value in the matter of sustenance and accommodation. The bar with its beamed ceiling and welcoming log fire exudes character, and excellent meals are served here or in a neat and tidy restaurant. A beer garden and patio are favourite places in which to relax in summer. Guest rooms have en suite facilities, television and tea and coffee-makers. *AA* ◆◆◆◆

3 BEDROOMS, ALL WITH PRIVATE BATHROOM; FREE HOUSE WITH REAL ALE; PETS WELCOME; BAR AND RESTAURANT MEALS; NON-SMOKING AREAS; LEYBURN 5 MILES; S££, D£.

---

The £ symbol when appearing at the end of the italic section of an entry shows the anticipated price, during 2005, for full Bed and Breakfast.

*Normal Bed & Breakfast rate per person (in single room)*

| PRICE RANGE | CATEGORY |
|---|---|
| **Under £25** | S£ |
| **£26-£35** | S££ |
| **£36-£45** | S£££ |
| **Over £45** | S££££ |

*Normal Bed & Breakfast rate per person (sharing double/twin room)*

| PRICE RANGE | CATEGORY |
|---|---|
| **Under £25** | D£ |
| **£26-£35** | D££ |
| **£36-£45** | D£££ |
| **Over £45** | D££££ |

This is meant as an indication only and does not show prices for Special Breaks, Weekends, etc. Guests are therefore advised to verify all prices on enquiring or booking.

## THE FORRESTERS ARMS HOTEL
Kilburn, North Yorkshire YO61 4AH
Tel & Fax: 01347 868386 • e-mail: paulcussons@forrestersarms.fsnet.co.uk
website: www.forrestersarms.fsnet.co.uk

Dating from the 12th century, this is one of England's oldest inns. The Henry Dee Bar still retains evidence of the days when it was the stable and the cosy lower bar has an unusual rounded stone chimney breast where log fires exude cheer in chilly weather. Both bars are furnished with the work of Robert Thompson (the 'Mouseman') who carved a tiny mouse on every piece of furniture produced. Real ale is available in convivial surroundings and ample and well-presented Yorkshire fare will more than satisfy the healthiest appetite. This is the heart of James Herriot Country, within the North York Moors National Park, and the hotel is well recommended as a touring base, having outstanding accommodation. *ETC* ♦♦♦, *AA* ★★

10 BEDROOMS, ALL WITH PRIVATE BATHROOM; FREE HOUSE WITH REAL ALE; HISTORIC INTEREST; CHILDREN AND PETS WELCOME; BAR AND RESTAURANT MEALS; NON-SMOKING AREAS; THIRSK 6 MILES; S£££, D£

## GEORGE AND DRAGON HOTEL
17 Market Place, Kirkbymoorside, North Yorkshire YO62 6AA
Tel: 01751 433334 • Fax: 01751 432933 • e-mail: georgeatkirkby@aol.com
website: www.georgedragon.com

Since the 17th century, this lovely old coaching inn has graced the centre of the picturesque little town of Kirkbymoorside. True, comforts and facilities have improved immeasurably over the years in line with contemporary demand but the time-honoured ambience remains unsullied. Acquaintance with the cosy, beamed bar confirms the warmth of hospitality. Enjoy a pint of one of the hand-pulled real ales or a choice malt or cognac and relax and wonder at the collection of sporting memorabilia that adorns the walls; no juke boxes or fruit machines disturb the reverie. Activated appetites will soon demand inspection of a mouth-watering list of 'blackboard specials' or maybe, in the evening, experience the chef's creative skills in a lovely candlelit restaurant. Fresh fish from Whitby, locally reared game and beef and home produce vie for attention amongst the stylishly presented dishes with an impressive selection of wines in attendance. Parting from such perfection is such sweet sorrow, so anticipate pleasures to come by booking accommodation at this multi-favoured hotel beforehand. Guest rooms are housed in a beautifully converted corn mill and rectory at the rear of the old inn. Superbly appointed with a tutored eye for elegance and harmonious colour co-ordinates, each delightful room has fine en suite facilities, remote-control colour television, clock radio, telephone and hospitality tray. Come and be spoilt! *ETC/AA* ★★

20 BEDROOMS, ALL WITH PRIVATE BATHROOM; FREE HOUSE WITH REAL ALE; HISTORIC INTEREST; CHILDREN AND PETS WELCOME; BAR AND RESTAURANT MEALS; NON-SMOKING AREAS; PICKERING 7 MILES; S££££, D£££.

---

A useful index of towns and counties appears at the back of this book on pages 173 – 174. Refer also to Contents Page 3.

## THE GENERAL TARLETON INN
Boroughbridge Road, Ferrensby, Knaresborough, North Yorkshire HG5 0PZ
Tel: 01423 340284 • Fax: 01423 340288 • e-mail: gti@generaltarleton.co.uk
website: www.generaltarleton.co.uk

Surrounded by glorious countryside, with Yorkshire's moors and dales awaiting discovery close at hand, this traditional 18th century coaching inn stands in the attractive village of Ferrensby, conveniently close to the A1. In the award-winning bar brasserie, imaginative pub 'special' dishes are enhanced by fine hand-pulled ales and selective wines, whilst a covered courtyard offers a complete contrast in surroundings. For formal occasions, a delightfully decorated dining room is also the setting for the ever-popular Sunday lunches. Restful en suite bedrooms are well appointed and pleasingly furnished. *AA* ★★★ *and Two Rosettes.*

14 BEDROOMS, ALL WITH PRIVATE BATHROOM; FREE HOUSE WITH REAL ALE; HISTORIC INTEREST; CHILDREN WELCOME;
BAR MEALS, RESTAURANT EVENINGS ONLY; NON-SMOKING AREAS; BOROUGHBRIDGE 4 MILES; S££££, D££££.

## GOLDEN LION HOTEL
Market Place, Leyburn, North Yorkshire DL8 5AS
Tel: 01969 622161 • Fax: 01969 623836 • e-mail: annegoldenlion@aol.com

At the gateway to Wensleydale, the attractive market town of Leyburn is surrounded by the picturesque undulating countryside of the Yorkshire Dales National Park of which there are spectacular views. At its very heart, this splendid hotel dates from 1765 although it has been tastefully modernised. With the oak-panelled bar and 70-cover restaurant furnished in clean-cut contemporary style, little evidence of former days exists but the facilities now available are of the highest class. Light meals and afternoon teas are served in the bars and, known for the quality of its extensive à la carte and table d'hôte menus, the restaurant with its picture windows and colourful murals is a popular venue; vegetarian and special diets are willingly catered for. For those intent on exploration of one of the most beautiful parts of the country, excellent accommodation is available in rooms with bathrooms en suite, television, telephone, radio and tea and coffee-makers. Rates are extremely competitive. A lift operates to all floors and many rooms are specially adapted to the needs of disabled guests. Within easy walking distance is the little town of Middleham on the River Ure with its ruined castle which has strong connections with Richard III and which is well known as a racehorse training centre. *ETC* ★, *AA, RAC. See also Colour Advertisement.*

15 BEDROOMS, ALL WITH PRIVATE BATHROOM; FREE HOUSE WITH REAL ALE; HISTORIC INTEREST;
CHILDREN AND PETS WELCOME; BAR AND RESTAURANT MEALS; NON-SMOKING AREAS; RICHMOND 8 MILES; S££, D££.

## THE STAR COUNTRY INN & RESTAURANT
Weaverthorpe, Malton, North Yorkshire YO17 8EY
Tel & Fax: 01944 738273 • www.starinn.net

In the heart of the Yorkshire Wolds, the original part of the 'Star' dates from the early 19th century. Owners, Mike and Kath Baker, have bought a cosy inn which was a row of adjacent cottages, the resultant attractive complex a magnet for those 'in the know' who come from far and wide to sample the chef's delectable cooking. The extensive menu offers a wide range of reasonably priced dishes. Here is Yorkshire hospitality at its best, the bars warmed by open fires from late summer to late spring and featuring several traditional hand-pulled beers. Accommodation is available on a Bed and Breakfast basis, most rooms having en suite facilities; all of them have television and tea and coffee-makers. *ETC* ♦♦♦

3 BEDROOMS, ALL WITH PRIVATE BATHROOM; FREE HOUSE WITH REAL ALE; CHILDREN WELCOME;
BAR AND RESTAURANT MEALS; NON-SMOKING AREAS; MALTON 10 MILES; S££, D££££.

---

Visit the **FHG** website
**www.holidayguides.com**
for details of the wide choice of accommodation
featured in the full range of FHG titles

## THE GOLDEN LION HOTEL
Duke Street, Settle, North Yorkshire BD24 9DU
Tel: 01729 822203 • Fax: 01729 824103 • e-mail: bookings@goldenlion.yorks.net
website: www.yorkshirenet.co.uk/stayat/goldenlion

Surrounded by a dramatic countryside of peaks and dales, caverns and castles, this traditional 17th century coaching inn lies in the market place of the homely little Ribblesdale town of Settle. A popular eating house for locals and visitors alike, the hostelry proffers a variety of appetising dishes, meals being taken either in the 70-seater restaurant or before an open log fire in the bar lounge. Virtually on the doorstep is the famous Settle-Carlisle railway and with the scenic delights of the Yorkshire Dales National Park close at hand, the hotel is a recommended place in which to take an extended break. Bedrooms in a variety of sizes await those acting upon this advice. Special deals for groups of ramblers. *ETC/AA/RAC* ◆◆◆◆

12 BEDROOMS, 10 WITH PRIVATE BATHROOM; THWAITES HOUSE WITH REAL ALE; HISTORIC INTEREST; CHILDREN AND PETS WELCOME; BAR AND RESTAURANT MEALS; NON-SMOKING AREAS; SKIPTON 13 MILES; S££/£££, D££££.

## CASTLE ARMS INN
Snape, Near Bedale, North Yorkshire DL8 2TB
Tel: 01677 470210 • Fax: 01677 470837 • e-mail: castlearms@aol.com

The sleepy village of Snape is the perfect location for an 'away from it all' break, of particular interest to those wishing to experience the scenic splendour of the Yorkshire Dales and North York Moors and also attractive to racing enthusiasts, for five of the principal Yorkshire racecourses (Ripon, Thirsk, Wetherby, Catterick and York) are within easy reach. Visitors to the area could do no better than base themselves at this neat and tidy inn, a Grade II Listed building which dates from the 14th century. Handsomely appointed bedrooms all have bath or shower rooms en suite, central heating, colour television and tea and coffee-making facilities. Lunches and dinners are served daily in a cosy restaurant where the emphasis is on traditional home cooking. *ETC/ AA* ◆◆◆◆

9 BEDROOMS, ALL WITH PRIVATE BATHROOM; FREE HOUSE WITH REAL ALE; HISTORIC INTEREST; CHILDREN WELCOME, PETS BY ARRANGEMENT; BAR AND RESTAURANT MEALS; NON-SMOKING AREAS; BEDALE 2 MILES; S£££, D££.

## THE ANGEL INN, COUNTRY INN, HOTEL & RESTAURANT
Long Street, Topcliffe, Thirsk, North Yorkshire YO7 3RW
Tel: 01845 577237 • Fax: 01845 578000

The Angel Inn, steeped in tradition, dates back to the early 17th century. Travellers would rest, take ale, food and change horses at The Angel on their journey north and on their return south. It has been tastefully extended in recent years into a charming quality country inn, renowned for a warm, friendly atmosphere, fine food and traditional Yorkshire ales. Amenities include en suite bedrooms, residents' lounge, three bar areas, games room, beer garden, water patio and large car park. *See also Colour Advertisement.*

15 BEDROOMS, ALL WITH PRIVATE BATHROOM; FREE HOUSE WITH REAL ALE; HISTORIC INTEREST; BAR MEALS; THIRSK 4 MILES.

# GOLDEN FLEECE HOTEL
Market Place, Thirsk, North Yorkshire YO7 1LL
Tel: 01845 523108 • Fax: 01845 523996
e-mail: goldenfleece@bestwestern.co.uk • website: www.goldenfleecehotel.com

Set in the heart of Herriot Country, the Golden Fleece Hotel is a 400-year-old coaching inn. This season's special "Mini Break" will provide you with local information on what to see and where to go around this delightful part of North Yorkshire. The Break is a dinner, bed and breakfast package and further information and current prices can be obtained by contacting the reception team at the hotel. *ETC/AA* ★★ *and Silver Award.*

23 BEDROOMS, ALL WITH PRIVATE BATHROOM; FREE HOUSE WITH REAL ALE; HISTORIC INTEREST; CHILDREN WELCOME, PETS BY ARRANGEMENT; BAR AND RESTAURANT MEALS; NON-SMOKING AREA; YORK 20 MILES, NORTHALLERTON 8; s££££, d£££.

# THE GANTON GREYHOUND
Ganton, Near Scarborough, North Yorkshire YO12 4NX
Tel: 01944 710116 • Fax: 01944 712705 • e-mail: gantongreyhound@supanet.com
website: www.gantongreyhound.com

The Branston Family are deservedly proud of their excellent reputation for providing good hospitality, good food, and a warm, friendly atmosphere. En suite bedrooms (double, twin, family and disabled) are tastefully furnished, with tea/coffee facilities and colour television, and there is a lounge for the exclusive use of guests. Drinks and meals can be enjoyed in the pleasant bar, where large open fireplaces and oak beams add to the welcoming ambience; meals are also available in the light and airy conservatory restaurant. Its location on the main A64 York to Scarborough road is ideal for exploring this scenic area; the North Yorkshire moors and several golf courses, including Ganton Championship Course, are within easy reach. *See also Colour Advertisement.*

18 BEDROOMS, 16 WITH PRIVATE BATHROOM; FREE HOUSE WITH REAL ALE; CHILDREN WELCOME;
BAR AND RESTAURANT MEALS; NON-SMOKING AREAS; FILEY 8 MILES; S£, D£.

# THE MARTON ARMS HOTEL
Thornton-in-Lonsdale, Ingleton, North Yorkshire LA6 3PB
Tel: 015242 41201 • Fax: 015242 42579 • e-mail: mail@martonarms.co.uk
website: www.martonarms.co.uk

Nestling beneath imposing Ingleborough (2373ft.), this appealing hostelry happily retains much of the character of its 13th century origins. Quietly situated in glorious countryside just off the Skipton to Kendal turnpike road, this is the perfect venue from which to explore the Yorkshire Dales and Lake District. A magnificent bar presents a staggering choice of no less than sixteen real ales and around 330 malts - a drinker's paradise! Cosy accommodation and hearty food make a visit to this lovely old inn a definite 'must'. Bedrooms charmingly converted from the former stable and hayloft have excellent modern facilities, including colour television and hospitality trays; two are on the ground floor for the convenience of the elderly and disabled. *ETC/AA* ◆◆◆◆, *RAC Sparking Diamond Award.*

12 BEDROOMS, ALL WITH PRIVATE BATHROOM; FREE HOUSE WITH REAL ALE; HISTORIC INTEREST; CHILDREN WELCOME;
BAR AND RESTAURANT MEALS; NON-SMOKING AREAS; KIRKBY LONSDALE 7 MILES; S£££, D£££.

## BLUE BELL INN
### Main Street, Weaverthorpe, North Yorkshire YO17 8EX
### Tel: 01944 738204 • Fax: 01944 738204

In a picturesque setting overlooking the village green, and delightfully placed for touring the North York Moors, Wolds and coast, this handsome Victorian country pub and restaurant is a recommended port of call and also a base for a plethora of pleasures. Scarborough, Bridlington and Filey may be reached in under half-an-hour, and the historic delights of York only slightly longer. Features of this well-run hostelry include a charismatic oak-beamed bar with an open fire, and Fishers Restaurant which offers à la carte and table d'hôte menus, plus a selection of daily 'blackboard specials' always available. This is a charmingly furnished holiday venue with well-appointed en suite bedrooms having colour television, radio alarm, hairdryer and tea and coffee-making facilities. *ETC* ◆◆◆

6 BEDROOMS, ALL WITH PRIVATE BATHROOM; FREE HOUSE WITH REAL ALE; CHILDREN AND PETS WELCOME;
BAR AND RESTAURANT MEALS (EVENINGS ONLY); NON-SMOKING AREAS; FILEY 15 MILES; S£££, D£££££.

## THE NEW INN MOTEL
### Main Street, Huby, York, North Yorkshire YO61 1HQ
### Tel: 01347 810219

Nine miles north of York in the village of Huby in the Vale of York, the Motel is an ideal base for a couple of nights away to visit York (15 minutes to the nearest long-stay car park), or a longer stay to visit the East Coast of Yorkshire, the Dales, the Yorkshire Moors, Herriot Country, Harrogate and Ripon. The Motel is situated behind the New Inn (a separate business) which, contrary to its name, is a 500-year old hostelry, originally an old coaching inn, and full of character. All rooms are en suite (singles, doubles, twin and family rooms), and have colour television and tea-making facilities. Good home cooking is served, including vegetarian meals, and a full English breakfast is a speciality. PETS ARE WELCOME (by arrangement). Special breaks always available. Telephone for brochure. *AA* ◆◆◆

8 BEDROOMS, ALL EN SUITE, WITH SHOWER; RESTAURANT MEALS; CHILDREN WELCOME; NON-SMOKING AREAS;
YORK 9 MILES; S££, D££.

---

# FHG
## Other specialised
## FHG PUBLICATIONS

Published annually: available in all good bookshops or direct from the publisher (post-free to addresses in the UK)

- **PETS WELCOME!**  £8.99
- **Recommended COUNTRY HOTELS of Britain**  £7.99
- **Recommended SHORT BREAK HOLIDAYS in Britain**  £7.99
- **THE GOLF GUIDE Where to Play/Where to Stay**  £9.99

### FHG PUBLICATIONS LTD,
Abbey Mill Business Centre,
Seedhill, Paisley, Renfrewshire PA1 1TJ
Tel: 0141-887 0428 • Fax: 0141-889 7204
e-mail: fhg@ipcmedia.com
website: www.holidayguides.com

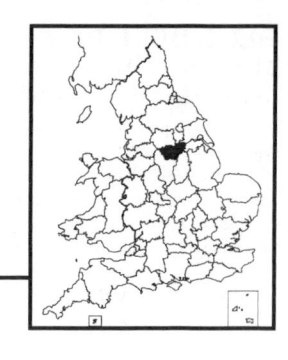

# South Yorkshire

## CUBLEY HALL
**Mortimer Road, Penistone, Sheffield, South Yorkshire S36 9DF**
**Tel: 01226 766086 • Fax: 01226 767335 • e-mail: cubley.hall@ukonline.co.uk**
**website: www.cubleyhall.co.uk**

Changing its shape and function over the years, this fascinating free house, restaurant and hotel claims an eventful past and the promise of an exciting future. Cloaked in history, Cubley Hall has evolved through the centuries from being a moorland farm on the Pennine packhorse routes of the 18th century to a fine gentleman's residence set in mature grounds during the reign of Queen Victoria. Following post-war duty as a children's home, it assumed the outline of its present role and, in 1990, saw the addition of the present renowned restaurant which was converted from the massive, oak-beamed stone barn. Extended in 1996 to incorporate full hotel facilities, loving care has been employed in retaining such architectural features as mosaic floors, stained glass, old oak panelling and ornate plaster ceilings. Add all the modern amenities expected of a distinguished country hotel and one has the complete up-to-date picture. Despite its wide range of services, this remains a convivial venue for both business and pleasure purposes, having retained its personal and friendly ambience. This is evident in the popular bar where traditional hand-pulled pints are as much in demand as the selection of malts, and particularly in the characterful restaurant with its high ceiling, massive beams and rustic furniture. Whether it is a romantic dinner for two or a function for 250, a professional staff and a team of talented chefs conjure up creations to satisfy the most discerning of diners. *ETC* ◆◆◆◆

12 BEDROOMS, ALL WITH PRIVATE BATHROOM; FREE HOUSE WITH REAL ALE; HISTORIC INTEREST; CHILDREN WELCOME; BAR MEALS, RESTAURANT WEEKENDS ONLY; NON-SMOKING AREAS; BARNSLEY 7 MILES; S£££users, D££££.

---

*The* **FHG**
**GOLF GUIDE**
*Where to Play*
*Where to Stay*

Available from most bookshops, **THE GOLF GUIDE** (published annually) covers details of every UK golf course – well over 2800 entries – for holiday or business golf. Hundreds of hotel entries offer convenient accommodation, accompanying details of the courses – the 'pro', par score, length etc.

*In association with 'Golf Monthly' and including Holiday Golf in Ireland, France, Portugal, Spain, The USA, South Africa and Thailand*

£9.99 from bookshops or from the publishers (postage charged outside UK) • FHG Publications, Abbey Mill Business Centre, Paisley PA1 1TJ

# West Yorkshire

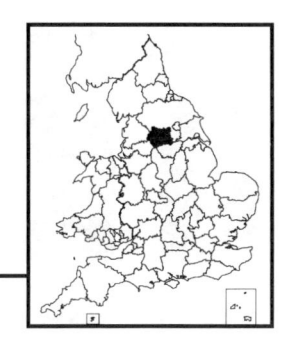

## THE THREE ACRES INN & RESTAURANT
Roydhouse, Shelley, Near Huddersfield, West Yorkshire HD8 8LR
Tel: 01484 602606 • Fax: 01484 608411 • e-mail: 3acres@globalnet.co.uk
website: www.3acres.com

Good cooking is the very heartbeat of this remarkable inn, the innovative menus combining the best of traditional English cooking with exotic and sophisticated dishes from all over the world. It is little surprise, therefore, to learn that the hostelry was designated as the 'Best Dining Pub in Britain - 2000' by a fellow publication. Set in the rolling Pennine foothills, this is a rewarding place to visit whilst exploring 'Last of the Summer Wine' country – Holmfirth is just down the road – for the neatly appointed bedrooms all have en suite facilities, television and telephone; ten of these are situated in the adjacent 'Cottages' annexe, all of which have their own gardens.

20 BEDROOMS, ALL WITH PRIVATE BATHROOM; FREE HOUSE WITH REAL ALE; CHILDREN WELCOME;
BAR AND RESTAURANT MEALS; HUDDERSFIELD 5 MILES; S££££, D££££.

## THE HOBBIT HOTEL
Hob Lane, Norland, Sowerby Bridge, Halifax, West Yorkshire HX6 3QL
Tel: 01422 832202 • Fax: 01422 835381 • www.londonandedinburghinns.com

Nestling on a hillside on the outskirts of Sowerby Bridge, overlooking the Calderdale Valley, these converted delvers' cottages are now The Hobbit Hotel and Rivendell Restaurant. 14 newly decorated en suite rooms, all with TV, telephone and tea/coffee making facilities, offer a perfect retreat from the daily hustle and bustle. There is always a friendly welcome, and the facility for bar food, a restaurant meal or a relaxed drink in the bar. Occasionally The Hobbit is a venue for weddings, murder mysteries, medieval banquets or tribute nights. *ETC* ★★ *See also Colour Advertisement.*

14 BEDROOMS, ALL WITH PRIVATE BATHROOM; REAL ALE; BAR AND BISTRO MEALS; NON-SMOKING AREAS;
HALIFAX 5 MILES.

# Ratings You Can Trust

## ENGLAND

The **English Tourism Council** (formerly the English Tourist Board) has joined with the **AA** and **RAC** to create a new, easily understood quality rating for serviced accommodation, giving a clear guide of what to expect.

**HOTELS** are given a rating from One to Five **Stars** – the more Stars, the higher the quality and the greater the range of facilities and level of services provided.

**GUEST ACCOMMODATION**, which includes guest houses, bed and breakfasts, inns and farmhouses, is rated from One to Five **Diamonds**. Progressively higher levels of quality and customer care must be provided for each one of the One to Five Diamond ratings.

**HOLIDAY PARKS, TOURING PARKS and CAMPING PARKS** are now also assessed using **Stars**. Standards of quality range from a One Star (acceptable) to a Five Star (exceptional) park.

Look out also for the new **SELF-CATERING** Star ratings. The more **Stars** (from One to Five) awarded to an establishment, the higher the levels of quality you can expect. Establishments at higher rating levels also have to meet some additional requirements for facilities.

## SCOTLAND

Star Quality Grades will reflect the most important aspects of a visit, such as the warmth of welcome, efficiency and friendliness of service, the quality of the food and the cleanliness and condition of the furnishings, fittings and decor.

**THE MORE STARS,
THE HIGHER THE STANDARDS.**

The description, such as Hotel, Guest House, Bed and Breakfast, Lodge, Holiday Park, Self-catering etc tells you the type of property and style of operation.

## WALES

Places which score highly will have an especially welcoming atmosphere and pleasing ambience, high levels of comfort and guest care, and attractive surroundings enhanced by thoughtful design and attention to detail

### STAR QUALITY GUIDE FOR

**HOTELS, GUEST HOUSES AND FARMHOUSES**
**SELF-CATERING ACCOMMODATION**
(Cottages, Apartments, Houses)
**CARAVAN HOLIDAY HOME PARKS**
(Holiday Parks, Touring Parks, Camping Parks)

★★★★★ Exceptional quality
★★★★ Excellent quality
★★★ Very good quality
★★ Good quality
★ Fair to good quality

*In England, Scotland and Wales, all graded properties are inspected annually by Tourist Authority trained Assessors.*

# Recommended Country Inns & Pubs
## of Britain 2005

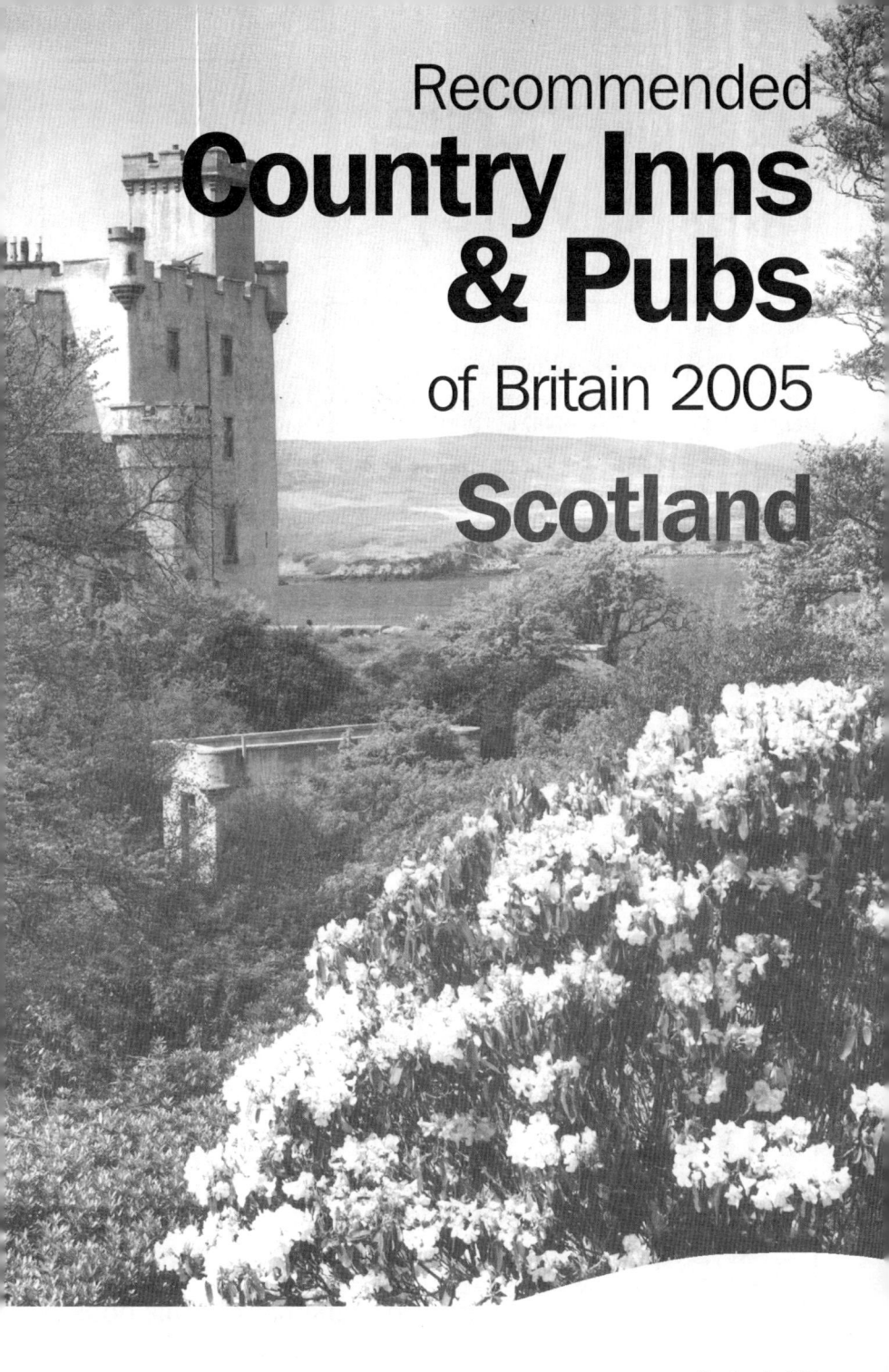

# Scotland

# Aberdeenshire, Banff & Moray

## GRANT ARMS HOTEL
The Square, Monymusk, Inverurie, Aberdeenshire AB51 7HJ
Tel: 01467 651226 • Fax: 01467 651494 • e-mail: ag@monymusk.com

This splendid former coaching inn of the 18th century has its own exclusive fishing rights on ten miles of the River Don, so it is hardly surprising that fresh salmon and trout are considered specialities of the restaurant, which is open nightly. Bar food is available at lunchtimes and in the evenings, and a pleasing range of fare caters for all tastes. Double and twin rooms, all with private facilities, accommodate overnight visitors, and some ground floor bedrooms are available, two of which have been specifically designed for wheelchair users. A traditional Scottish welcome and a real interest in the welfare of guests makes a stay here a particular pleasure. *RAC* ◆◆

11 BEDROOMS, ALL WITH PRIVATE BATHROOM; FREE HOUSE WITH REAL ALE; HISTORIC INTEREST; CHILDREN WELCOME; BAR AND RESTAURANT MEALS; NON-SMOKING AREAS; ABERDEEN 18 MILES; S£££££, D££.

## KILDRUMMY INN
Kildrummy, Alford, Aberdeenshire AB33 8QS
Tel & Fax: 01975 571287 • website: www.kildrummyinn.co.uk

This small family-run inn is situated in the Grampian Highlands, within easy reach of several good golf courses and ideal for touring, fishing, hill walking and pony trekking. Accommodation is available in two family and two double bedrooms, all with washbasins, tea-making facilities and television. There is a residents' dining room, a lounge bar serving lunches and evening meals, a public bar with several draught beers on tap and a good range of whisky, and a sun lounge where meals, coffees, snacks etc are also served. The inn is situated on the A97 Strathdon to Huntly road, with easy access and good parking facilities, and is a good base for scenic round trips. A Caravan & Camping Club licensed site is available for up to five caravans.

4 BEDROOMS, 1 WITH PRIVATE BATHROOM; FREE HOUSE WITH REAL ALE; CHILDREN AND PETS WELCOME; BAR LUNCHES, RESTAURANT EVENINGS ONLY; NON-SMOKING AREAS; ALFORD 6 MILES; S££, D£££££.

# FHG

## FHG PUBLICATIONS
publish a large range of well-known accommodation guides. We will be happy to send you details or you can use the order form at the back of this book.

# Argyll & Bute

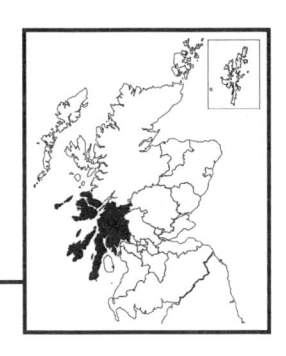

## THE GALLEY OF LORNE INN
Ardfern, By Lochgilphead, Argyll PA31 8QN
Tel: 01852 500284 • website: www.galleyoflorne.co.uk

Beautifully situated overlooking Loch Craignish, this warmly welcoming free house is particularly noted for its restaurant which offers excellent menus featuring Scottish specialities, charcoal-grilled steaks and seafood fresh from the loch; a substantial range of bar meals is also available, along with a good selection of malt whiskies. Those seeking accommodation will find spick-and-span, nicely furnished guest rooms, all with private bathrooms, central heating, colour television, and tea and coffee facilities; most have stunning views of the loch. A wide range of sporting and leisure activities in this area make this an ideal base for a Highland holiday at any time. *STB* ★★★ *Inn*.

7 BEDROOMS, ALL WITH PRIVATE BATHROOM; FREE HOUSE; HISTORIC INTEREST; CHILDREN AND DOGS WELCOME;
BAR MEALS, RESTAURANT EVENINGS ONLY; NON-SMOKING AREAS; LOCHGILPHEAD 12 MILES; S£££/££££, D£££/££££.

## CAIRNDOW STAGECOACH INN
Cairndow, Argyll PA26 8BN
Tel: 01499 600286 • Fax: 01499 600220

Amidst the beautiful scenery which characterises the upper reaches of Loch Fyne, this historic stagecoach inn enjoys a spectacular sheltered position. In the delightful restaurant one may dine well by candlelight from the table d'hôte and à la carte menus; bar meals are served all day. There is also a new functions bar and games room. Bedrooms are centrally heated, with radio, television, direct-dial telephone, baby listening, and tea-making facilities. There are two de luxe rooms with two-person spa baths, king-size beds and 20" television! This is an ideal spot for touring Oban, the Western Highlands, Glencoe, the Trossachs, the Cowal Peninsula, Kintyre and Campbeltown. The inn is under the personal supervision of hosts Mr and Mrs Douglas Fraser, and the area offers opportunities for many outdoor pursuits and visits. Lochside beer garden, exercise room, sauna and solarium. *STB* ★★★ *Inn*. ***See also Colour Advertisement.***

12 BEDROOMS, ALL EN SUITE; FREE HOUSE WITH REAL ALE; HISTORIC INTEREST; CHILDREN WELCOME;
BAR AND RESTAURANT MEALS; NON-SMOKING AREAS; ARROCHAR 12 MILES, INVERARAY 10; S££, D££.

---

See the ***Family-Friendly Pubs & Inns***
Supplement on pages 163-171 for establishments
which really welcome children

## CLACHAIG INN
Glencoe, Argyll PH49 4HX
Tel: 01855 811252 • Fax: 01855 812030 • e-mail: inn@clachaig.com
website: www.clachaig.com

Whether touring, participating in the wide range of outdoor activities that the area offers or just seeking a relaxing break in the clean mountain air, this superb hostelry provides all the requirements for a memorable stay. Hospitality second to none is backed by facilities of the highest calibre: there are three bars invariably buzzing with animated conversation and a beer garden. Food is served all day and there is a generous selection of whiskies and Scottish real ales. Beer festivals are held from time to time and live music is featured every Saturday night throughout the year – a place of infinite good cheer. Excellent dinners are served from an imaginative à la carte menu and packed lunches are supplied on request. Beautifully placed at the heart of the glen, this outstanding inn is the perfect base for hill walking, climbing, sailing, mountain biking and ski-ing, all amidst the most dramatic scenery. Walks particularly worthy of recommendation are the Lochan Walk, adjacent to Glencoe village, which gives 12 hours of unexacting exercise, the Lost Valley Walk (two hours) and the Forest Walk to the Signal Rock with its associations with the famous Glencoe massacre of 1692. Today, all is positive and cheerful at this well-favoured retreat and the recently refurbished accommodation is of a high standard of comfort and convenience. There are also several well-equipped self-contained units in the grounds. STB ★★ *Inn*.

23 BEDROOMS, ALL WITH PRIVATE BATHROOM; FREE HOUSE WITH REAL ALE; HISTORIC INTEREST; CHILDREN WELCOME; PETS BY ARRANGEMENT; BAR AND RESTAURANT MEALS; NON-SMOKING AREAS; KINLOCHLEVEN 5 MILES; S£££, D£££.

## WIDE MOUTHED FROG
Dunstaffnage Bay, Near Oban, Argyll PA37 1PX • e-mail: frogenqs@aol.com
Tel: 01631 567205 • Fax: 01631 571044 • website: www.widemouthedfrog.com

The "Frog" is ideally situated at Dunstaffnage Marina, just three miles north of Oban and the ferry terminal to the Isles, and owners, Linda and Stuart Byron, concentrate on providing a casual and relaxed atmosphere. There is an all-day food service, with menus featuring the best of local produce and specialising in fresh seafood, and the bars offer a varied selection of refreshments. Accommodation is available in ten new en suite bedrooms, all with satellite colour television, direct-dial telephone and tea/coffee making facilities; bathrooms have bath and power shower. Major credit cards accepted. STB ★★★ *Restaurant with Rooms. See also Colour Advertisement.*

10 BEDROOMS, ALL WITH PRIVATE BATHROOM; FREE HOUSE WITH REAL ALE; CHILDREN WELCOME; BAR AND RESTAURANT MEALS; NON-SMOKING AREAS; CONNEL 2 MILES; S£££, D£££.

## WEST LOCH HOTEL
By Tarbert, Loch Fyne, Argyll PA29 6YF
Tel: 01880 820283 • Fax: 01880 820930
e-mail: westlochhotel@btinternet.com

An attractive, family-run, 18th century coaching inn of character, the West Loch Hotel is well situated for a relaxing holiday on the west coast of Scotland. The hotel is renowned for outstanding food, whether in the elegant Waterfalls Restaurant, or, more informally, in the bar areas. After dining, guests can relax in front of an open fire, perhaps sampling on the many local malt whiskies. With glorious scenery, the area is excellent for hill-walking and enjoying the wide variety of wildlife. Visits to Islay, Jura, Arran and Gigha can be pleasant day trips, and there are many attractions in the area, such as castles, distilleries, gardens and sandy beaches. Fishing, golf and boat hire can be arranged.

8 BEDROOMS, 7 WITH PRIVATE BATHROOM; FREE HOUSE WITH REAL ALE; CHILDREN AND PETS WELCOME; BAR AND RESTAURANT MEALS; NON-SMOKING AREAS; CAMPBELTOWN 32 MILES; S££, D££.

---

**FHG PUBLICATIONS** publish a large range of well-known accommodation guides.
We will be happy to send you details or you can use the order form at the back of this book.

# Ayrshire & Arran

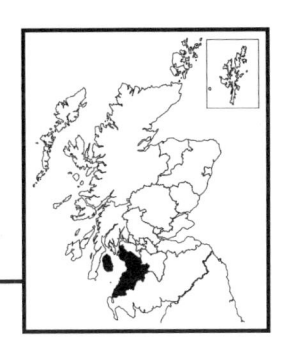

## THE KIRKTON INN
**1 Main Street, Dalrymple, By Ayr, Ayrshire KA6 6DF**
Tel: 01292 560241 • Fax: 01292 560835 • e-mail: kirkton@cqm.co.uk
website: www.kirktoninn.co.uk

Exuding the very essence of Scottish hospitality, this picturesque inn is renowned for its worthy range of generously-served dishes and its selection of some 60 single malt whiskies in the Malt Room adjacent to the Poachers traditional village bar. All food is freshly prepared and special diets are willingly catered for. The inn is conveniently situated for a variety of sporting diversions which include horse-racing at Ayr, golf at Troon and Turnberry, and numerous opportunities for fishing and walking. The admirable en suite accommodation takes the form of double and twin hotel rooms or triple, twin and family studios at ground level. First-rate facilities exist for social functions and meetings. *STB* ★★ *Inn, AA* ◆◆◆

11 BEDROOMS, ALL WITH PRIVATE BATHROOM; FREE HOUSE; HISTORIC INTEREST; CHILDREN AND PETS WELCOME; BAR AND RESTAURANT MEALS; NON-SMOKING AREAS; AYR 5 MILES; S£££, D£££.

---

**Visit the FHG website**
**www.holidayguides.com**
for details of the wide choice of accommodation
featured in the full range of FHG titles

# Borders

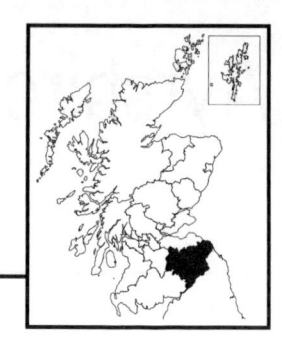

## THE BORDER HOTEL
The Green, Kirk Yetholm, Kelso, Roxburghshire TD5 8PQ
Tel: 01573 420237 • Fax: 01573 420549 • website: www.theborderhotel.com
e-mail: BorderHotel@aol.com

Nestling on the northern slopes of the Cheviots and but a mile from the Scotland-England border, this attractive hotel with its distinctive black and white facade is situated at the end of the 268-mile Pennine Way. The surrounding undulating countryside supports an abundance of wildlife, and nature lovers, be they walkers, cyclists or car drivers, find this a convenient and comfortable port of call and appreciate the recently upgraded refreshment and accommodation facilities. Good ale and good company may be sought in a bright and friendly bar and there is a beer garden popular on sunny days. Delightfully furnished rooms with en suite facilities await overnight guests. *STB* ★★★ *Hotel. See also Colour Advertisement.*

5 BEDROOMS, ALL WITH PRIVATE BATHROOM; FREE HOUSE WITH REAL ALE; HISTORIC INTEREST; CHILDREN AND PETS WELCOME; BAR AND RESTAURANT MEALS; NON-SMOKING AREAS; KELSO 7 MILES; S£££, D£££.

---

## • • *Some Useful Guidance for Guests and Hosts* • •

Every year literally thousands of holidays, short breaks and overnight stops are arranged through our guides, the vast majority without any problems at all. In a handful of cases, however, difficulties do arise about bookings, which often could have been prevented from the outset.

*It is important to remember that when accommodation has been booked, both parties – guests and hosts – have entered into a form of contract. We hope that the following points will provide helpful guidance.*

### GUESTS:
- When enquiring about accommodation, be as precise as possible. Give exact dates, numbers in your party and the ages of any children.
- State the number and type of rooms wanted and also what catering you require – bed and breakfast, full board etc. Make sure that the position about evening meals is clear – and about pets, reductions for children or any other special points.
- Read our reviews carefully to ensure that the proprietors you are going to contact can supply what you want. Ask for a letter confirming all arrangements, if possible.
- If you have to cancel, do so as soon as possible. Proprietors do have the right to retain deposits and under certain circumstances to charge for cancelled holidays if adequate notice is not given and they cannot re-let the accommodation.

### HOSTS:
- Give details about your facilities and about any special conditions. Explain your deposit system clearly and arrangements for cancellations, charges etc. and whether or not your terms include VAT.
- If for any reason you are unable to fulfil an agreed booking without adequate notice, you may be under an obligation to arrange suitable alternative accommodation or to make some form of compensation.

*While every effort is made to ensure accuracy, we regret that FHG Publications cannot accept responsibility for errors, omissions or misrepresentations in our entries or any consequences thereof. Prices in particular should be checked because we go to press early. We will follow up complaints but cannot act as arbiters or agents for either party.*

# Dumfries & Galloway

## ANCHOR HOTEL
**Kippford, Dalbeattie, Kirkcudbrightshire DG5 4LN**
**Tel & Fax: 01556 620205**

Kippford is a pretty village on the shores of Rough Firth which itself opens out into the Solway Firth. It is a popular resort of yachtsmen who make a point of patronising this splendid hotel, the Seafarers Bar of which has great atmosphere. Refurbished in bright and attractive style, the 'Anchor' offers an extensive range of dishes at lunchtime and in the evening and also excellent accommodation in variably sized rooms, some of which overlook the Marina. Children are more than welcome and there is a games room with pool, board games and other diversions to suit all ages. There is a quiet, sandy bay just 10 minutes from the hotel. *STB* ★★ *Hotel.*

6 BEDROOMS, ALL WITH PRIVATE BATHROOM; FREE HOUSE WITH REAL ALE; CHILDREN WELCOME; PETS IN BAR AREA ONLY; BAR MEALS; NON-SMOKING AREAS; DALBEATTIE 4 MILES; S£££, D££.

## BLACK BULL HOTEL
**Churchgate, Moffat, Dumfriesshire DG10 9EG**
**Tel: 01683 220206 • Fax: 01683 220483 • e-mail: hotel@blackbullmoffat.co.uk**
**website: www.blackbullmoffat.co.uk**

Much care has been taken to preserve the authentic atmosphere of this famous, 16th century inn. Many colourful characters have sat within these hospitable walls taking food and drink amongst convivial company, most notably, one Rabbie Burns, a regular patron, who complemented his mood by writing the famous 'Epigram to a Scrimpit Nature' here and possibly other whimsies. The warm welcome is still there with good real ale and a selection of bar snacks available, whilst the Claverhouse Restaurant is renowned for its top quality food and friendly service. Excellent fishing and golf may be enjoyed locally, further reasons for taking advantage of the high standard of modern accommodation. *STB* ★★★ *Hotel.*

13 BEDROOMS, ALL WITH PRIVATE BATHROOM; FREE HOUSE WITH REAL ALE; HISTORIC INTEREST; CHILDREN WELCOME; PETS NOT ALLOWED IN BEDROOMS; BAR AND RESTAURANT MEALS; NON-SMOKING AREAS; DUMFRIES 19 MILES; S£££, D£££.

## CRIFFEL INN
**2 The Square, New Abbey, Near Dumfries, Dumfriesshire DG2 8BX**
**Tel: 01387 850244**

*Attractions such as first-class food served in the bar and dining room featuring fresh local produce and home baking, neat bedrooms (including four en suite) with colour television and tea making facilities, and a pretty garden patio for fine weather relaxation make this an ideal spot for rest and refreshment whatever the season. Set in the beautiful Scottish Borders, the village of New Abbey is famed as the site of the 13th century Sweetheart Abbey and is a most convenient base for exploring this unspoiled part of the country. Leisure activities available locally include golf, sea angling, and river and loch fishing. STB ★★ Inn.*

4 BEDROOMS, ALL WITH PRIVATE BATHROOM; FREE HOUSE WITH REAL ALE; HISTORIC INTEREST;
CHILDREN AND PETS WELCOME; BAR AND RESTAURANT MEALS; NON-SMOKING AREAS; DUMFRIES 6 MILES; S£, D£.

## THE WATERFRONT HOTEL & BISTRO
**North Crescent, Portpatrick, Wigtownshire DG9 8SX**
**Tel: 01776 810800 • Fax: 01776 810850**
**e-mail: WaterfrontHotel@aol.com • website: www.waterfronthotel.co.uk**

*The Waterfront is a stylish new hotel, furnished to a very high specification and situated opposite the picturesque harbour of Portpatrick. With eight en suite bedrooms and an elegant restaurant serving a delicious selection of dishes and wines, The Waterfront is perfectly located for that golfing break, with Portpatrick (Dunskey) and Lagganmore Golf Clubs being within one mile and Stranraer Golf Club within eight miles. Individual or group golfing packages at favourable rates available on request. 'We look forward to welcoming you". STB ★★★ See also Colour Advertisement.*

8 BEDROOMS, ALL WITH PRIVATE BATHROOM; BAR AND RESTAURANT MEALS; STRANRAER 8 MILES.

---

The £ symbol when appearing at the end of the italic section of an entry shows the anticipated price, during 2005, for full Bed and Breakfast.

*Normal Bed & Breakfast rate per person per person (in single room)*

*Normal Bed & Breakfast rate (sharing double/twin room)*

| PRICE RANGE | CATEGORY | PRICE RANGE | CATEGORY |
|---|---|---|---|
| **Under £25** | S£ | **Under £25** | D£ |
| **£26-£35** | S££ | **£26-£35** | D££ |
| **£36-£45** | S£££ | **£36-£45** | D£££ |
| **Over £45** | S££££ | **Over £45** | D££££ |

This is meant as an indication only and does not show prices for Special Breaks, Weekends, etc. Guests are therefore advised to verify all prices on enquiring or booking.

# Highlands

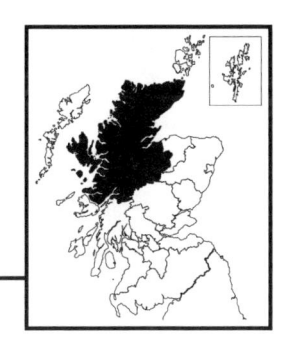

## THE GUN LODGE HOTEL
**High Street, Ardersier, Inverness-shire IV2 7QB**
**Tel & Fax: 01667 462754 • e-mail: availability@gunlodgehotel.co.uk**
**website: www.gunlodgehotel.com**

Situated on the Moray Firth coast with easy access to rugged Highland scenery and forested areas to the south, this unpretentious family-run hotel offers food and shelter in a warm and friendly atmosphere. In addition to tasty bar food, there is a full à la carte menu in the cosy restaurant, prices being extremely reasonable. Fishing, shooting, hill walking and golf are activities that can be enjoyed locally and historians will be fascinated by the colossal fortress of Fort George, 1½ miles away and the famous battlefield of Culloden (10 miles) where Bonnie Prince Charlie was defeated in 1746. Comfortable overnight accommodation is available, including two en suite family rooms with a full range of support facilities for young children and babies. *See also Colour Advertisement.*

SOME BEDROOMS WITH PRIVATE BATHROOM; CHILDREN WELCOME; BAR AND RESTAURANT MEALS; NON-SMOKING AREAS; INVERNESS 11 MILES.

## THE INN AT ARDGOUR
**Ardgour, Fort William, Inverness-shire PH33 7AA**
**Tel: 01855 841225 • Fax: 01855 841214 • e-mail: theinn@ardgour.biz**
**website: www.ardgour.biz**

Ideally placed for walking, fishing and touring the West Highlands, this bonny, wide-fronted inn at the entrance to the Great Glen is the place to visit for good company, real ales and an impressive range of malt whiskies to be savoured in the bars: a sense of proportion is advised as the drams are 35ml measures! Close by is the slipway of the Corran Ferry which makes the short crossing of Loch Linnhe every half-hour. Splendid à la carte dinners are served in a charming little restaurant, specially featuring venison from the hills and seafood from the loch. There is a choice of en suite guest rooms, five of which are on the ground floor; all have colour television, radio, beverage-makers and fabulous views. STB ★★★ *Small Hotel.*

10 BEDROOMS, ALL WITH PRIVATE BATHROOM; FREE HOUSE WITH REAL ALE; HISTORIC INTEREST; CHILDREN AND PETS WELCOME; BAR MEALS, RESTAURANT EVENINGS ONLY; NON-SMOKING AREAS; FORT WILLIAM 10 MILES; S£££, D£££.

## THE ROWAN TREE COUNTRY HOTEL
**Loch Alvie, by Aviemore, Inverness-shire PH22 1QB**
**Tel & Fax: 01479 810207 • e-mail: enquiries@rowantreehotel.com**
**website: www.rowantreehotel.com**

Our award-winning, small, friendly Country Hotel is the ideal location for a holiday or short break in the Highlands. The hotel is very easy to get to and is centrally located for visiting the many activities and attractions in the area. The Rowan Tree offers you a stunning setting, comfortable, individually decorated, en suite bedrooms, cosy lounges and bar, crackling fires and great Taste of Scotland home-cooked dinners; special diets a pleasure. There are drying and storage rooms and ample parking. We also welcome well-behaved dogs. STB ★★★ *Small Hotel, Inn of the Year 2001, Taste of Scotland Accredited.*

11 ROOMS, 10 EN SUITE, 1 WITH PRIVATE BATH AND WC; SMOKING RESTRICTED TO BAR ONLY, CHILDREN WELCOME; ALL BEDROOMS NON-SMOKING; AVIEMORE 2 MILES; S£££, D£££.

## LOCH LEVEN HOTEL
Old Ferry Road, North Ballachulish, Inverness-shire PH33 6SA
Tel: 01855 821236 • Fax: 01855 821550 • website: www.lochlevenhotel.co.uk
e-mail: reception@lochlevenhotel.co.uk

The Loch Leven Hotel was originally built more than 300 years ago. It now combines the best of old and new. It is owned and run by Hilary and John who provide comfort in a friendly and informal setting. All 11 rooms are en suite and most have spectacular views of the loch and the magnificent mountains beyond. There is an extensive menu and daily-changing specials, all freshly prepared to order using the best of Scottish produce. The comfortable lounge bar offers an impressive display of over 50 different malts, and the public bar has an open fire and lots of atmosphere. There is also a family/games room for more relaxed dining. Dogs are allowed in their owner's bedroom, the public bar and the games/family room, and there are ample opportunities for safe off-road walking.

11 BEDROOMS, ALL WITH PRIVATE BATHROOM; FREE HOUSE; HISTORIC INTEREST; CHILDREN AND PETS WELCOME;
BAR AND RESTAURANT MEALS; NON-SMOKING AREAS; BALLACHULISH 2 MILES; S£££, D££.

## THE TRENTHAM HOTEL
The Poles, Dornoch, Sutherland IV25 3HZ
Tel: 01862 810551 • Fax: 01862 811426 • e-mail: thetrenthamhotel@yahoo.co.uk

Whether visiting this neat and tidy inn just off the A9 as a convenient overnight stay en route to the Orkneys, or as a touring, golfing or fishing holiday base set amidst magnificent scenery, this well-organised retreat has numerous attributes to commend it. Food is a speciality, especially the 'real steak sizzlers' and there is an elegantly furnished public bar with a real old-world atmosphere; residents have their own sumptuously appointed lounge. Originally an 18th century coaching inn, the 'Trentham' has been tastefully updated and offers attractively equipped bedrooms with colour television and beverage-makers. The resort of Dornoch with its extensive sands is within walking distance. STB ★★ *Inn*.

6 BEDROOMS; FREE HOUSE; CHILDREN AND PETS WELCOME; BAR LUNCHES, RESTAURANT EVENINGS ONLY;
NON-SMOKING AREAS; BONAR BRIDGE 12 MILES; S£, D£.

## MOORINGS HOTEL
Banavie, Fort William, Inverness-shire PH33 7LY
Tel: 01397 772797 • Fax: 01397 772441

The long low facade of this attractive hostelry emphasises the dominance of Ben Nevis which looms in the background. The loch and mountain scenery is impressive, as are the splendid facilities offered by this delightful retreat by the Caledonian Canal. The award-winning Jacobean-style restaurant features choice (and reasonably-priced) Scottish produce on its imaginative à la carte and table d'hôte menus and the food selection in the Mariners Bar is almost as tempting; here, the wide selection of malt whiskies and beers is much appreciated. Guest rooms are well appointed and the residents' lounge is a comfortable place in which to spend quiet moments. There is a fine leisure complex within easy reach at Fort William. STB ★★★★, AA ★★★ and Rosette, RAC ★★★, *Taste of Scotland*.

28 BEDROOMS, ALL WITH PRIVATE BATHROOM; FREE HOUSE; CHILDREN AND PETS WELCOME;
BAR MEALS; RESTAURANT EVENINGS ONLY; FORT WILLIAM 2 MILES; £££.

---

*The* **FHG**
**GOLF GUIDE**
*Where to Play*
*Where to Stay*

Available from most bookshops, **THE GOLF GUIDE** (published annually) covers details of every UK golf course – well over 2800 entries – for holiday or business golf. Hundreds of hotel entries offer convenient accommodation, accompanying details of the courses – the 'pro', par score, length etc.

In association with 'Golf Monthly' and including Holiday Golf in Ireland, France, Portugal, Spain, The USA, South Africa and Thailand

£9.99 from bookshops or from the publishers (postage charged outside UK) • FHG Publications,
Abbey Mill Business Centre, Paisley PA1 1TJ

## GLENELG INN
**Glenelg, By Kyle of Lochalsh, Ross-shire IV40 8JR**
**Tel: 01599 522273 • Fax: 01599 522283 • website: www.glenelg-inn.com**
**e-mail: christophermain7@glenelg-inn.com**

Where the strait narrows between the Scottish mainland and the Isle of Skye, this hospitable and delightfully furnished inn welcomes visitors to an area of unspoilt beauty, a land of quiet sea lochs, remote beaches, secret places and an abundance of wildlife. Standing in extensive grounds, the genial Glenelg Inn lies a short distance south of the ferry (and infamous bridge!) to Skye and in the area there are opportunities for pony trekking, golf, fishing, birdwatching and hill walking. Visitors and locals can meet in the cosy and welcoming public bar in the lively atmosphere of the ceilidh, where the traditional music of the pipe and the fiddle are the order of the evening. Fresh seafood specialities are served every night in the dining room. *STB* ★★★ *Inn, AA.*

7 BEDROOMS, ALL WITH PRIVATE BATHROOM; FREE HOUSE; HISTORIC INTEREST; CHILDREN AND PETS WELCOME; BAR LUNCHES, RESTAURANT EVENINGS ONLY; SHIEL BRIDGE 10 MILES; S££££, D££££.

## KINLOCHEWE HOTEL
**Kinlochewe, Wester Ross IV22 2PA**
**Tel: 01445 760253 • e-mail: kinlochewehotel@tinyworld.co.uk**

This 10-bedroom hotel, surrounded by the magnificent Torridon Mountains, is ideally situated for walking, climbing, birdwatching, or touring the North West of Scotland. The Beinn Eighe Nature Reserve, the Inverewe National Trust Gardens, the spectacular Applecross Peninsula and the Isle of Skye are all within easy reach. The hotel has an excellent reputation for home-cooked food and a varied menu, at reasonable prices. For climbers and walkers, there are over 20 Munros within 20 miles, and guides can be arranged for all levels of experience.

10 BEDROOMS; BAR MEALS; CHILDREN WELCOME; NON-SMOKING AREAS; ACHNASHEEN 9 MILES; S££, D££.

## THE NIP INN
**Main Street, Lairg, Sutherland IV27 4DB**
**Tel: 01549 402243 • Fax: 01549 402593 • e-mail: info@nipinn.co.uk**

Lying in the centre of the village of Lairg, The Nip Inn is an ideal base from which to tour the North of Scotland. Superb, home-cooked food, using the best local ingredients, is served in the elegant restaurant and in the attractive setting of the lounge bar. All meals can be complemented by a bottle of wine from a comprehensive list. All six bedrooms are individual in character, and furnished to a high standard, with en suite facilities, colour TV and tea/coffee hospitality tray. The popular lounge bar, boasting some fine malt whiskies and good draught beers, is just the place to unwind and relax. Among the many attractions of this scenic area are fishing, boating, sailing and golf, including Royal Dornoch nearby. Local places of interest include the Falls of Shin, Dunrobin Castle and Clynelish Distillery. *STB* ★★★ *Hotel. See also Colour Advertisement.*

6 BEDROOMS, ALL WITH PRIVATE BATHROOM; CHILDREN WELCOME; BAR AND RESTAURANT MEALS; GOLSPIE 17 MILES.

## CASTLE ARMS HOTEL
**Mey, By Thurso, Caithness KW14 8XH**
**Tel & Fax: 01847 851244 • e-mail: info@castlearms.co.uk**
**website: www.castlearms.co.uk**

This former 19th century coaching inn on the John O'Groats peninsula is set in six acres of parkland, close to the Queen Mother's former Highland home, the Castle of Mey. Fully modernised, the hotel has eight centrally heated en suite bedrooms with colour television and tea making facilities; the spacious Pentland Suite offers a double and family room with en suite bathroom. Locally caught salmon, crab and other fine Highland produce feature on the varied table d'hôte and grill menus available in the Garden Room, while lighter meals and snacks can be enjoyed in the cosy Pentland Lounge. A warm Highland welcome awaits you. *STB* ★★ *Hotel.*

8 BEDROOMS, ALL WITH PRIVATE BATHROOM; FREE HOUSE; HISTORIC INTEREST; CHILDREN AND PETS WELCOME;
BAR AND RESTAURANT MEALS; NON-SMOKING AREAS; JOHN O' GROATS 6 MILES; S£££, D££.

## ORD ARMS HOTEL
**Great North Road, Muir of Ord, Ross-shire IV6 7XR**
**Tel: 01463 870286 • Fax: 01463 870048 • e-mail: ordarmshotel@hotmail.com**

One of life's greatest pleasures must surely be dining before a log fire on a chilly autumn evening - particularly when the cuisine is of the standard to be found at this lovely old Highland hotel just thirteen miles north of Inverness. Local salmon, venison, lamb and other fresh produce is carefully prepared and imaginatively presented in the spacious dining room, while lighter appetites are catered for in the friendly informality of the lounge bar. Here a value for money range of bar snacks is served all day, plus of course a comprehensive selection of Scotch whiskies and other refreshments. Bedrooms at the Ord Arms are mainly en suite, and have colour television, tea and coffee facilities, radio and direct-dial telephone; decor and furnishings are just as charming and comfortable as in the spick and span public rooms. Fishing and Highland safari trips can be arranged at reception, and ponytrekking, sailing, water skiing, golf and bowling are but a short distance away from this village which until last century was the main centre for Scottish cattle dealing. Those wishing merely to relax and enjoy the wonderful air and scenery, however, may rest assured that they will be allowed to do precisely that.

8 BEDROOMS, 5 WITH PRIVATE BATHROOM; FREE HOUSE WITH REAL ALE; CHILDREN AND PETS WELCOME;
BAR AND RESTAURANT MEALS; NON-SMOKING AREAS; BEAULY 3 MILES; S££, D££.

## AURORA HOTEL AND ITALIAN RESTAURANT
**2 Academy Street, Nairn IV12 4RJ**
**Tel: 01667 453551 • Fax: 01667 456577**
**e-mail: aurorahotelnairn@aol.com • www.aurorahotel.co.uk**

At the Aurora Hotel we aim to ensure that all our guests can relax, feel at home and enjoy their stay, whether staying on business or pleasure. You can be assured of a warm welcome and comfortable surroundings, with the personal attention of the resident owners. All en suite bedrooms are tastefully decorated, with tea/coffee making facilities, colour TV and central heating. The hotel is close to all local amenities, including the town centre and shopping, as well as the beach, harbour, championship golf courses and leisure centre. During your stay why not dine in our restaurant, which is renowned for its extensive menu of traditional Italian dishes and wide variety of reasonably priced wines. Nairn is an ideal base for exploring the delights of the Highlands. Historic Culloden Moor and Cawdor Castle and Gardens are close by, with legendary Loch Ness and Urquhart Castle a little further away. It is also ideally placed for those wanting to follow the Speyside Whisky Trail. *STB* ★★ *Hotel.* **See also Inside Back Cover.**

10 BEDROOMS, ALL WITH PRIVATE BATHROOM; FREE HOUSE; CHILDREN AND PETS WELCOME;
RESTAURANT MEALS, EVENINGS ONLY; INVERNESS 15 MILES; S££, D££.

---

**FHG** Free or reduced rate entry to Holiday Visits and Attractions - see our **READERS' OFFER VOUCHERS** on pages 21-40

# Perth & Kinross

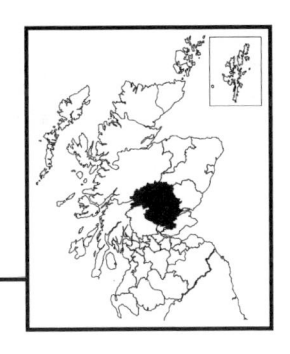

## FOULFORD INN
**By Crieff, Perthshire PH7 3LN**
**Tel & Fax: 01764 652407**

Set amongst the Perthshire hills, Foulford Inn is a long-established resting place for travellers - there has been an inn here since 1785! The inn has been owned by the same family since 1912 and, over the years, has been totally transformed to provide comfortable, modern accommodation at affordable rates. Because of its central location, there are lots of interesting places within easy driving distance, and lots of golf courses to choose from. The inn has its own! The inn has a well deserved reputation for tasty food – local produce, freshly prepared, is a recipe that takes some beating. *STB* ★★ *Inn*.

9 BEDROOMS, 7 WITH PRIVATE BATHROOM; CHILDREN AND PETS WELCOME; NON-SMOKING AREAS; PERTH 16 MILES; S£, D£.

## THE MUIRS INN KINROSS
**49 Muirs, Kinross, Perth & Kinross KY13 8AU**
**Tel & Fax: 01577 862270 • e-mail: themuirsinn@aol.com**
**website: www.themuirsinnkinross.com**

Open all year round and listed as one of Scotland's best pubs, it is a traditional Scottish Country Inn – at its best. With all bedrooms en suite it is full of character and boasts its own award-nominated restaurant which serves home-cooked fresh country cuisine at sensible prices every day. Scottish real ales and malt whiskies are a speciality at this charming inn where you spend time and not a fortune. Historic Kinross is ideal for business or for pleasure and is a superb holiday centre with 130 golf courses and all major cities within driving distance. This Inn is simply something special. Details of special mid-week and weekend breaks sent on request.

5 BEDROOMS, ALL WITH PRIVATE BATHROOM; FREE HOUSE WITH REAL ALE; HISTORIC INTEREST; CHILDREN WELCOME; BAR AND RESTAURANT MEALS; DUNFERMLINE 9 MILES; S££, D££.

# Scottish Islands

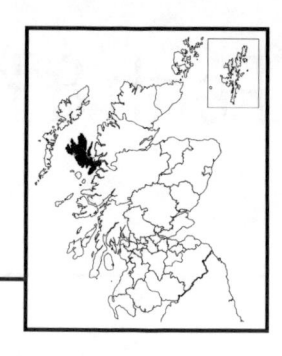

## ARDVASAR HOTEL
Ardvasar, Sleat, Isle of Skye IV45 8RS
Tel: 01471 844223 • Fax: 01471 844495 • www.ardvasarhotel.com
e-mail: richard@ardvasar-hotel.demon.co.uk

Since the 1700s this solid white-washed hotel has gazed over the Sound of Sleat to the Knoydart Mountains and the beautiful Sands of Morar, and as well as being one of the oldest coaching inns on the west coast, it is surely one of the most idyllically situated. Not surprisingly, seafood features extensively on the menu here, together with local venison and other fine Scottish produce, and tasty bar lunches and suppers are offered as an alternative to the more formal cuisine served in the restaurant. A private residents' lounge is furnished to the same high standard of comfort as the cosy guest rooms, all of which have private facilities. STB ★★★ Hotel, AA ★★

10 BEDROOMS, ALL WITH PRIVATE BATHROOM; FREE HOUSE WITH REAL ALE; HISTORIC INTEREST; CHILDREN AND PETS WELCOME; BAR MEALS, RESTAURANT EVENINGS ONLY; NON-SMOKING AREAS; BROADFORD 16 MILES; S££££, D£££.

## THE OLD INN
Carbost, Isle of Skye IV47 8SR
Tel: 01478 640205 • Fax: 01478 640325 • e-mail: spencer@oldinn.f9.co.uk
website: www.carbost.f9.co.uk

For those with the impelling urge to get away from it all, this fine inn on the shores of Loch Harport, on the remote westermost part of the island, is the perfect answer. With splendid views of the Cuillins, this attractively appointed free house is popular with hill walkers and climbers; excellent Bed and Breakfast accommodation is provided for them in well-appointed en suite rooms. Alternatively, those of more pioneering frame of mind, may stay in the new 24-bed bunkhouse with its own kitchen and balcony overlooking the beauty of the loch. Terms are moderate in the extreme. Great food and ale is served all day all year round. STB ★, AA.

6 BEDROOMS, ALL WITH PRIVATE BATHROOM + 24 BUNKBEDS; FREE HOUSE WITH REAL ALE; HISTORIC INTEREST; CHILDREN AND PETS WELCOME; BAR AND RESTAURANT MEALS; PORTREE 18 MILES; S££, D££.

# Recommended Country Inns & Pubs of Britain 2005

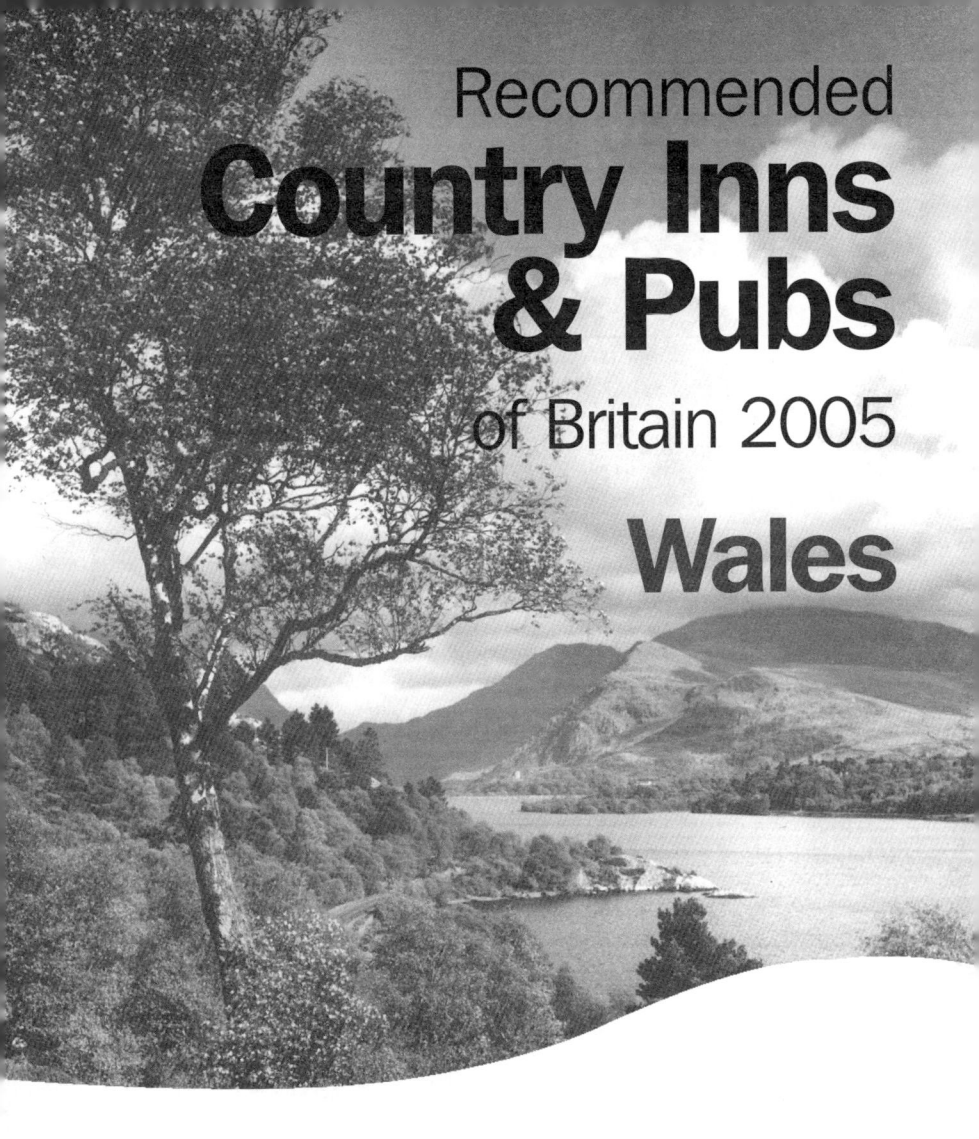

## Wales

---

**WELSH HISTORIC INNS**
Caeathro, Caernarfon, Gwynedd LL55 2SS
Tel: 01286 676115 • Fax: 01286 674831 • e-mail: office@welsh-historic-inns.com
website: www.welsh-historic-inns.com

Stay in these individual and historic Inns, which reflect their locality and unique Welsh history. They all offer quality, value for money and a friendly atmosphere.

**The White Lion Royal Hotel, Bala**, Gwynedd • Tel: 01678 520314 • Fax: 01678 521798
e-mail: whitelion@welsh-historic-inns.com

**The Bull Hotel, Llangefni,** Anglesey • Tel: 01248 722119 • Fax: 01248 750488
e-mail: bullhotel@welsh-historic-inns.com

**The Black Boy Inn, Caernarfon**, Gwynedd • Tel: 01286 673604 • Fax: 01286 674955
e-mail: blackboy@welsh-historic-inns.com

WELSH HISTORIC INNS

# Anglesey & Gwynedd

## HARP INN
Llandwrog, Caernarfon, Gwynedd LL54 5SY
Tel: 01286 831071 • Fax: 01286 830279 • website: www.welcome.to/theharp
e-mail: management@theharp.globalnet.co.uk

Traditionally Welsh right down to its foundations, although it is run by Scots, Colin and Madeleine Downie, this solid, stone-built inn has innate character and is a good place for family parties to enjoy an authentic taste of Wales in food and custom. Children under 14 are welcome in the parlour, restaurant and games room and there is also a large beer garden and patio with beautiful views of the mountains. As a contrast from the lofty attractions of Snowdonia, the beach at Dinas Dinlle is only a mile away and the Lleyn Peninsula is within easy reach. The Harp is well worthy of a casual or extended visit to experience good food in some variety, good company and accommodation at moderate outlay. WTB ★★★ Inn.

4 BEDROOMS, ALL WITH PRIVATE BATHROOM; FREE HOUSE WITH REAL ALE; HISTORIC INTEREST; CHILDREN WELCOME, PETS IN BAR ONLY; BAR AND RESTAURANT MEALS (NOT MON.); NON-SMOKING AREAS; CAERNARFON 5 MILES; S££, D£.

## GWESTY MINFFORDD HOTEL
Talyllyn, Gwynedd LL36 9AJ
Tel: 01654 761265 • Fax: 01654 761517 • e-mail: hotel@minffordd.com
website: www.minffordd.com

A 17th century Drovers' Inn that offers today's traveller all the modern comforts. A mixture of old and new style bedrooms with central heating, three lounges with log fires to relax in after having enjoyed one of Minffordd dinners. The dinners for which their reputation grows use local Welsh produce, organic vegetables, Welsh flavourings and are cooked on an Aga. With the Cader Idris path starting from the door this Hotel is the centre for everyone whether be it walking, just touring or sightseeing. The Talyllyn lake, Dolgoch falls and the Centre for Alternative Technology are within five miles. Further afield there are beaches and fishing ports, but whatever your taste you will find a real welcome (or Croeso in Welsh) upon your return. Perhaps that is why guests return year after year. Hosts, Gordon and Michelle Holt. WTB ★★★ Hotel, Founder Member Taste of Wales.

7 BEDROOMS, ALL WITH PRIVATE BATHROOM; FREE HOUSE; HISTORIC INTEREST; CHILDREN AND PETS WELCOME; BAR MEALS, RESTAURANT EVENINGS ONLY + SUN. LUNCH; NON-SMOKING AREAS; DOLGELLAU 8 MILES; S£££, D£££.

**For our guide to Pet-Friendly Pubs, Inns & Hotels see pages 149-162**

# Ceredigion

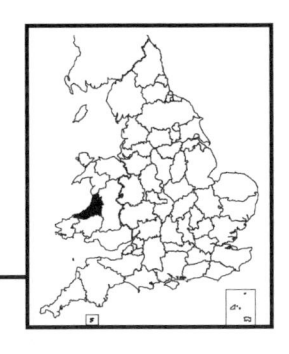

## BLACK LION HOTEL
**High Street, Cardigan, Ceredigion SA43 1HJ**
**Tel: 01239 612532 • Fax: 01239 621509 • e-mail: blionhotel@tiscali.co.uk**

Still retaining its classic 18th century frontage, this old hostelry has a long and colourful history. It was established on the site in 1105 as a one-roomed 'Grogge Shoppe' and is probably the oldest inn in Wales. In 1635, it was enlarged and improved and became the residence of a local squire. When Cardigan became an overnight stopover on the main route between North and South Wales, the 'Black Lion' became an important coaching inn. The mews entrance may still be seen leading off the High Street. Many interesting people have stayed here over the years: during Assize week, the judge would stay and the Assize banquet was held in the upstairs Long Room, popular with the local gentry for their meetings and balls in the 19th century. In the latter years of that century the hotel played host to a thriving cycling club – a new craze! Although still blessed with considerable old-world charm, the hotel has been brought gently into line with the requirements of the 20th and 21st century. Its historic bars thrum with the buzz of convivial conversation whilst serving Tomos Watkin Ltd's Welsh ales and the restaurant provides a selection of fine fare. Guest rooms now have en suite facilities, colour television, telephone and tea and coffee-makers and social events and functions are expertly catered for. For touring the Teifi Valley and the coast of West Wales, this is the ideal base. *WTB* ★★ *Inn.*

14 BEDROOMS, ALL WITH PRIVATE BATHROOM; CELTIC INNS HOUSE WITH REAL ALE; HISTORIC INTEREST;
CHILDREN WELCOME; BAR AND RESTAURANT MEALS; NON-SMOKING AREAS; ABERYSTWYTH 34 MILES; S££, D£££.

---

**FHG** **FHG PUBLICATIONS** publish a large range of well-known accommodation guides. We will be happy to send you details or you can use the order form at the back of this book.

# Pembrokeshire

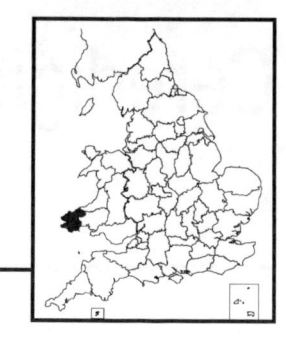

## THE DIAL INN
Lamphey, Pembroke, Pembrokeshire SA71 5NU
Tel: 01646 672426

The Dial Inn is situated in Lamphey village, two miles east of Pembroke, and only a stone's throw from the Bishop's Palace. This elegant, interesting and deceptively large village pub has excellent bar food, a daily blackboard menu, and an imaginative dining room menu. All food is freshly prepared and cooked. Also available are fine wines and cask-conditioned ales, and the inn is open for coffee, lunch, dinner and bar meals. It is listed in all the best food and beer guides including 'Which?' and the AA. *CAMRA*.

5 BEDROOMS, ALL WITH PRIVATE BATHROOM; FREE HOUSE WITH REAL ALE; HISTORIC INTEREST; CHILDREN WELCOME; BAR AND RESTAURANT MEALS; NON-SMOKING AREAS; PEMBROKE 2 MILES; S££, D££.

## TREWERN ARMS HOTEL
Nevern, Newport, Pembrokeshire SA42 0NB
Tel: 01239 820395 • Fax: 01239 820173

Set deep in a forested and secluded valley on the banks of the River Nevern, this picturesque, 16th century hostelry has a warmth of welcome that is immediately apparent in the interestingly-shaped Brew House Bar with its original flagstone floors, stone walls, old settles and beams decorated with an accumulated collection of bric-a-brac. Bar meals are served here from a popular grill area. By contrast, the Lounge Bar is furnished on cottage lines and the fine restaurant has received many accolades from far and wide for its culinary delights. The tranquil village of Nevern is ideally placed for Pembrokeshire's historic sites and uncrowded, sandy beaches and the accommodation offered at this recommended retreat is in the multi-starred class. *WTB* ★★★ *Inn*

10 BEDROOMS, ALL WITH PRIVATE BATHROOM; FREE HOUSE WITH REAL ALE; CHILDREN WELCOME; BAR MEALS, RESTAURANT THURS/FRI/SAT EVENINGS ONLY; NON-SMOKING AREAS; NEWPORT 2 MILES; S££, D££

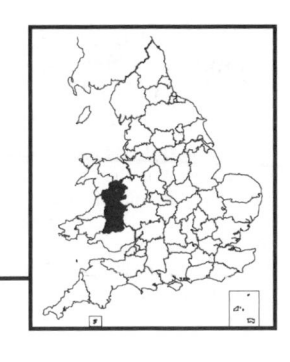

# Powys

## CAIN VALLEY HOTEL
**High Street, Llanfyllin, Powys SY22 5AQ**
**Tel: 01691 648366 • Fax: 01691 648307 • website: www.cainvalleyhotel.co.uk**

A family-run old coaching inn dating from the early 17th century, the Cain Valley Hotel is a Grade II Listed building of great character with many period features, including a Jacobean staircase, oak panelling and many old beams. Having full central heating and en suite rooms with colour television and tea/coffee making facilities, this is a first class centre from which to explore the mountains, lakes and waterfalls of Mid and North Wales. Real ales and light meals are served in the lounge bar, and the Birches Restaurant presents an à la carte menu and an extensive wine list, with the emphasis on freshly prepared food using local produce where possible. There is a private car park at the rear of the hotel. *WTB/AA* ★★ *Hotel, CAMRA.*

13 BEDROOMS, ALL EN SUITE; FREE HOUSE WITH REAL ALE; HISTORIC INTEREST; CHILDREN AND PETS WELCOME; BAR AND RESTAURANT MEALS; NON-SMOKING AREAS; WELSHPOOL 9 MILES; S£££, D££.

## BLACK LION HOTEL
**Llangurig, Powys SY18 6SG**
**Tel: 01686 440223 • e-mail: blacklion@llangurig.org.uk**
**website: www.llangurig.org.uk/**

Originally a 16th century shooting lodge, this is a friendly little inn-cum-hotel on the upper reaches of the River Wye and in the heart of a lovely village, the highest in Wales. On the A44 Aberystwyth road and right in the centre of Wales, it is an ideal base for exploring Wales itself and for walking, fishing and bird watching in the locality. Refreshment is plentifully available in a cosy bar warmed by an open fire in cool weather, an extensive menu including many tempting home-made dishes served at lunchtime and in the evening. Fully centrally heated, the hotel has several well-appointed guest rooms and there is a large comfortable lounge with colour television. *WTB* ★★ *Inn.*

8 BEDROOMS, 5 WITH PRIVATE BATHROOM; FREE HOUSE WITH REAL ALE; HISTORIC INTEREST; CHILDREN AND PETS WELCOME; BAR AND RESTAURANT MEALS; NON-SMOKING AREAS; LLANIDLOES 4 MILES; S£, D£.

## THE BLUE BELL INN
**Llangurig, Powys SY18 6SG**
**Tel: 01686 440254 • Fax: 01686 440337 • e-mail: info@theblue-bell.inn.com**
**website: www.theblue-bellinn.com**

The Blue Bell Inn is situated on the main A44 road to Aberystwyth opposite the Llangurig village church. At the rear of the church runs the River Wye, its source just ten miles away. The area is ideal for angling, walking, cycling, bird-watching, clay pigeon shooting, horse riding and golf. The inn serves very good food and the menu extends from a sandwich to a Prime Welsh steak. The menu also includes a good selection of vegetarian dishes. The inn is a free house and serves a wide variety of real ales and lagers. This friendly pub has a very good reputation for food and drink, and visitors always get a warm welcome from Gwlithyn, Jo and all the staff and regular customers. *WTB* ★ *Inn. See also Colour Advertisement.*

8 BEDROOMS, 4 WITH PRIVATE BATHROOM; REAL ALE; HISTORIC INTEREST; CHILDREN WELCOME; BAR AND RESTAURANT MEALS; NON-SMOKING AREAS; LLANIDLOES 4 MILES; S£, D£.

# THE RED LION INN
**Llanfihangel Nant Melan, New Radnor, Powys LD8 2TN**
**Tel & Fax: 01544 350220 • e-mail: theredlioninn@tiscali.co.uk**
**website: www.theredlioninn.net**

For escape from the tribulations of the urban world, the spectacular terrain of mid-Wales provides an answer, made perfect by a visit to this splendid country inn on the A44, just west of New Radnor. Hospitality is epitomised by good liquid and solid refreshment in a homely bar warmed by a wood burning fire, and an informal eating area where an extensive menu is calculated to suit all tastes and pockets. The beauty of the area is enhanced by facilities for numerous outdoor pursuits, particularly fishing, golf and riding. The pub has a 'sun trap' garden and for complete revivification of body and soul, this friendly retreat is well recommended. Accommodation comprises comfortable en suite rooms, all with radio alarm, colour television and tea and coffee-makers. *WTB* ★★★ *Inn.*

6 BEDROOMS, ALL WITH PRIVATE BATHROOM; FREE HOUSE WITH REAL ALE; HISTORIC INTEREST; CHILDREN AND PETS WELCOME; BAR LUNCHES AND RESTAURANT MEALS; NON-SMOKING AREAS; PRESTEIGNE 10 MILES; S££, D££.

# THE CASTLE COACHING INN
**Trecastle, Brecon, Powys LD3 8UH**
**Tel: 01874 636354 • Fax: 01874 636457 • e-mail: guest@castle-coaching-inn.co.uk**
**website: www.@castle-coaching-inn.co.uk**

Set in the heart of the spectacular Brecon Beacons National Park, the former Georgian coaching inn makes a perfect base for exploring the many attractions of the area and, for the energetic, there are many leisure activities available, such as golf, pony trekking, rambling and climbing, whilst opportunities for fishing are excellent. Rooms of varying sizes and capacities all have en suite facilities, colour television, direct-dial telephone, hairdryer and tea and coffee-making facilities. Menus in the à la carte restaurant are firmly based on the rich variety of produce for which Wales is famous; alternatively, lighter meals are obtainable in a convivial bar where cask ales are served and whose popularity with the locals is recommendation enough. *WTB* ★★★ *Inn.*

9 BEDROOMS, ALL WITH PRIVATE BATHROOM; FREE HOUSE WITH REAL ALE; HISTORIC INTEREST; CHILDREN WELCOME, PETS IN PUBLIC AREAS ONLY; BAR AND RESTAURANT MEALS; NON-SMOKING AREAS; LLANDOVERY 8 MILES; S££££, D££.

---

The £ symbol when appearing at the end of the italic section of an entry shows the anticipated price, during 2005, for full Bed and Breakfast.

*Normal Bed & Breakfast rate per person (in single room)*

| PRICE RANGE | CATEGORY |
|---|---|
| **Under £25** | *S£* |
| **£26-£35** | *S££* |
| **£36-£45** | *S£££* |
| **Over £45** | *S££££* |

*Normal Bed & Breakfast rate per person (sharing double/twin room)*

| PRICE RANGE | CATEGORY |
|---|---|
| **Under £25** | *D£* |
| **£26-£35** | *D££* |
| **£36-£45** | *D£££* |
| **Over £45** | *D££££* |

This is meant as an indication only and does not show prices for Special Breaks, Weekends, etc. Guests are therefore advised to verify all prices on enquiring or booking.

# South Wales

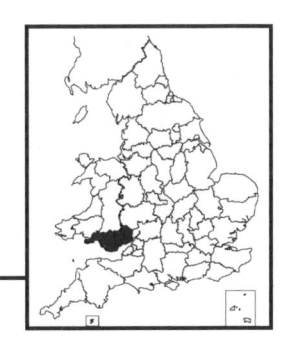

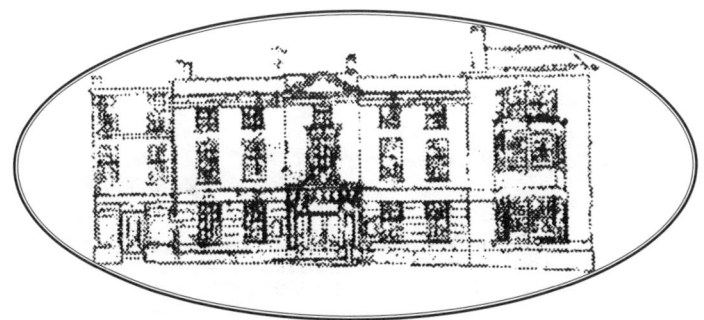

## THE ANGEL HOTEL
**15 Cross Street, Abergavenny, South Wales NP7 5EN**
**Tel: 01873 857121 • Fax: 01873 858059 • www.angelhotelabergavenny.com**
**e-mail: mail@angelhotelabergavenny.com**

This historic, comfortable, Georgian town house hotel in Abergavenny was once one of the great coaching inns on the busy London to Fishguard road. The Angel makes an ideal base for exploring the Brecon Beacons and the Wye Valley, with the wide range of leisure and sporting activities available. The hotel has recently been refurbished with antiques and original artwork, and the restaurant has acquired a reputation for excellent food using local produce. The Foxhunter Bar is popular for light meals or drinks, including real ales, and The Courtyard is open during the summer months for al fresco dining. Delicious afternoon teas are served throughout the year. Guest rooms all have private bathroom, colour television, direct-dial telephone, and tea and coffee making facilities. *WTB* ★★★ *Hotel, AA* ★★★ *and Rosette.*

29 BEDROOMS, ALL WITH PRIVATE BATHROOM; REAL ALE; HISTORIC INTEREST; CHILDREN AND PETS WELCOME;
BAR AND RESTAURANT MEALS; NON-SMOKING AREAS; PONTYPOOL 9 MILES; S££££, D£££.

## YE OLDE CROWN INN
**Old Hereford Road, Pant-y-Gelli, Abergavenny, Monmouthshire NP7 7HR**
**Tel & Fax: 01873 853314**

A friendly welcome awaits all to our 15th century Coaching Inn situated on the lower slopes of the Sugar Loaf within the Brecon Beacons National Park. All bedrooms have tea and coffee facilities and enjoy magnificent views of the Holy Mountain. Sample our range of real ales (CAMRA Millennium Pub Guide) or try one of our numerous malts whilst browsing over our bar, special or restaurant menus featuring many tempting dishes created by our full time chef and team using local produce including game, lamb, pork and trout. Traditional dishes on our bar snack menu include the old favourites such as steak and ale, liver and onions, and faggots and peas. Our restaurant menu offers more exotic, international and traditional choices. There are many activities throughout the area and your hosts will be only too happy to advise.

4 BEDROOMS, WITH GUESTS' BATHROOM; FREE HOUSE WITH REAL ALE; CHILDREN AND PETS WELCOME;
BAR AND RESTAURANT MEALS; NON-SMOKING AREAS; ABERGAVENNY 2 MILES; S£, D££.

# HALF MOON INN
## Llanthony, Abergavenny, Monmouthshire NP7 7NN
### Tel: 01873 890611 • e-mail: halfmoonllanthony@talk21.com

Set amidst the beautiful scenery of the Vale of Ewyas and dominated by the slopes of the Black Mountains, this attractive inn on the winding B4423 is a welcome sight. Inside, a bar virtually unchanged over the years confirms the welcome, serving traditional ales, cider and good food. In an area popular with enthusiastic ramblers and hill walkers, this is a favourite port of call, the boot and drying room being much appreciated. Close by are the fascinating remains of 12th century Llanthony Priory and a partly ruined 19th century monastery, with several Norman border castles within easy reach. Wholesome Bed and Breakfast accommodation is available.

9 BEDROOMS, ALL WITH WASHBASINS; FREE HOUSE WITH REAL ALE; CHILDREN AND PETS WELCOME; BAR MEALS; NON-SMOKING AREAS; ABERGAVENNY 9 MILES; S£, D£.

# THE CLYTHA ARMS
## Clytha, Near Abergavenny, South Wales NP7 9BW
### Tel & Fax: 01873 840206 • e-mail: clythaarms@tiscali.co.uk
### website: www.clytha-arms.com

A converted Dower House set in its own grounds alongside the old Abergavenny to Raglan road (B4598), the Clytha Arms is known primarily for its superb food; furthermore, it is very unpublike in its appearance and its facilities equate more to a distinguished country hotel. Indeed, the accommodation, limited though it may be, is of the highest calibre, the en suite rooms prettily decorated and sumptuously appointed. Nevertheless, this lovely retreat, in the hands of Andrew and Bev Canning, still maintains traditions of a wayside inn with real ales and snacks available in the public bar. However, it is culinary art and expertise that is the big attraction here – imaginative fare, delightfully presented.

4 BEDROOMS, ALL WITH PRIVATE BATHROOM; FREE HOUSE WITH REAL ALE; CHILDREN WELCOME;
BAR AND RESTAURANT MEALS; NON-SMOKING AREAS; RAGLAN 3 MILES, ABERGAVENNY 6 MILES; S££££, D£££.

---

# PLEASE NOTE

All the information in this book is given in good faith in the belief that it is correct. However, the publishers cannot guarantee the facts given in these pages, neither are they responsible for changes in policy, ownership or terms that may take place after the date of going to press. Readers should always satisfy themselves that the facilities they require are available and that the terms, if quoted, still apply.

Pet-Friendly Pubs

# Pet-Friendly Pubs, Inns & Hotels

Please note that these establishments may not feature in the main section of this book

## ENGLAND

### BEDFORDSHIRE

**The Farmer's Boy 01582 872207**

* Family country pub. * Large garden. * Children's play area. * Home made food. * Fullers real ales. * Pets allowed in pub, drinking water supplied.

*Mrs Laverty, The Farmers Boy, 216 Common Road, Kensworth LU6 2PJ*

### BERKSHIRE

**The Greyhound ★ Eton Wick ★ Tel: 01753 863925**

A picturesque pub with plenty of walks close by. Food served daily. Kia the Shepherd and Harvey the Retriever are the resident pets.
• Sunday lunch only £5.95 between 12.00pm - 3.30pm. •

**UNCLE TOM'S CABIN**
Hills Lane, Cookham Dean, Berkshire (01628 483339).
**Dogs allowed throughout.**
*Pet Regulars: Flossie and Ollie (Old English Sheepdog). Free dog biscuit pub.*

**THE GREYHOUND (known locally as 'The Dog')**
The Walk, Eton Wick, Berkshire (01753 863925).
**Dogs allowed throughout the pub.**
*Pet Regulars: Harvey (Retriever), retrieves anything, including Beer mats. KIA - German Shepherd.*

**THE SWAN**
9 Mill Lane, Clewer, Windsor, Berkshire (01753 862069).
**Dogs allowed throughout the pub.**
*Pet Regulars: Mollie and Lucy (Jack Russells).*

**THE TWO BREWERS**
Park Street, Windsor, Berkshire (01753 855426).
**Dogs allowed, public and saloon bars.**
*Pet Regulars: Harry (Pyrenean) and his mate Molly (Newfoundland) take up the whole bar, 'Bear' (Black Labrador), Tessa (Cocker Spaniel), Rufus (Springer Spaniel), Mr Darcy (Poodle), Mr Darcy (Great Dane), Rosie (Chocolate Labrador), Jessie (Labrador/German Shepherd) and Jemma (Golden Retriever).*

Please mention *Country Inns & Pubs* when enquiring about accommodation featured in these pages.

## BUCKINGHAMSHIRE

**WHITE HORSE**
Village Lane, Hedgerley, Buckinghamshire SL2 3UY (01753 643225).
**Dogs allowed at tables on pub frontage, beer garden (on leads), public bar.**

**FROG AT SKIRMETT**
Skirmett, Henley-on-Thames, Buckinghamshire RG9 6TG (01491 638996)
**Dogs welcome, pet friendly.**
*Pet Regular: Resident cat "Cleo".*

**GEORGE AND DRAGON**
High Street, West Wycombe, Buckinghamshire HP14 3AB (01494 464414)
**Pet friendly.**

## CAMBRIDGESHIRE

**YE OLD WHITE HART**
Main Street, Ufford, Peterborough, Cambridgeshire (01780 740250).
**Dogs allowed in non-food areas.**

## CHESHIRE

**THE GROSVENOR ARMS**
Chester Road, Aldford, Cheshire CH3 6HJ (01244 620228)
**Pet friendly.**
*Pet Regulars: resident dog "Sadie" (Labrador).*

**JACKSONS BOAT**
Rifle Road, Sale, Cheshire (0161 973 8549).
**Dogs allowed throughout on lead.**

## CORNWALL

**DRIFTWOOD SPARS HOTEL**
Trevaunance Cove, St Agnes, Cornwall (01872 552428).
**Dogs allowed everywhere except the restaurant.**
*Pet Regulars: Buster (Cornish Labrador cross with a Seal) - devours anything.*

**JUBILEE INN**
Pelynt, Near Looe, Cornwall PL13 2JZ (01503 220312).
**Dogs allowed in all areas except restaurant; accommodation for guests with dogs.**

**THE MILL HOUSE INN**
Trebarwith Strand, Tintagel, Cornwall PL34 0HD (01840 770200).
**Pet friendly.**

**THE MOLESWORTH ARMS HOTEL**
Molesworth Street, Wadebridge, Cornwall PL27 7DP (01208 812055).
**Dogs allowed in all public areas and in hotel rooms.**
*Pet Regulars: Thomson Cassidy (Black Lab), Ruby Cassidy and Lola (Black Lab).*

Pet-Friendly Pubs

## CUMBRIA

**GRAHAM ARMS HOTEL** Longtown, Near Carlisle, Cumbria CA6 5SE
180-year-old former Coaching Inn situated six miles from the M6 (J44) and Gretna Green. Ideal overnight stop or perfect touring base for Scottish Borders, English Lakes, Hardian's Wall and more. Meals and snacks served throughout the day. Real ales and fine selection of malt whiskies.
Pets welcome with well behaved owners!
Tel & Fax: 01228 791213 • office@grahamarms.com • www.grahamarms.com

**Brackenrigg Inn**    Watermillock, Ullswater, Penrith CA11 0LP
Tel: 01768 486206 • Fax: 01768 486945
This 18th century coaching inn is an informal port of call with a cheerful bar warmed by an open fire and a reputation for excellent food. A bar menu is available for lunch and dinner, with a table d'hôte menu added in the evenings; the chef inspired fayre can be enjoyed in the bar, lounge or restaurant. Fabulous panorama of lake and fells, comfortable guest rooms with en suite facilities. Wheelchair access. Pets welcome.   AA ◆◆◆◆
E-mail: enquiries@brackenrigginn.co.uk • Website: www.brackenrigginn.co.uk

### THE BRITANNIA INN
Elterwater, Ambleside, Cumbria LA22 9HP (015394 37210).
**Dogs allowed in all areas except dining room and residential lounge.**
Pet Friendly.

### THE MORTAL MAN HOTEL
Troutbeck, Windermere, Cumbria LA23 IPL (015394 33193).
**Pets allowed everywhere except restaurant.**

### STAG INN
Dufton, Appleby, Cumbria (017683 51608).
**Dogs allowed in non-food bar, beer garden, village green plus B&B and cottage.**
Pet Regulars: Toffee (cross between Saluki and Golden Setter); Willow (cross between Great Dane and an Old English Sheepdog); Kim (Weimaraner), best bitter drinker; Toffee (cross between Chihuahua and Papillon – likes beef dinner. Seb 'chats up' Toffee.

### WATERMILL INN
School Lane, Ings, Near Staveley, Kendal, Cumbria (01539 821309).
**Dogs allowed in beer garden, Wrynose bottom bar.**
Pet Regulars: Blot (sheepdog) and Scruffy (mongrel). Both enjoy a range of crisps and snacks. Scruffy regularly drinks Cheaston Best Bitter. Pub dog Shelley (German Shepherd). Owners cannot walk dogs past pub, without being dragged in! Biscuits and water provided.

## DERBYSHIRE

### THE GEORGE HOTEL
Commercial Road, Tideswell, Near Buxton, Derbyshire SK17 8NU (01298 871382).
**Dogs allowed in snug and around the bar, water bowls provided.**

### DOG AND PARTRIDGE COUNTRY INN & MOTEL
Swinscoe, Ashbourne, Derbyshire (01335 343183).
**Dogs allowed throughout, except restaurant.**
Pet Regulars: Include Mitsy (57); Rusty (Cairn); Spider (Collie/GSD) and Rex (GSD).

### DEVONSHIRE ARMS
Peak Forest, Near Buxton, Derbyshire SK17 8EJ (01298 23875)
**Dogs allowed in bar.**

Pet-Friendly Pubs

*DEVON*

## The Foxhunters Inn   West Down, Near Ilfracombe EX34 8NU
300 year-old coaching Inn conveniently situated for beaches and country walks. Serving good local food. En suite accommodation. Pets allowed in bar areas and beer garden, may stay in accommodation by prior arrangement. Water bowls provided.
**Tel: 01271 863757 * Fax: 01271 879313 * Web: www.foxhuntersinn.co.uk**

### THE SHIP INN
Axmouth, Devon EX12 4AF (01297 21838).
**A predominantly catering pub, so dogs on a lead please.**
*Pet Regulars: Charlie (Labrador), Kym (Boxer), Soxy (cat). Also resident Tawny Owl.*

### BRENDON HOUSE
Brendon, Lynton, North Devon EX35 6PS (01598 741206).
**Dogs very welcome and allowed in tea gardens, guest bedrooms by arrangement.**
*Owner's dogs - Drummer (Labrador) and Piper (Labrador).*

### THE BULLERS ARMS
Chagford, Newton Abbot, Devon (01647 432348).
**Dogs allowed throughout pub, except dining room/kitchen. "More than welcome".**

### CROWN AND SCEPTRE
2 Petitor Road, Torquay, Devon TQ1 4QA (01803 328290).
**Dogs allowed in non-food bar, family room, lounge. All dogs welcome.**
*Pet Regulars: Two Jack Russells - Scrappy Doo and Minnie Mouse.*

### THE JOURNEY'S END INN
Ringmore, Near Kingsbridge, South Devon TQ7 4HL (01548 810205).
**Dogs allowed throughout the pub except in the dining room, must be on a lead.**

### PALK ARMS INN
Hennock, Bovey Tracey, Devon TQ13 9QS (01626 836584).
**Pets welcome.**

### THE ROYAL OAK INN
Dunsford, Near Exeter, Devon EX6 7DA (01647 252256).
**Dogs allowed in bars, beer garden, accommodation for guests with dogs.**
*Pet Regulars: Cleo and Kizi.*

### THE POLSHAM ARMS
Lower Polsham Road, Paignton, Devon (01803 558360).
**Dogs allowed throughout the pub.**
*Pet Regulars: Stella (German Shepherd), pub dog; C.J. (West Highland Terrier) loves pork scratchings; Patch, owner brings his supply of dog biscuits, and Bracken (German Shepherd).*

### THE SEA TROUT INN
Staverton, Near Totnes, Devon TQ9 6PA (01803 762274).
**Dogs welcome in lounge and public bar, beer garden, owners' rooms (but not on beds).**
*Pet Regulars: Buster (resident dog) partial to beer drip trays.*

### THE DEVONSHIRE INN
Sticklepath, Okehampton, Devon EX20 2NW (01837 840626).
**Dogs allowed in non-food bar, car park, beer garden, family room and guest rooms.**
*Pet Regulars: Clarrie and Rosie (Terriers).*

# Pet-Friendly Pubs

**THE TROUT & TIPPLE**
(A386 - Tavistock to Okehampton Road), Parkwood Road, Tavistock, Devon PL10 0JS (01822 618886)
**Dogs welcome at all times in bar, games room and patio.**
*Pet regulars include: Jet (black Labrador) likes biscuits and his two sons Connor and Fenrhys - sometimes misbehave. Alf (GSD) visits occasionally - but has to stay off the Guinness. Casey (Bronze Springer) - always after food. Border, Chaos and Mischief (Border Collies). Also, our own two dogs Borgia (GBD 57) and Morgan (no brain lurcher).*

## DORSET

**THE ANVIL HOTEL**
Sailsbury Road, Pimperne, Blandford, Dorset DT11 8UQ (01258 453431).
**Pets allowed in bar, lounge and bedrooms.**

**THE SQUARE AND COMPASS**
Swanage, Dorset BH19 3LF (01929 439229).
**Well-behaved dogs allowed - but beware of the chickens!**

**THE NOTHE TAVERN**
Barrack Road, Weymouth, Dorset DT4 8TZ (01305 839255).
**Pet friendly - well known for allowing pets.**
*Pet Regulars: get a warm welcome from the pub Alsatian.*

**DRUSILLA'S INN**
Wigbeth, Horton, Dorset (01258 840297).
**Well-behaved dogs welcome.**

## DURHAM

**MOORCOCK INN**
Hill Top, Eggleston, Teesdale, County Durham DL12 9AU (01833 650395).
*Pet Regulars: Thor, the in-house hound dog, and Raymond, the resident hack, welcome all equine travellers; Gem (Jack Russell); Arnie (Ginger Tom); Poppy (Jack Russell); Haflinger - the horse.*

**TAP AND SPILE**
27 Front Street, Framwellgate Moor, Durham DH1 5EE (0191 386 5451).
**Dogs allowed throughout the pub.**

**THE ROSE TREE**
Low Road West, Shincliff, Durham DH1 2LY (0191-386 8512).
**Pets allowed in bar area only.**
*Pet Regulars: "Benson" (Boxer), "Ben" (Miniature White Poodle) and "Oliver" (King Charles).*

**THE SEVEN STARS**
High Street North, Shincliff, Durham (0191-384 8454).
**Dogs welcome in bar area only.**

---

Visit the **FHG** website
# www.holidayguides.com
for details of the wide choice of accommodation featured in the full range of FHG titles

## ESSEX

### WHITE HARTE
The Quay, Burnham-on-Crouch, Essex CM0 8AS (01621 782106).
**Pets welcome.**
*Pet Regulars: Resident dog "Tilly" (Collie).*

### THE OLD SHIP
Heybridge Basin, Heybridge, Maldon, Essex (01621 854150).
**Dogs allowed throughout pub.**

## GLOUCESTERSHIRE

### THE OLD STOCKS HOTEL
The Square, Stow on the Wold, Gloucestershire GL54 1AF (01451 830666).
**Dogs allowed in the beer garden, accommodation for dogs and their owners also available.**
*Pet Regulars: Ben (Labrador) enjoys bitter from the drip trays and Oscar (Doberman) often gets carried out as he refuses to leave.*

### THE OLD CROWN
The Green, Uley, Gloucestershire GL11 5SN (01453 861070).
**Pets allowed throughout the pub.**

## GREATER LONDON

### THE PHOENIX
28 Thames Street, Sunbury on Thames, Middlesex (01932 785358).
**Dogs allowed on lead in non-food bar, beer garden, family room. Capability 2 Grading.**
*Pet Regulars: Sammy (Black Labrador), Billy and Ellie (Lhasa).*

### THE TIDE END COTTAGE
Ferry Road, Teddington, Middlesex (0208 977 7762).
**Dogs allowed throughout the pub.**
*Pet Regulars: Mimi (Labrador).*

---

*The* **FHG**
**GOLF GUIDE**
*Where to Play*
*Where to Stay*
**2005**

Available from most bookshops, the 2005 edition of **THE GOLF GUIDE** covers details of every UK golf course – well over 2800 entries – for holiday or business golf. Hundreds of hotel entries offer convenient accommodation, accompanying details of the courses – the 'pro', par score, length etc.

In association with 'Golf Monthly' and including Holiday Golf in Ireland, France, Portugal, Spain, The USA, South Africa and Thailand .

**£9.99 from bookshops or from the publishers (postage charged outside UK) • FHG Publications, Abbey Mill Business Centre, Paisley PA1 1TJ**

Pet-Friendly Pubs

## HAMPSHIRE

**PLOUGH INN** Sway Road, Tiptoe, Lymington SO41 6FQ

17th century New Forest Inn. Large garden and plenty of parking. Children's play area. Good range of traditional ales. Home made food. Dogs welcome. Dog biscuits on every visit, water bowls available.

Lynne & Nigel Griggs *01425 610185* or e-mail: *ngriggs@ploughtiptoe.fsbusiness.co.uk*

### THE SUN
Sun Hill, Bentworth, Alton, Hampshire GU34 5JT (01420 562338)
**Pets welcome throughout the pub.**
*Pet Regulars: "Rover" (Black Labrador) and "Dilweed" the cat.*

### HIGH CORNER INN
Linwood, Near Ringwood, Hampshire BH24 3QY (01425 473973).
**Dogs, and even horses, are catered for here.**

### THE CHEQUERS
Ridgeway Lane, Lower Pennington, Lymington, Hants (01590 673415).
**Dogs allowed in non-food bar, outdoor barbecue area (away from food).**
*Pet Regulars: Rusty Boyd - parties held for him. Resident pet - D'for (Labrador).*

### THE VICTORY
High Street, Hamble-le-Rice, Southampton, Hampshire (023 80 453105).
**Dogs allowed.**

## HERTFORDSHIRE

### THE BLACK HORSE
Chorley Wood Common, Dog Kennel Lane, Rickmansworth, Herts (01923 282252).
**Dogs very welcome and allowed throughout the pub, on a lead.**

### THE RED LION
Chenies Village, Rickmansworth, Hertfordshire WD3 6ED (01923 282722).
**Pets welcome in bar area only.**
*Pet Regulars: Resident dog "Bobby" (Terriers mixture), "Moss" and "Luke" (Boxer).*

### THE ROBIN HOOD AND LITTLE JOHN
Rabley Heath, near Codicote, Hertfordshire (01438 812361).
**Dogs allowed in non-food bar, car park tables, beer garden.**
*Pet Regulars: Bonnie (Labrador), beer-mat catcher. The locals of the pub have close to 50 dogs between them, most of which visit from time to time. The team includes a two Labrador search squad dispatched by one regular's wife to indicate time's up. When they arrive he has five minutes' drinking up time before all three leave together.*

**FHG PUBLICATIONS LIMITED**
publish a large range of well-known accommodation guides. We will be happy to send you details or you can use the order form at the back of this book.

*Pet-Friendly Pubs*

### KENT

**THE FOX & HOUNDS**   Mike or Kay Garman 01959 525428
A traditional country pub dating back to the 17th century, serving fine ales and wholesome home made food. Set close to the North Downs Way, an ideal area for hikers and ramblers.
★ *Water bowls available both on beer patio and in beer garden.* ★

**KENTISH HORSE**
Cow Lane, Mark Beech, Edenbridge, Kent (01342 850493).
**Dogs allowed in reserved area.**

**THE OLD NEPTUNE**
Marine Terrace, Whitstable, Kent CT5 lEJ (01227 272262).
**Dogs allowed in beach frontage.**

**THE SWANN INN**
Little Chart, Kent TN27 0QB (01233 840702).
**Dogs allowed - everywhere except restaurant.**

### LANCASHIRE

**House Without a Name**
75-77 Lea Gate, Harwood, Bolton BL2 3ET

- Judith Rowlands & Gary Bennett, 01204 300063 -
A warm welcome awaits, with friendly bar staff and excellent cask ales in a traditional environment. Also find us in the CAMRA Good Beer Guide!!
*Pets get lots of attention, and can either sit outside in our Beer Garden or inside, with fresh water and doggie buiscuits.*

**ASSHETON ARMS**
Downham, Clitheroe, Blackburn, Lancashire BB7 4BJ (01200 441227).
**Dogs welcome.**

**MALT'N HOPS**
50 Friday Street, Chorley, Lancashire PR6 0AH (01257 260967).
**Dogs allowed throughout pub if kept under control.**
*Pet Regulars: Mork – says please for bag of crisps.*

### LINCOLNSHIRE

**THE HAVEN INN**
Ferry Road, Barrow Haven, North Lincolnshire DN19 7EX (01469 530247).
**Dogs allowed in the public bar, beer garden, and bedrooms on their own bed/blanket.**

**THE BLUE DOG INN**
Main Street, Sewstern, Grantham, Lincs NG33 5QR (01476 860097).
**Dogs allowed.**
*Pet Regulars: The Guv'nor (Great Dane), best draught-excluder in history; Cassie (Scottie) shares biscuits with pub cats; Nelson – Terrier. Also two cats: Fred and Brahms.*

## MERSEYSIDE

**THE SCOTCH PIPER**
Southport Road, Lydiate, Merseyside (0151 526 0503).
**Dogs allowed throughout the pub.**

## MIDLANDS

**AWENTSBURY HOTEL**
21 Serpentine Road, Selly Park, Birmingham B29 7HU (0121 472 1258).
**Dogs allowed.**
*Pet Regulars: Well-behaved dogs welcome.*

## NORFOLK

**THE OLD RAILWAY TAVERN**
Eccles Road, Quidenham, Norwich, Norfolk NR16 2JG (01953 888223).
**Dogs allowed, must be on lead.**
*Pet Regulars: Roscow (Poodle) and pub dogs Flo (Scottish Terrier) and Benji (Jack Russell).*

**THE HOSTE ARMS**
The Green, Burnham Market, King's Lynn, Norfolk PE31 8HD (01328 738777).
**Dogs allowed throughout the pub.**
*Pet Regulars: "Augustus" and "Sweep" (Black Labradors).*

**THE ROSE AND CROWN**
Nethergate Street, Harpley, King's Lynn, Norfolk (01485 520577).
**Dogs allowed in non-food bar, car park tables.**

## OXFORDSHIRE

**THE BELL**
Shenington, Banbury, Oxfordshire OX15 6NQ (01295 670274).
**Pets allowed throughout.**
*Pet Regulars: Resident pub dogs "Oliver" (Great Dane) and "Daisy" (Labrador).*

**THE PLOUGH INN**
High Street, Finstock, Chipping Norton, Oxfordshire (01993 868333).
**Dogs more than welcome.**
*Pet Regulars: Resident dogs - "Jodi", "Charlie" and "Rosie" (Poodles); "Henry", "Gertie" (Beagles) and "Zac" (Sheepdog) are regular visitors.*

**THE BELL INN**
High Street, Adderbury, Oxon (01295 810338).
**Dogs allowed throughout the pub with the exception of the restaurant and letting rooms.**
*Owner's dog: Elsa (Black Labrador).*

---

See the ***Family-Friendly Pubs & Inns***
Supplement on pages 163-171 for establishments
which really welcome children

## SHROPSHIRE

**THE INN AT GRINSHILL** High Street, Grinshill, Shrewsbury SY4 3BL (01939 220410)
Set at the base of Grade II Listed Grinshill Hill, where wonderful walks can be enjoyed, nestles this newly refurbished inn. Dogs on leads are welcome in the Elephant and Castle bar, which has a separate non-smoking family room. Enjoy local fresh food from the bistro or the daily specials menu, complemented by a choice of real ales, new world wines, non-alcoholic beverages, tea, or coffee made fresh from the bean. Dog bowl and water; garden, car parking, disabled access toilet facilities available. Credit Cards welcome. Situated 7 miles north of Shrewsbury, signposted just off the A49 Whitchurch Road.
e-mail: theinnatgrinshill@hotmail.com • website: www.theinnatgrinshill.co.uk

### THE TRAVELLERS REST INN
Church Stretton, Shropshire (01694 781275).
**Well-mannered pets welcome - but beware of the cats!**

### LONGMYND HOTEL
Cunnery Road, Church Stretton, Shropshire SY6 6AG (01694 722244).
**Dogs allowed in owners' hotel bedrooms but not in public areas.**
Pet Regulars: Bruno and Frenzie; and owner's dogs, Sam and Sailor.

## SOMERSET

### CASTLE OF COMFORT HOTEL
Dodington, Nether Stowey, Bridgwater, Somerset TA5 1LE (01278 741264).
**Pet friendly.**

### THE SPARKFORD INN
High Street, Sparkford, Somerset BA22 7JN (01963 440218).
**Dogs allowed in bar areas but not in restaurant; safe garden and car park.**

### THE BUTCHERS ARMS
Carhampton, Somerset (01643 821333).
**Dogs allowed in bar. B&B accommodation available.**

### HOOD ARMS
Kilve, Somerset TA5 1EA (01278 741210)
**Pets welcome.**

### THE SHIP INN
High Street, Porlock, Somerset (01643 862507).
**Dogs allowed throughout and in guests' rooms.**
Pet Regulars: Include Silver (Jack Russell); Sam (Black Lab) and Max (Staffordshire). Monty (Pug), resident pet.

## FHG PUBLICATIONS

FHG publish a large range of well-known accommodation guides. We will be happy to send you details or you can use the order form at the back of this book.

## SUFFOLK

**The Harbour Inn** Blackshore, Southwold, Suffolk IP18 6TA • Tel: 01502 722381
Riverside location, one mile walk from town centre. Paved area to front, grassed section to rear offering views over the marshes to Southwold town. Two welcoming bars; extension into a former grain store provides extra dining space. Children welcome before 9pm.

### THE KINGS HEAD
High Street, Southwold, Suffolk IP18 6AD (01502 724517).
**Well-behaved dogs welcome.**

### SIX BELLS AT BARDWELL
The Green, Bardwell, Bury St Edmunds, Suffolk IP31 1AW (01359 250820).
**Dogs allowed in guest bedrooms but not allowed in bar and restaurant.**

## SURREY

### THE PLOUGH
South Road, Woking, Surrey GU21 4JL (01483 714105).
**Pets welcome in restricted areas.**

### THE SPORTSMAN
Mogador Road, Mogador, Surrey (01737 246655).
**Adopted dogs congregate at this pub.**
*Pet Regulars: "Daisy" (Mongrel) and "Max" (German Shepherd).*

### THE CRICKETERS
12 Oxenden Road, Tongham, Farnham, Surrey (01252 333262).
**Dogs allowed in beer garden on lead.**

## SUSSEX

### THE FORESTERS ARMS
High Street, Fairwarp, Near Uckfield, East Sussex TN22 3BP (01825 712808).
**Dogs allowed in the beer garden and at car park tables, also inside.**
*Dog biscuits always available.*

### THE PLOUGH
Crowhurst, Near Battle, East Sussex TN33 9AY (01424 830310).
**Dogs allowed in non-food bar, car park tables, beer garden.** .

### QUEENS HEAD
Village Green, Sedlescombe, East Sussex (01424 870228).
**Dogs allowed throughout the pub.**

### THE SLOOP INN
Freshfield Lock, Haywards Heath, West Sussex RH17 7NP (01444 831219).
**Dogs allowed in public bar and garden.**

Pet-Friendly Pubs

## THE SMUGGLERS' ROOST
125 Sea Lane, Rustington, West Sussex BN16 2SG (01903 785714).
**Dogs allowed in non-food bar, at car park tables, in beer garden, family room.**
*Pet Regulars: Skip; Malcolm (Bull Mastiff); PJ and Mel (Staffs); Leo (Border Terrier), forms instant affections with anyone who notices him; Tim (King Charles Spaniel), quite prepared to guard his corner when food appears. The landlord owns an Alsatian.*

## THE SPORTSMAN'S ARMS
Rackham Road, Amberley, Near Arundel, West Sussex BN18 9NR (01798 831787).
**Dogs allowed in the bar area.**

## *WILTSHIRE*

## THE HORSE AND GROOM
The Street, Charlton, Near Malmesbury, Wiltshire (01666 823904).
**Dogs welcome in bar.**
*Pet Regulars: Buster (Basset Hound); Troy (black Labrador).*

## THE PETERBOROUGH ARMS
Dauntsey Lock, Near Chippenham, Wiltshire SN15 4HD (01249 890409).
**All pets welcome in bar.**
*Resident pets - Poppy, Holly and Lilly (3 generations of Jack Russell).*

## THE THREE HORSESHOES
High Street, Chapmanslade, Near Westbury, Wiltshire (01373 832280).
**Dogs allowed in non-food bar and beer garden.**
*Resident Pets: Include Oscar (dog) and one cat. Three horses overlooking the beer garden.*

## *YORKSHIRE*

## BARNES WALLIS INN
North Howden, Howden, East Yorkshire (01430 430639).
**Guide dogs only**

## KINGS HEAD INN
Barmby on the Marsh, East Yorkshire DN14 7HL (01757 630705).
**Dogs allowed in non-food bar.**
*Pet Regulars: Many and varied!*

## THE FORESTERS ARMS
Kilburn, North Yorkshire YO6 4AH (01347 868386).
**Dogs allowed throughout, except restaurant.**
*Pet Regulars: Ainsley (Black Labrador).*

## NEW INN HOTEL
Clapham, Near Settle, North Yorkshire LA2 8HH (015242 51203).
**Dogs allowed in bar, beer garden, bedrooms.**

## SIMONSTONE HALL
Hawes, North Yorkshire DL8 3LY (01969 667255).
**Dogs allowed except dining area.**
*Dogs of all shapes, sizes and breeds welcome.*

## THE SPINNEY
Forest Rise, Balby, Doncaster, South Yorkshire DN4 9HQ (01302 852033).
**Dogs allowed throughout the pub.**
*Pet Regulars: Shamus (Irish Setter), pub thief - fair game includes pool balls, beer mats, crisps, beer, coats, hats - jumped 15 feet off pub roof with no ill effect; Wyn (Labrador) a guide dog and Buster (Staff).*

Pet-Friendly Pubs

**THE ROCKINGHAM ARMS**
8 Main Street, Wentworth, Rotherham, South Yorkshire S62 7LO (01226 742075).
**Pets welcome.**
Pet Regulars: Sheeba (Springer Spaniel), Charlie and Gypsy (Black Labradors), Sally (Alsatian) and Rosie (Jack Russell).

**THE GOLDEN FLEECE**
Lindley Road, Blackley, near Huddersfield, West Yorkshire (01422 372704).
**Dogs allowed in non-food bar.**
Pet Regulars: Holly and Honey (Border Collies).

*CHANNEL ISLANDS/JERSEY*

**LA PULENTE INN**
La Pulente, St Brelade, Jersey (01534 744487).
**Dogs allowed in public bar.**

# WALES

*ANGLESEY & GWYNEDD*

**THE GRAPES HOTEL**
Maentwrog, Blaenau Ffestiniog, Gwynedd LL41 4HN (01766 590365).
**Pets allowed in bar area only.**

**THE BUCKLEY HOTEL**
Castle Street, Beaumaris, Isle of Anglesey LL58 8AW (01248 810415).
**Dogs allowed throughout the pub, except in the dining room and bistro.**
Pet Regulars: Cassie (Springer Spaniel) and Rex (mongrel), dedicated 'companion' dogs, also Charlie (Spaniel).

*NORTH WALES*

**THE WEST ARMS HOTEL**
Llanarmon Dyffryn Ceiriog, Llangollen, North Wales LL20 7LD (01691 600665).
**Welcome pets.**

*CARMARTHENSHIRE*

**FISHERS ARMS**
TEL: 01994 241329 FAX: 01994 241371
EMAIL: shazsteve@tiscali.co.uk
MR AND MRS STEPHEN JONES, FISHERS ARMS, SPRING GARDENS, WHITLAND SA34 0HH

Small friendly pub with touring caravan and camping site. Water and dog chews available free!! Large field to walk the dogs and we offer lots of cuddles!!!

*PEMBROKESHIRE*

**THE FARMERS**
14-16 Goat Street, St David's, Pembrokeshire (01437 721666).
**Pets welcome in the pub area only.**

## POWYS

### SEVERN ARMS HOTEL
Penybont, Llandrindod Wells, Powys LD1 5UA (01597 851224).
**Dogs allowed in the bar, but not the restaurant, and in the rooms - but not on the beds.**

# SCOTLAND

## ABERDEEN, BANFF & MORAY

### THE CLIFTON BAR
Clifton Road, Lossiemouth, Moray (01343 812100).
**Dogs allowed in beer garden only.**

### ROYAL OAK
Station Road, Urquhart, Elgin, Moray (01343 842607).
**Dogs allowed throughout pub.**
*Pet Regulars: Jack (Collie).*

## ARGYLL & BUTE

### CAIRNDOW STAGECOACH INN
Cairndow, Argyll PA26 8BN (01499 600286).
*Pet regulars: Our own dog Rocky is a Golden Labrador.*

### THE BALLACHULISH HOTEL
Ballachulish, Argyll PA39 4JY (01855 811606).
**Dogs allowed in the lounge, beer garden and guests' bedrooms, excluding food areas.**

## EDINBURGH & LOTHIANS

### JOHNSBURN HOUSE
Johnsburn Road, Balerno, Lothians EH14 7BB (0131-449 3847).
**Pets welcome in bar area only.**
*Pet Regulars: Resident dog "Topaz" (Great Dane).*

### LAIRD & DOG
Lasswade, Midlothian (0131-663 9219).
**Dogs allowed in bar.**
*Pet Regulars: Many pet regulars. Drinking bowls.*

## PERTH & KINROSS

### FOUR SEASONS HOTEL
St Fillans, Perthshire (01764 685333).
**Dogs allowed in all non-food areas.**

### THE MUNRO INN
Main Street, Strathyre, Perthshire FK18 8NA (01877 384333).
**Dogs allowed throughout pub, lounge, games room, beer garden and bedrooms (except restaurant).**
*Pet Regulars: Residents Jess (black mongrel with brown eyes) and Jules (white lurcher with blue eyes) have many local pals who visit including Rory, Cally, Kerry and Robbie. Bring your dog to visit! Water and dog biscuits always available.*

# FHG

# "Family-Friendly"
## Pubs, Inns & Hotels

This is a selection of establishments which make an extra effort to cater for parents and children. The majority provide a separate children's menu or they may be willing to serve small portions of main course dishes on request; there are often separate outdoor or indoor play areas where the junior members of the family can let off steam while Mum and Dad unwind over a drink. For more details, please see individual entries under county headings.

*NB: Many other inns, pubs and hotels listed in the main section of the book but not included in this Supplement also welcome children – please see individual entries.*

Family-Friendly Pubs & Inns

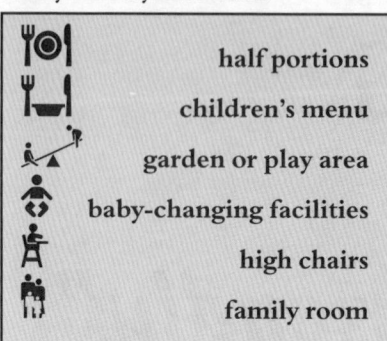

- 🍽 half portions
- 🍴 children's menu
- 🛝 garden or play area
- 👶 baby-changing facilities
- 🪑 high chairs
- 👨‍👩‍👧 family room

### DIFFERENT DRUMMER HOTEL
94 High Street, Stony Stratford
Milton Keynes, Bucks MK11 1AH
Tel: 01908 564733 • Fax: 01908 260646

### ROYAL OAK INN
Duke Street, Lostwithiel,
Cornwall PL22 0AG
Tel: 01208 872552
www.royaloaklostwithiel.co.uk

### THE GODOLPHIN ARMS
West End, Marazion,
Cornwall TR17 0EN
Tel: 01736 710202
www.godolphinarms.co.uk

### CORNISHMAN INN
Tintagel,
Cornwall PL34 0DB
Tel: 01840 770238
www.cornishmaninn.com

### NEW INN
Tresco, Isles Of Scilly,
Cornwall TR24 0QE
Tel: 01720 422844
www.tresco.co.uk

### THE BURNMOOR INN
Boot, Eskdale,
Cumbria CA19 1TG
Tel: 019467 23224
www.burnmoor.co.uk

### THE GILPIN BRIDGE INN & HOTEL
Bridge End, Levens, Near Kendal,
Cumbria LA8 8EP
Tel: 015395 52206
www.gilpinbridgeinn.co.uk

**Family-Friendly Pubs & Inns**

## BRACKENRIGG INN
Watermillock, Ullswater,
Penrith, Cumbria CA11 0LP
Tel: 01768 486206
Fax: 01768 486945

## THE RISING SUN INN
Woodland, Ashburton,
Devon, TQ13 7JT
Tel: 01364 652544
www.risingsunwoodland.co.uk

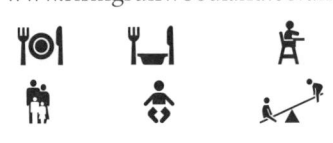

## THE POACHER'S POCKET
Burlescombe, Near Tiverton,
Devon EX16 7JY
Tel: 01823 672286
www.poacherspocket.co.uk

## MILDMAY COLOURS INN
Holbeton, Plymouth,
Devon PL8 1NA
Tel: 01752 830248
www.mildmay-colours.co.uk

## KING'S ARMS INN
Tedburn St Mary, Exeter,
Devon EX6 6EG
Tel: 01647 61224
www.kingsarmsinn.co.uk

## THREE HORSESHOES INN
Running Waters, Sherburn House,
Durham DH1 2SR
Tel: 0191 372 0286
www.activehotels.com

## FERRY BOAT INN
North Fambridge,
Essex CM3 6LR
Tel: 01621 740208
www.ferryboatinn.net

## BECKFORD INN HOTEL
Beckford, Near Tewkesbury,
Gloucestershire GL20 7AN
Tel: 01386 881532
www.beckfordinn.co.uk

165

**Family-Friendly Pubs & Inns**

### THE KINGS'S ARMS HOTEL
The Square, Chipping Campden,
Gloucestershire GL55 6AW
Tel: 01386 840256
www.thekingsarmshotel.com

### THE BELL INN
High Street, Moreton-in-Marsh,
Gloucestershire GL56 0AF
Tel: 01608 651688

### THE HOLLOW BOTTOM
Guiting Power, Cheltenham,
Gloucestershire GL54 5UX
Tel: 01451 850392
www.hollowbottom.com

### THE WYNDHAM ARMS HOTEL
Clearwell, Near Coleford,
Gloucestershire GL16 8JT
Tel: 01594 833666
www.thewyndhamhotel.co.uk

### THE COMPASSES INN
Damerham, Near Fordingbridge,
Hampshire SP6 3HQ
Tel: 01725 518231
www.compassesinn.net

### THE BELL INN HOTEL
Brook, Lyndhurst,
Hampshire
Tel: 023 8081 2214
www.bramshaw.co.uk

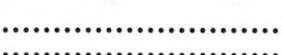

### THE NEW INN
St Owen's Cross,
Herefordshire HR2 8LQ
Tel: 01989 730274
www.newinn.net

### THE SWINGATE INN
Deal Road, Dover,
Kent CT15 5DP
Tel: 01304 204043
www.swingate.com

**Family-Friendly Pubs & Inns**

### THE FARMER'S ARMS
Heskin, Near Chorley,
Lancashire PR7 5NP
Tel: 01257 451276
www.farmersarms.co.uk

### HARK TO BOUNTY INN
Slaidburn, Near Clitheroe,
Lancashire BB7 3EP
Tel: 01200 446246
www.harktobounty.co.uk

### RAM JAM INN
Stretton, Oakham,
Rutland LE15 7QX
Tel: 01780 410776
www.ramjaminn.co.uk

### THE POACHERS COUNTRY HOTEL
Swineshead Road, Kirton Holme,
Lincolnshire PE20 1SQ
Tel: 01205 290310

### THE BLUE COW INN AND BREWERY
South Witham, Grantham,
Lincolnshire NG33 5QB
Tel: 01572 768432
www.thebluecowinn.co.uk

### THE ANGEL INN
Larling, Norwich,
Norfolk NR16 2QU
Tel: 01953 717963

### THE CROWN HOTEL
Wells-next-the-Sea,
Norfolk NR23 1EX
Tel: 01328 710209
www.thecrownhotelwells.co.uk

### QUEEN'S HEAD HOTEL
Townfoot, Rothbury,
Northumberland NE65 7SR
Tel: 01669 620470
www.queensheadrothbury.com

**Family-Friendly Pubs & Inns**

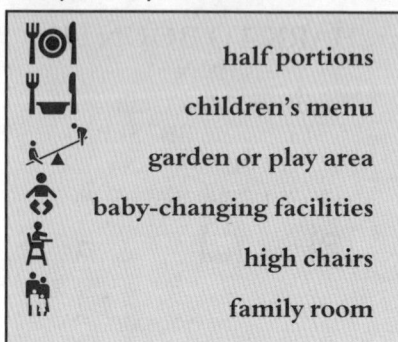

- half portions
- children's menu
- garden or play area
- baby-changing facilities
- high chairs
- family room

### FOUR ALLS INN
Woodseaves, Market Drayton
Shropshire TF9 2AG
Tel: 01630 652995
www.thefouralls.com

### THE CROSSWAYS INN
West Huntspill, Near Highbridge,
Somerset TA9 3DQ
Tel: 01278 783756
www.crossways-inn.com

### HALFWAY HOUSE INN
Chilthorne Domer, Yeovil
Somerset BA22 8RE
Tel: 01935 840350
www.halfwayhouseinn.com

### SPARKFORD INN
Sparkford, Yeovil,
Somerset BA22 7JN
Tel: 01963 440218

### THE CROWN HOTEL
104 High Street, Bildeston,
Suffolk IP7 7EB
Tel: 01449 740510

### THE SHIP INN
Dunwich, Near Saxmundham,
Suffolk IP17 3DT
Tel: 01728 648219

### THE ANCHOR INN
Barcombe, Near Lewes,
East Sussex BN8 5BS
Tel: 01273 400414
www.anchorinnandboating.co.uk

**Family-Friendly Pubs & Inns**

### THE BELL ALDERMINSTER
Shipston Road, Stratford-upon-Avon,
Warwickshire CV37 8NY
Tel: 01789 450414
www.thebellald.co.uk

### CASTLE INN HOTEL
Castle Combe, Chippenham,
Wiltshire SN14 7HN
Tel: 01249 783030
www.castle-inn.info

### THE BOOT INN
Radford Road, Flyford Flavell,
Worcestershire WR7 4BS
Tel: 01386 462658
www.thebootinn.com

### THE ADMIRAL RODNEY
Berrow Green, Martley,
Worcestershire WR6 6PL
Tel: 01886 821375
www.admiral-rodney.co.uk

### THE BAY HORSE INN
Green Hammerton, York,
North Yorkshire YO26 8BN
Tel: 01423 330338
www.thebayhorseinn.info

### GEORGE & DRAGON HOTEL
Kirkbymoorside,
North Yorkshire YO62 6AA
Tel: 01751 433334
www.georgedragon.com

### THE MARTON ARMS
Thornton-in-Lonsdale, Ingleton,
North Yorkshire LA6 3PB
Tel: 015242 41281
www.martonarms.co.uk

### CUBLEY HALL
Penistone, Sheffield,
South Yorkshire S36 9DF
Tel: 01226 766086
www.cubleyhall.co.uk

Family-Friendly Pubs & Inns

## THE THREE ACRES INN & RESTAURANT
Roydhouse, Near Huddersfield,
West Yorkshire HD8 8LR
Tel: 01484 602606
www.3acres.com

## KILDRUMMY INN
Kildrummy, Alford,
Aberdeenshire AB33 8QS
Tel: 01975 571227
www.kildrummyinn.co.uk

## CLACHAIG INN
Glencoe,
Argyll PH49 4HX
Tel: 01855 811252
www.clachaig.com

## THE KIRKTON INN
1 Main Street, Dalrymple,
By Ayr, Ayrshire KA6 6DF
Tel: 01292 560241
www.kirktoninn.co.uk

## CRIFFEL INN
2 The Square, New Abbey,
Dumfriesshire DG2 8BX
Tel: 01387 850244

## THE INN AT ARDGOUR
Ardgour, Fort William,
Inverness-shire PH33 7AA
Tel: 01855 841225
www.ardgour.biz

## GLENELG INN
Glenelg, By Kyle Of Lochalsh,
Ross-shire IV40 8JR
Tel: 01599 522273
www.glenelg-inn.com

## TRENTHAM HOTEL
The Poles, Dornoch
Sutherland IV25 3HZ
Tel: 01862 810551

## Family-Friendly Pubs & Inns

### THE MUIRS INN KINROSS
49 Muirs, Kinross,
Perth & Kinross KY13 8AU
Tel: 01577 862270
www.themuirsinnkinross.com

### ARDVASAR HOTEL
Ardvasar, Sleat,
Isle Of Skye IV45 8RS
Tel: 01471 844223
www.ardvasarhotel.com

### THE OLD INN
Carbost,
Isle Of Skye IV47 8SR
Tel: 01478 640205
www.carbost.f9.co.uk

### HARP INN
Llandwrog, Caernarfon,
Gwynedd LL54 5SY
Tel: 01286 831071
www.welcome.to/theharp

### BLACK LION HOTEL
High Street, Cardigan,
Ceredigion SA43 1HJ
Tel: 01239 612532

### THE RED LION INN
Llanfihangel Nant Melan,
New Radnor, Powys LD8 2TN
Tel: 01544 350220
www.theredlioninn.net

### THE ANGEL HOTEL
15 Cross Street, Abergavenny,
South Wales NP7 5EN
Tel: 01873 857121
www.angelhotelabergavenny.com

### THE CLYTHA ARMS
Clytha, Near Abergavenny,
South Wales NP7 9BW
Tel: 01873 840206
www.clytha-arms.com

# THE FHG DIPLOMA

## HELP IMPROVE BRITISH TOURIST STANDARDS

You are choosing holiday accommodation from our very popular FHG Publications. Whether it be a hotel, guest house, farmhouse or self-catering accommodation, we think you will find it hospitable, comfortable and clean, and your host and hostess friendly and helpful.

Why not write and tell us about it?

As a recognition of the generally well-run and excellent holiday accommodation reviewed in our publications, we at FHG Publications Ltd. present a diploma to proprietors who receive the highest recommendation from their guests who are also readers of our Guides. If you care to write to us praising the holiday you have booked through FHG Publications Ltd. – whether this be board, self-catering accommodation, a sporting or a caravan holiday, what you say will be evaluated and the proprietors who reach our final list will be contacted.

The winning proprietor will receive an attractive framed diploma to display on his premises as recognition of a high standard of comfort, amenity and hospitality. FHG Publications Ltd. offer this diploma as a contribution towards the improvement of standards in tourist accommodation in Britain. Help your excellent host or hostess to win it!

-------------------------------------------------------------------------------

**FHG DIPLOMA**

We nominate

Because

Name ....................................................................................................................

Address................................................................................................................

..............................................................................................................................

Telephone No............................................

**FHG**

| | | | |
|---|---|---|---|
| Abberley | WORCESTERSHIRE | Danby | NORTH YORKSHIRE |
| Abergavenny | SOUTH WALES | Devizes | WILTSHIRE |
| Abingdon | OXFORDSHIRE | Didmarton | GLOUCESTERSHIRE |
| Alderminster | WARWICKSHIRE | Dorchester | DORSET |
| Ambleside | CUMBRIA | Dornoch | HIGHLANDS |
| Ardersier | HIGHLANDS | Dover | KENT |
| Ardfern | ARGYLL & BUTE | Dulverton | SOMERSET |
| Ardgour | HIGHLANDS | Dunsford | DEVON |
| Ardvasar | SCOTTISH ISLANDS/SKYE | Dunwich | SUFFOLK |
| Arkengarthdale | NORTH YORKSHIRE | Durham | DURHAM |
| Armathwaite | CUMBRIA | East Haddon | NORTHAMPTONSHIRE |
| Ashbourne | DERBYSHIRE | Eaton | CHESHIRE |
| Ashburton | DEVON | Eckington | WORCESTERSHIRE |
| Ashprington | DEVON | Elterwater | CUMBRIA |
| Avergavenny | SOUTH WALES | Ennerdale Bridge | CUMBRIA |
| Aviemore | HIGHLANDS | Escrick | NORTH YORKSHIRE |
| Aysgarth | NORTH YORKSHIRE | Ewerby | LINCOLNSHIRE |
| Ballachulish | HIGHLANDS | Flyford Flavell | WORCESTERSHIRE |
| Barcombe | EAST SUSSEX | Forest of Bowland | LANCASHIRE |
| Barham | KENT | Fort William | HIGHLANDS |
| Beckermet | CUMBRIA | Froxfield | HAMPSHIRE |
| Beckford | GLOUCESTERSHIRE | Glastonbury | SOMERSET |
| Bedale | NORTH YORKSHIRE | Glencoe | ARGYLL & BUTE |
| Bedford | BEDFORDSHIRE | Glenelg | HIGHLANDS |
| Bildeston | SUFFOLK | Grassington | NORTH YORKSHIRE |
| Bilsborrow | LANCASHIRE | Great Ayton | NORTH YORKSHIRE |
| Birch Vale | DERBYSHIRE | Green Hammerton | NORTH YORKSHIRE |
| Bishop's Castle | SHROPSHIRE | Grittleton | WILTSHIRE |
| Bledington | OXFORDSHIRE | Guiting Power | GLOUCESTERSHIRE |
| Blockley | GLOUCESTERSHIRE | Hartington | DERBYSHIRE |
| Boot | CUMBRIA | Haslemere | SURREY |
| Brampton | CUMBRIA | Hawes | NORTH YORKSHIRE |
| Brimfield | SHROPSHIRE | Hertford | HERTFORDSHIRE |
| Briston | NORFOLK | Heskin | LANCASHIRE |
| Buckland | OXFORDSHIRE | Hexworthy | DEVON |
| Burlescombe | DEVON | Holbeton | DEVON |
| Buxton | DERBYSHIRE | Holt | WILTSHIRE |
| Cairndow | ARGYLL & BUTE | Hope Valley | DERBYSHIRE |
| Carbost | SCOTTISH ISLANDS/SKYE | Hubberholme | NORTH YORKSHIRE |
| Cardigan | CEREDIGION | Hunton | NORTH YORKSHIRE |
| Carlisle | CUMBRIA | Ide | DEVON |
| Castle Cary | SOMERSET | Inverurie | ABERDEEN, BANFF & MORAY |
| Castle Combe | WILTSHIRE | Kelso | BORDERS |
| Castleton | DERBYSHIRE | Kempsey | WORCESTERSHIRE |
| Chagford | DEVON | Kilburn | NORTH YORKSHIRE |
| Chalfont St Giles | BUCKINGHAMSHIRE | Kildrummy | ABERDEEN, BANFF & MORAY |
| Chipping Campden | GLOUCESTERSHIRE | Kingston-upon-Thames | SURREY |
| Chop Gate | NORTH YORKSHIRE | Kinlochewe | HIGHLANDS |
| Clearwell | GLOUCESTERSHIRE | Kinross | PERTH & KINROSS |
| Clytha | SOUTH WALES | Kintbury | BERKSHIRE |
| Coniston | CUMBRIA | Kirkbymoorside | NORTH YORKSHIRE |
| Corton | WILTSHIRE | Kirton Holme | LINCOLNSHIRE |
| Cotebroke | CHESHIRE | Knaresborough | NORTH YORKSHIRE |
| Cowes | ISLE OF WIGHT | Lairg | HIGHLANDS |
| Crieff | PERTHSHIRE | Lamphey | PEMBROKESHIRE |
| Dacre Banks | NORTH YORKSHIRE | Langport | SOMERSET |
| Dalbeattie | DUMFRIES & GALLOWAY | Larling | NORFOLK |
| Dalrymple | AYRSHIRE & ARRAN | Leadenham | LINCOLNSHIRE |
| Damerham | HAMPSHIRE | Ledbury | HEREFORDSHIRE |

**FHG** Free or reduced rate entry to Holiday Visits and Attractions - see our **READERS' OFFER VOUCHERS** on pages 21-40

| | |
|---|---|
| Leek | STAFFORDSHIRE |
| Leighton Buzzard | BEDFORDSHIRE |
| Lerryn | CORNWALL |
| Levens | CUMBRIA |
| Leyburn | NORTH YORKSHIRE |
| Lichfield | STAFFORDSHIRE |
| Llandwrog | ANGLESEY & GWYNEDD |
| Llanfyllin | POWYS |
| Llangurig | POWYS |
| Llanymynech | SHROPSHIRE |
| Lostwithiel | CORNWALL |
| Ludlow | SHROPSHIRE |
| Lydford | DEVON |
| Lyndhurst | HAMPSHIRE |
| Lynmouth | DEVON |
| Maidstone | KENT |
| Malton | NORTH YORKSHIRE |
| Market Drayton | SHROPSHIRE |
| Marsham | NORFOLK |
| Martley | WORCESTERSHIRE |
| Mells | SOMERSET |
| Mey | HIGHLANDS |
| Mickleham | SURREY |
| Milton Keynes | BUCKINGHAMSHIRE |
| Moffat | DUMFRIES & GALLOWAY |
| Molland | DEVON |
| Monkton Combe | SOMERSET |
| Montacute | SOMERSET |
| Moreton-in-Marsh | GLOUCESTERSHIRE |
| Mortehoe | DEVON |
| Muir of Ord | HIGHLANDS |
| Munslow | SHROPSHIRE |
| Nairn | HIGHLANDS |
| New Abbey | DUMFRIES & GALLOWAY |
| New Radnor | POWYS |
| Newark | NOTTINGHAMSHIRE |
| Newbury | BERKSHIRE |
| Newport | PEMBROKESHIRE |
| North Bovey | DEVON |
| North Fambridge | ESSEX |
| Nunney | SOMERSET |
| Oban | ARGYLL & BUTE |
| Odiham | HAMPSHIRE |
| Okehampton | DEVON |
| Painswick | GLOUCESTERSHIRE |
| Parkend | GLOUCESTERSHIRE |
| Patterdale | CUMBRIA |
| Penistone | SOUTH YORKSHIRE |
| Penzance | CORNWALL |
| Piddletrenthide | DORSET |
| Port Isaac | CORNWALL |
| Portpatrick | DUMFRIES & GALLOWAY |
| Ringwood | HAMPSHIRE |
| Ross-on-Wye | HEREFORDSHIRE |
| Rothbury | NORTHUMBERLAND |
| Rowarth | DERBYSHIRE |
| Rowlands Castle | HAMPSHIRE |
| Rushall | NORFOLK |
| Scarborough | NORTH YORKSHIRE |
| Settle | NORTH YORKSHIRE |
| Shalfleet | ISLE OF WIGHT |
| Shelley | WEST YORKSHIRE |
| Shipston-on-Stour | WARWICKSHIRE |
| Slaidburn | LANCASHIRE |
| Snape | NORTH YORKSHIRE |
| South Witham | LINCOLNSHIRE |
| Sowerby Bridge | WEST YORKSHIRE |
| Sparkford | SOMERSET |
| Spilsby | LINCOLNSHIRE |
| St Agnes | CORNWALL |
| St Neot | CORNWALL |
| St Owen's Cross | HEREFORDSHIRE |
| Staple Fitzpaine | SOMERSET |
| Stow-on-the-Wold | GLOUCESTERSHIRE |
| Stratford-upon-Avon | WARWICKSHIRE |
| Stretton | LEICESTERSHIRE & RUTLAND |
| Talyllyn | ANGLESEY & GWYNEDD |
| Tarbert | ARGYLL & BUTE |
| Tedburn St Mary | DEVON |
| Temple Grafton | WARWICKSHIRE |
| Thirsk | NORTH YORKSHIRE |
| Thornham | NORFOLK |
| Thornton-in-Lonsdale | NORTH YORKSHIRE |
| Thorpeness | SUFFOLK |
| Tintagel | CORNWALL |
| Totnes | DEVON |
| Trecastle | POWYS |
| Tresco | CORNWALL (ISLES OF SCILLY) |
| Troutbeck | CUMBRIA |
| Truro | CORNWALL |
| Ullswater | CUMBRIA |
| Weaverthorpe | NORTH YORKSHIRE |
| Wells-next-the-Sea | NORFOLK |
| Weobley | HEREFORDSHIRE |
| West Huntspill | SOMERSET |
| Willersey | WORCESTERSHIRE |
| Wimborne | DORSET |
| Winchcombe | GLOUCESTERSHIRE |
| Wing | LEICESTERSHIRE & RUTLAND |
| Yeovil | SOMERSET |
| York | NORTH YORKSHIRE |

# FHG

**FHG PUBLICATIONS** publish a large range of well-known accommodation guides. We will be happy to send you details or you can use the order form at the back of this book.

# OTHER FHG TITLES FOR 2005

FHG Publications have a large range of attractive holiday accommodation guides for all kinds of holiday opportunities throughout Britain. They also make useful gifts at any time of year. Our guides are available in most bookshops and larger newsagents but we will be happy to post you a copy direct if you have any difficulty. POST FREE for addresses in the UK. We will also post abroad but have to charge separately for post or freight.

**£7.99**

The original
**Farm Holiday Guide to COAST & COUNTRY HOLIDAYS** in England, Scotland, Wales and Channel Islands. Board, Self-catering, Caravans/Camping, Activity Holidays.

**£6.99**

**BED AND BREAKFAST STOPS**
Over 1000 friendly and comfortable overnight stops. Non-smoking, Disabled and Special Diets Supplements.

**£5.99**

**BRITAIN'S BEST HOLIDAYS**
A quick-reference general guide for all kinds of holidays.

**£8.99**

**PETS WELCOME!**
The original and unique guide for holidays for pet owners and their pets.

**£7.99**

Recommended
**COUNTRY HOTELS**
of Britain
Including Country Houses, for the discriminating.

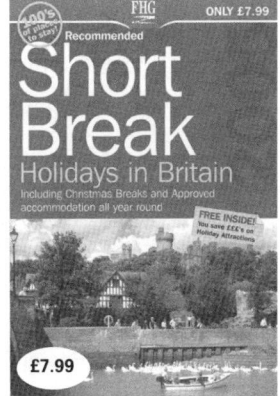

**£7.99**

Recommended
**SHORT BREAK HOLIDAYS IN BRITAIN**
"Approved" accommodation for quality bargain breaks.

*175*

**CHILDREN WELCOME!**
Family Holidays and Days Out guide.
Family holidays with details of amenities for children and babies.

The FHG Guide to
**CARAVAN & CAMPING HOLIDAYS,**
Caravans for hire, sites and holiday parks and centres.

**SELF-CATERING HOLIDAYS**
in Britain
Over 1000 addresses throughout for self-catering and caravans in Britain.

**The GOLF GUIDE –**
**Where to play  Where to stay**
In association with GOLF MONTHLY. Over 2800 golf courses in Britain with convenient accommodation. Holiday Golf in France, Portugal, Spain, USA, South Africa and Thailand.

£9.99

Tick your choice and send your order and payment to ..........................

FHG PUBLICATIONS, ABBEY MILL BUSINESS CENTRE, SEEDHILL, PAISLEY PA1 1TJ
TEL: 0141- 887 0428; FAX: 0141- 889 7204
e-mail: fhg@ipcmedia.com
Deduct 10% for 2/3 titles or copies; 20% for 4 or more.

Send to:  NAME .............................................................................
         ADDRESS .......................................................................
         ......................................................................................
         ......................................................................................
         POST CODE ............................
I enclose Cheque/Postal Order for £ ..................................................
         SIGNATURE...........................................DATE ...............................

Please complete the following to help us improve the service we provide. How did you find out about our guides?:

☐ Press    ☐ Magazines    ☐ TV/Radio    ☐ Family/Friend    ☐ Other